The Story of
Black Rock, Utah

Michael R. Kelsey

Kelsey Publishing
456 E. 100 N.
Provo, Utah, USA, 84606
Tele & Fax 1-801-373-3327

First Edition April, 1996

Copyright © 1996 Michael R. Kelsey
All Rights Reserved

Library of Congress Catalog Card Number 96-075103
ISBN 0-944510-12-4

Distributors for Kelsey Publishing
Primary Distributor All of Michael R. Kelsey's books are sold by this company. If you'd like to order any book, please write to the following address:
Wasatch Book Distribution, P.O. Box 11776, 268 S., 200 E., Salt Lake City, Utah, USA, 84147-0776, Tele. 1-801-575-6735, or orders from bookstores, 1-800-786-6715, Fax 1-801-575-6834.

Some of Kelsey's books are sold by the following distributors.
Alpenbooks, 3616 South Road, Building C, Suite 1, Mukilteo, Washington, 98275, Tele. 1-206-290-8587, or 1-800-290-9898. Fax 1-206-290-9461
Canyon Country Publications, P. O. Box 963, Moab, Utah, 84532, Tele. 1-801-259-6700.
Canyonlands Publications, 4999 East Empire, Unit A, Flagstaff, Arizona, 86004, 1-602-527-0730.
Crown West Books(Library Service), 575 E. 1000 S., Orem, Utah, 84058, Tele. 1-801-224-1455.
Northern Arizona News, 1709 North, East Street, Flagstaff, Arizona, 86004, Tele. 1-602-774-6171.
Many Feathers, 2626 West, Indian School Road, Phoenix, Arizona, 85012, Tele. 1-602-266-1043.
Nevada Publications, 4135 Badger Circle, Reno, Nevada, 89509, Tele. 1-702-747-0800.
Mountain 'N Air Books, 7251 Foothill Blvd., Tujunga, California, 91042, Tele. 1-818-951-4150, or for bookstores, 1-800-446-9696
Peregrine Outfitters, P.O. Box 1500, Williston, Vermont, 05495-1500, Tele. 1-802-860-2977, Fax 1-802-860-2978.
Recreational Equipment, Inc.(R.E.I.), P.O. Box C-88126, Seattle, Washington, 98188, Tele. 1-800-426-4840(or check at any of their local stores).

For the UK and Europe, and the rest of the world contact:
CORDEE, 3a De Montfort Street, Leicester, England, UK, LE1 7HD, Tele. 0116-254-3579, Fax 0116-247-1176.

Printed by Bookcrafters, Chelsea, Michigan, USA

All fotos by the author, unless otherwise stated
All maps & floor plans drawn by the author.

Front Cover

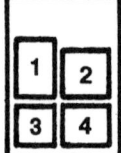

Front Cover
1. AG James and 1928 Buick, in the 1930's.
2. Walter & Helen James Family, daughters L to R, Benita, Helen(Babe), and Thekla, about 1920.
3. Old Railroad Depot, before 1926.
4. Black Rock Store & Hotel, 1890's.

Back Cover

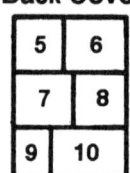

Back Cover
5. Shearing Sheep, early 1900's
6. Big House at the Black Rock Ranch, early or mid-1900's.
7. S. P. L. A. & S. L. steam engine, early 1900's.
8. James Girls, Benita, top, Thekla & Babe, about 1904.
9. The old Black Rock Store & Hotel Cellar, 1996.
10. New Railroad Depot, after 1926.

Table of Contents

Acknowledgments and the Author 4
Map Symbols and Abbreviations 5
Metric Conversion Table 6
Location Map 7
Chapter 1--Preface or Introduction **8**
Chapter 2--History of the Region: Up to 1879 .... **9**
Chapter 3--History of the Black Rock Region: From 1880 to about 1901 .. **14**
Chapter 4--Black Rock from about 1901 until 1916 .... **27**
    The Black Rock School 29   Dry Farming and Mining 33
    The Railroad 31   The Entire James Family History 34
Chapter 5--Black Rock from about 1917 to 1944 .... **44**
    Store & Hotel, and The Ranch 44   John, Dan and Albert(Bert) James 87
    The Black Rock School 52   Last Days of Sheep Shearing 89
    The Railroad 57   Other Important Residents 90
    Dry farming, BB, Mining, Oil Wells 60   Black Rock CCC Camp 97
    The Walter James Family 64   Walter James Dies 99
    The AG James Family 77
Chapter 6--Black Rock from 1944 to 1957 .... **104**
    The Walter James Family 104   The Railroad 116
    Oil Wells 109   Other Events at Black Rock 121
    The AG James Family 111   The Black Rock Ranch is Sold 123
    Sheep Shearing & Shipping Sheep. 115
Chapter 7--Black Rock from 1957 to 1996 .... **126**
    The Kaufman Ranch 126   Last Residents 149
    The Original Settlers Die 137   Maps, & Things to See Near B. Rock. 150
    Crystal Peak Minerals 146
Known Railroad Agents & Postmasters at Black Rock **158**
Further Reading **159**
Other Guidebooks by the Author & Distributors for Kelsey Publishing ... **160**

List of Maps, Floor Plans & School Teachers

Area Map--Black Rock Townsite, Railway Sidings, Area Mines & Volcanos 7
Old 1875 Map: Black Rock Region, Stagecoach Stations and Utah's West Desert 13
Black Rock Store, Hotel & Post Office Floor Plan--1930's 48
Black Rock School Teachers, 1899--1942, Number of Students & Population of BR 54
Black Rock, Antelope Spring, and Walter James' Oil Wells & Mines at Antelope Point .. 68
Black Rock Ranch and Townsite--About 1932 to 1942 69
Black Rock Townsite--Store-Hotel, Shearing Barns, Railway D., School-1925 to 1945 . 81
Black Rock Railroad Depot Floor Plan--1926 to 1972 118
Black Rock Ranch--1996 128
Black Rock School & 1908 Ranch House Floor Plan(1996) 129

Acknowledgments

It's impossible to recall all the many people who helped with this book, but special thanks should go to the following people: Robert Barber of Delta, who worked on the railroad in the Black Rock area. Hamp Burke(deceased), who married Benita James, daughter of Walter James. Deon Gillen of Oasis, who helped tear down the Black Rock store & hotel. Mae Labrum(deceased) & Della Labrum Madsen of Meadow, who worked at Black Rock in the 1920's & 1930's. Donetta Hardy of Delta, who lived at Black Rock in 1946-47. Anna Mae James Robison of Salt Lake, and Bobbie James of Milford who knew the James families of Black Rock and had a number of old pictures. Inez Kelly & Dawn Kelly Anderson of Oasis, and Jim Kelly of Las Vegas, Nevada, all of whom knew about the Black Rock CCC Camp. Nola Miller of Bountiful who married Wally Miller, son of Merrill & Thekla James Miller. Elise McMillen Brougham, from Wheat Ridge, Colorado, daughter of Helen (Babe) James. Garnetta & Dude Hollis of Milford & Minersville, who lived at Black Rock. Beryl Gillen Sorensen of St. George, who supplied some fotos and genealogy of the AG & Velora James family. Mildred Fitch of Ventura California, who supplied Velora James' life story and several old pictures. Jack Stahl of Washington, Utah, & Donna Stahl Smith of West Jordan, who gave information about, and pictures of, Horace A. Stahl. Christine Rogers Mathews & Frances Rogers Green, whose mother Rose Rogers taught school in Black Rock. Inez Bertoldi Travers Beers of Craig, Colorado, who was married to Jack Travers; and Walter James (Jim) Travers, the second son of Jack Travers presently of Kanab, Utah. Gilbert McCulley of Milford, who lived at Black Rock and knows railroads. Victor & Dorothy Kaufman, the couple who bought the Black Rock Ranch in 1957; and their son and daughter-in-law, Jim & Cynthia Kaufman. And last, Larry Sower of Milford, who remembered the history of the Crystal Peak Minerals and its work on the Sevier Dry Lake Bed.

Also, La Preal Wilson of Richfield, Lee Barton of Manti, Warren G.(Sonny) Allsop of Salt Lake, Nels Bogh, Legrand Law of Delta, Elmo Gillen of Oasis, Gladys Whittaker, Rosalie Koch Cook Burke, Ida Hardy Beitz, Richard Jefferson, Elroy Nelson and Judy Briscoe of Milford.

And many thanks goes to my mother, Venetta B. Kelsey who looks after my small publishing business when I'm on the road and who helped proof-read this manuscript.

The Author

The author, who was born in 1943, experienced his earliest years of life in eastern Utah's Uinta Basin, namely around the town of Roosevelt. Then the family moved to Provo, and he graduated from Provo High in 1961, and later went to Brigham Young University, where he earned a B.S. degree in Sociology. Shortly thereafter he discovered that was the wrong subject, so he attended the University of Utah, where he received his Master of Science degree in Geography, finishing that in June, 1970.

It was then real life began, for on June 9, 1970, he put a pack on his back and started traveling for the first time. Since then he has seen 186 countries, republics, islands, or island groups. All this wandering has resulted in a number of books being written and published by himself: *Climber's and Hiker's Guide to the World's Mountains(3rd Ed.), Utah Mountaineering Guide, and the Best Canyon Hikes(2nd Ed.); China on Your Own and the Hiking Guide to China's Nine Sacred Mountains(3rd Ed.); Canyon Hiking Guide to the Colorado Plateau(3rd Edition); Hiking and Exploring Utah's San Rafael Swell(2nd Ed.); Hiking and Exploring Utah's Henry Mountains and Robbers Roost(Revised Edition); Hiking and Exploring the Paria River(Updated Edition); Hiking and Climbing in the Great Basin National Park(Wheeler Peak, Nevada); Boater's Guide to Lake Powell--Featuring Hiking, Camping, Geology, History and Archaeology(Updated Edition); Climbing and Exploring Utah's Mt. Timpanogos; River Guide to Canyonlands National Park & Vicinity; and Hiking, Biking and Exploring Canyonlands National Park & Vicinity.*

He also helped his mother Venetta B. Kelsey write a book about the town she was born and raised in, **Life on the Black Rock Desert--A History of Clear Lake, Utah.**

Map Symbols & Abbreviations

Buildings, City or Town
Railroad Sidings
Railway Line
Black Rock School
Black Rock Hotel
Interstate Highway
US Highway
Utah State Highway
Mile Post Markers
County Road, Graveled
Other Dirt Roads

Mountain Peak
Volcanos
Running Water, River
Dry Stream Bed
Lake, or Dry Lake Bed
Mine
Spring
Elevation Point, in Meters
Bench--Escarpment, Ridge
Corral or Fence Line
Radio or Microwave Tower

Kilometer .... km   Kilometers .... kms

All elevations on maps are given in meters

Antelope Spring, located southeast of Black Rock. Winter of 1995-96. This is the site of an old stagecoach station dating from about 1870.

Metric Conversion Table

1 Centimeter = 0.39 Inch
1 Inch = 2.54 Centimeters
1 Meter = 39.37 Inches
1 Foot = 0.3048 Meter
1 Kilometer = 0.621 Mile

1 Mile = 1.609 Kilometers
100 Miles = 161 Kilometers
100 Kilometers = 62.1 Miles
1 Liter = 1.056 Quarts(US)
1 Kilogram = 2.205 Pounds

1 Pound = 453 Grams
1 Quart(US) = 0.946 Liter
1 Gallon(US) = 3.785 Liters
1 Acre = 0.405 Hectare
1 Hectare = 2.471 Acres

METERS TO FEET (Meters x 3.2808 = Feet)

100 m = 328 ft.	2500 m = 8202 ft.	5000 m = 16404 ft.	7500 m = 24606 ft.
500 m = 1640 ft.	3000 m = 9842 ft.	5500 m = 18044 ft.	8000 m = 26246 ft.
1000 m = 3281 ft.	3500 m = 11483 ft.	6000 m = 19686 ft.	8500 m = 27887 ft.
1500 m = 4921 ft.	4000 m = 13124 ft.	6500 m = 21325 ft.	9000 m = 29527 ft.
2000 m = 6562 ft.	4500 m = 14764 ft.	7000 m = 22966 ft.	

FEET TO METERS (Feet ÷ 3.2808 = Meters)

1000 ft. = 305 m	9000 ft. = 2743 m	16000 ft. = 4877 m	23000 ft. = 7010 m
2000 ft. = 610 m	10000 ft. = 3048 m	17000 ft. = 5182 m	24000 ft. = 7315 m
3000 ft. = 914 m	11000 ft. = 3353 m	18000 ft. = 5486 m	25000 ft. = 7620 m
4000 ft. = 1219 m	12000 ft. = 3658 m	19000 ft. = 5791 m	26000 ft. = 7925 m
5000 ft. = 1524 m	13000 ft. = 3962 m	20000 ft. = 6096 m	27000 ft. = 8230 m
6000 ft. = 1829 m	14000 ft. = 4268 m	21000 ft. = 6401 m	28000 ft. = 8535 m
7000 ft. = 2134 m	15000 ft. = 4572 m	22000 ft. = 6706 m	29000 ft. = 8839 m
8000 ft. = 2438 m			30000 ft. = 9144 m

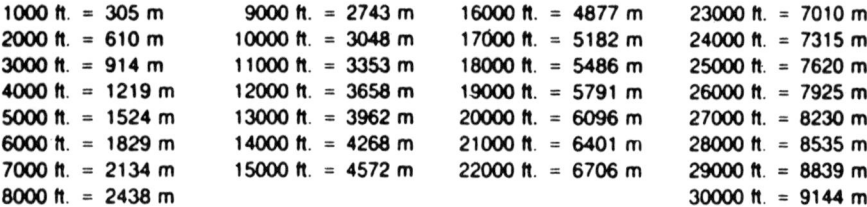

CENTIMETERS / INCHES

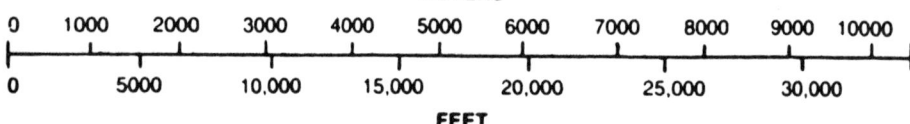

METERS / FEET

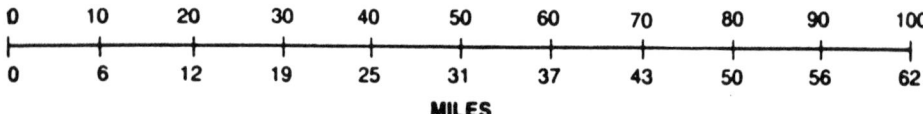

KILOMETERS / MILES

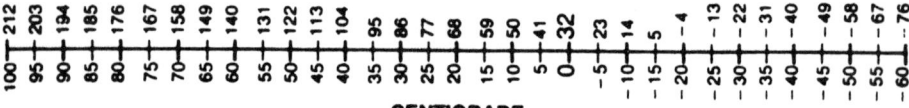

FAHRENHEIT / CENTIGRADE

Area Map--Black Rock Townsite, Railway Sidings, Area Mines & Volcanos

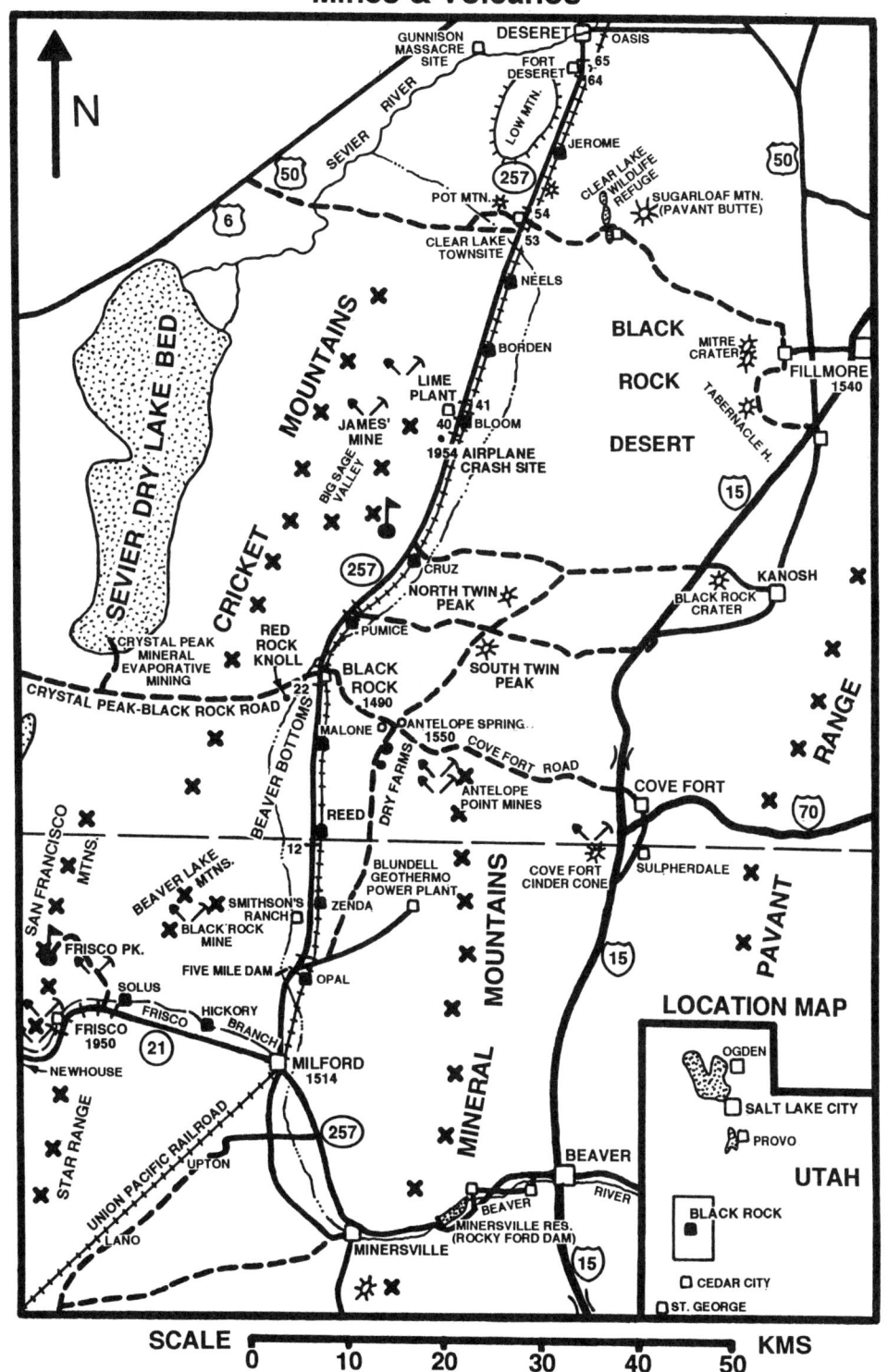

Chapter 1
Preface or Introduction

The story of how I got involved with this book began with my mother's family, Hyrum and Lovina Bond, and their move to and life in the little town of Clear Lake. It's a ghost town now, but it was located on the railroad line south of Delta and Deseret, west of Holden, and northwest of Fillmore. It was also the first town north of Black Rock. The town died in the mid-1930's, and everyone moved away. But most of mother's family stayed close by, and several members of her family worked on the railroad at or near Black Rock.

My first recollections of the region are of visiting Grandmother Bond in Meadow, and the black lava flows on the way to the old abandoned townsite of Clear Lake. This was back in the late 1940's when our family lived in Roosevelt. Besides the Bonds, my family roots on my mother's side have names like Adams, Bushnell, Brockbank and Dame, many of whom were early-day pioneers of Central Utah.

In the mid-1980's, I began urging my mother, Venetta Bond Kelsey, to do a little story on her home town. One reason for this was, all the books in print which have mentioned Clear Lake, had its history all wrong. Some dates were as much as 20-25 years off, and little of anything else was right. Also, everyone who had grown up there was getting old, and when they die, so goes the history. So she finally undertook the challenge and after 5 years of struggle, her book, **Life on the Black Rock Desert: A History of Clear Lake, Utah**, came out.

After that, I began urging her to do something on another little town just down the railway line a ways. Black Rock was also on the railroad, and settled about the same time as Clear Lake. Both towns were at or near a large desert spring which kept each town and one big ranch alive. Both were about the same size and both began and died about the same time. There were also only a few people alive who had lived or worked at Black Rock who could remember the place and who could help. The only problem was, Mother was heavily involved in writing her own family history, and that was more important.

Also, while doing the Clear Lake book, we found that one of the old timers who had owned the Clear Lake Hotel before the Bonds moved there in 1905, had left a dozen diaries with one of his grandchildren. This man's name was Jack Watson. He had been in Clear Lake in 1903 and ran the hotel for a time. He had also been out on the West Desert and built a cabin & store for sheepmen. He called the place **Ibex**, apparently after the Asian mountain goat or sheep. Jack's son, Tom Watson, married mother's cousin Mae Dame, so there was a tie between the two families after 1917.

With all these factors in mind, I finally decided to go ahead and do a book on the West Desert of Millard County myself. The center of attention was to be Jack Watson, his little sheep herder's cabin & store called Ibex, and the early day sheepmen of the desert. My original thoughts were to also include the histories of Black Rock, the Hermit of Marjum-- Bob Stinson, the Antelope Spring CCC Camp, the latest information on the Gunnison Massacre, and maybe repeat some history of Clear Lake and the volcanos of the Black Rock Desert. Also, a hiking and geology guide to west Millard County would be included. As it turned out, Black Rock didn't quite fit in with the West Desert so as of the beginning of 1996, I decided to do a small book just on the history of the little town Black Rock.

Hopefully at sometime in the future, a book on Jack Watson's Ibex and the West Desert of Millard County will be written, perhaps in the summer of 1996. That book will also include the Bob Stinson story, history of the Antelope CCC Camp, geology & fossils of the West Desert, and a hiking & mountaineering guide to West Millard County.

Chapter 2
History of the Region:
Up to 1879

Black Rock was a small railroad, sheep shearing, and ranching community located about 37 kms north of Milford. What's left of the town is next to the railroad tracks and Highway 257, both of which run between Milford on the south, and Deseret, Hinckley and Delta to the north. The town itself was built next to the railway, which runs north-south about one km west of several large springs. This waterhole has long been known as **Black Rock Springs.** It got that name because it comes out from under an ancient lava flow. This source of good water was the reason the land was homesteaded by white settlers early on, then for building the town after the railway passed through the region. Here then is the history of **Black Rock, Utah.**

The first people to live around the Black Rock Springs were Native Americans. Evidence of this is found along the low cliffs or bench under which several springs issue. These early travelers left a number of petroglyphs etched into the black lava rock. Most of these are located at or near the several springs and on the property of the Black Rock Ranch. Therefore this ancient graffiti is not accessible to the public. The first people who camped or lived at Black Rock were likely the ancestors of the Kanosh, Pavant, or Piute Indians, who live at or near Kanosh today.

Besides water for people, this spot would have provided a drinking place for wild animals such as deer, antelope, coyotes and foxes, as well as waterfowl. It must have been a little green paradise with shade trees and undoubtedly some edible plants. There may have been fish such as minnows as well, since these springs today put out about 3 second/feet of water, the equivalent of which will fit into an average irrigation ditch.

The first white men to see these springs may have been members of the **Dominguez & Escalante Expedition.** They set out from Santa Fe, New Mexico on July 29, 1776 and headed north through western Colorado, then west into Utah's Uinta Basin. Then it was up and over the Strawberry Country and down to Utah Lake by the end of September. They then headed south and camped in the vicinity of Clear Lake on October 1st and 2nd. By October 5, 1776, they camped the first of three nights near **Red Rock Knoll**, which is about 7 kms directly west of the Black Rock Springs.

However, this writer believes whoever translated the expedition's diary into English, then went out looking for these campsites, may have made a slight mistake. This is a desert location and while the best and easiest landmark to describe may have been Red Rock Knoll, it seems unimaginable that they would have camped so far away from the Black Rock Springs. During the first week of October, there likely wouldn't have been any water in the nearby Beaver River; or in the Beaver Bottoms, which is just south of Red Rock Knoll. The expedition camped in this area for 3 nights, **October 5, 6, and 7,** and surely their only source of water was from these springs. So it's likely they camped closer to Black Rock than to Red Rock Knoll.

From this campsite the expedition changed its plans because of a big snow storm and headed back to Santa Fe. They never reached their intended goal which was Southern California.

The first time Mormons knew of the existence of these springs may have been in the late 1860's. Keep in mind the Utah settlers had almost continuous troubles with Indians up until about 1868. That was the year which signaled the end of the **Black Hawk War**, which started in 1865. So up until 1868, there was hardly any exploring beyond the original settlements throughout Utah. Everybody stayed pretty close to home in those days because of the conflict with the Indians. On an 1866 map of the state of Utah, the only road shown in this entire region was the main track running from Salt Lake City south through the colonies to St. George; plus another minor track running from Fillmore to Deseret. Black Rock Springs isn't even shown on that map, indicating it may not have been known to the Mormons at that time(?).

In several books written about early Millard County history, it's mentioned that in about 1870, people from Fillmore and Beaver sent some of their milk cows out to Black Rock Springs to graze during the summer months. According to Benita James Burke, they used the cold spring water to preserve the milk until it could be made into butter or cheese. The first documented evidence of this comes from Volney King's diary. One paragraph states:

In June 1869. It was concluded to improve the premises at Black Springs on the sink of Beaver, & Fillmore sent 4 men with their teams to take large heavy poles like house logs down there with which to make large stock corrals. These 4 men were F. M. Lyman, Lorenzo Lyman, E. P. Marquandson & Wm Hatton. They went via Cove Creek where they loaded the poles & were gone 10 days. Mr. Ira N. Hinckley & John King living at Cove Creek rendered assistance.

It wasn't long after the first corrals were built and cows grazed at Black Rock Springs that someone decided to take up a homestead at the site. On an 1870 territorial survey map of the region, it shows a corral and a cabin and the name "Murdock Corral", located at the southern-most spring(now called the Big Spring, or sometimes the Railroad Spring), while at the northern spring(Tie House Spring), it shows a cabin and the name "Rodgers".

Regarding the name Murdock, Jim Kaufman who is presently part owner of the Black Rock Ranch, has a letter in his possession from a **John C. Murdock** dated June 18, 1957. John was a grandson of the fellow who built that corral and he originally sent the letter to Benita James Burke. Part of that letter gives us a peek into the life of the man who built that corral. It went like this:

My grandfather, as you probably are aware, had entered into a patriarchal marriage arrangement with two women, besides my grandmother, about 1862, and before he came to Beaver. When US Marshals were scouring that area for those guilty of unlawful cohabitation, it seems grandpa kept a fine high-spirited horse capable of endurance, and when he would receive wind from the underground that the marshals were about, he would mount his said charger and make his way with the utmost dispatch to Black Rock, there to keep discreetly out of sight until the danger had subsided.

Nothing more is known about this polygamist Murdock, but next to the Big Spring today, are some ruins of something that could be very old. Still standing next to the spring are three walls of a rock cabin, partially hidden down in the willows below the rim and in the little alcove from which the spring drains out of. It looks the same now as it did in pictures from 1949. This could well be Murdock's Cabin. Also, just upon the rim, maybe 20 meters away, is a bunch of rocks forming a square, which appears to be a foundation of some kind of building. This could also be rather old and possibly something belonging to Murdock(?).

In the Millard County courthouse records showing the land ownership of Section 22, T24S, R10W, the first name recorded was that of **Ammon L. Rappleye**. The entry shows he was given a Patent Deed by the United States on April 15, 1876. A **Patent Deed** means the very first deed issued by the US government, usually upon completion of homestead requirements. In those days, a family or individual had to live on and make significant improvement to 160 acres of land for 5 years, before a Patent Deed was issued. Going by this, Rappleye must have settled at Black Rock sometime in about 1871(?). After 5 years, the deed was then recorded for the first time. The next courthouse entry shows Rappleye selling his 160 acres to Millard County Cooperative Stock Company on December 2, 1876.

It was about this same time, around 1870, that the Black Rock Springs became an important waterhole and campsite for miners heading into the region surrounding what is today Milford. In the first years after the termination of the Black Hawk War, prospectors began roaming the West Desert of Utah looking for precious metals. The very first mineral discoveries in the Milford area were in the San Francisco Mountains southwest of Black Rock and northeast of the ghost town of Newhouse. The claims were made in 1870 and

Part of an old stone cabin next to the Big Spring. This could date from about 1870(?). The roof of the headhouse covering the Big Spring is in the upper left hand corner.

they later became the Cactus Mine in Copper Gulch. Most other mining districts in this region were set up or founded in 1871. In the winter of 1873-74, the first stamp mill was set up in the area that is today Milford, but it wasn't until the late 1870's that the region really began to boom. So gradually, beginning in the early 1870's, wagon roads began to appear for the first time around Black Rock..

The next maps of Utah were printed in 1874 and 1875. See the 1875 map Utah's West Desert on page 13. Both of these show Black Rock Springs, as well as several wagon roads. Also shown are the dozen or so mining districts, a proposed railway route, and a number of stagecoach stations marking the main route from Fillmore southwest to the mining areas in the Milford region, as well as to the towns of Panaca and Pioche in eastern Nevada. The springs at Black Rock were apparently not on the main stage route, but freighters were undoubtedly using it as a campsite at least as early as 1870 or 1871.

To better understand how Black Rock fit into the road system in those early days, let's look at the situation in eastern Nevada. Some time during the winter of 1863-64, William Hamblin, brother of Jacob Hamblin, was led by Indians to some mineral deposits in the mountains near present-day **Pioche**. In March, 1864, Hamblin returned with a group of miners and they immediately staked out several claims, then beat it for Salt Lake City to file them. At that time their claims were in the Utah Territory, but in 1866, the Utah-Nevada territorial boundary was changed to where it is today, putting Pioche in Nevada.

Also, in May of 1864, a group of Mormons from Southern Utah arrived in Meadow Valley, which is south of Pioche and north of present-day Caliente. They settled near some springs at the head of the valley and called the place **Panaca**. In the very beginning, the supply base for Panaca was Cedar City and St. George, but a short time later supplies began coming from Salt Lake City. Because of limited water supplies, Panaca never got very big, only 200-300 people throughout it's history; but they had a school, lumber and grist mill and a store by 1868. Here's a quote from the book, *A Century in Meadow Valley: 1864-1964:*

The settlers joined in organizing a co-op store which kept a complete stock of goods. Henry Lee recorded that merchandise "was brought from Salt Lake City, Utah, a distance of 350 miles [560 kms], by mule teams. Four teams of six mules each were on the road constantly as a month was required to make the trip to Salt Lake and return." This indicates there was some kind of a wagon road from Pioche and Panaca through the Black Rock area to Fillmore as early as 1868.

Pioche first got a smelter in 1869, which marked the beginning of mining. In 1870 the boom began. The mines reached their high water mark in 1873, then came the bust by 1876. Since that time, Pioche has been up and down throughout its history, but the first half of the 1870's was its real boom period. Going by the figures quoted in the book, *Lincoln County, Nevada: 1864-1909*, it's believed the first stages began rolling out of eastern Nevada in the early 1870's. Freighting to and from Salt Lake also increased greatly at this same time.

By looking at the map on page 13, we see stagecoach stations along the route. It appears Black Rock was not on this main road, but was undoubtedly used by freighters going to various mining districts in the immediate area. The closest stagecoach station to Black Rock was at **Antelope Spring**, which is located about 10 kms to the southeast. According to Hampton(Hamp) Burke, the man who married Benita James of Black Rock: *Nothing was there when I came here in 1929, but before I came they used to have a great big barn, a stagecoach station, a saloon and whore house. It wasn't a ranch, just a stage stop. They had hay and grain there for the teams. The road used to come down through Meadow, Kanosh, and into Antelope Springs and then crossed someplace right up through here[Milford], and went to Pioche. That was the old stage route.*

Other sources generally agree with Hamp Burke about Antelope Spring, but most leave out the part about the whore house! Also, at a later date the main stage route was changed and it went through Petersburg, near present-day Hatton, rather than past White Mountain, as is indicated on the 1874 and 1875 maps.

With major stage and freight wagon roads established, the next big event to happen at Black Rock, was the coming of the railroad. One reason for bringing the railroad to this region was the heavy concentration of valuable ore bodies and mining. Very briefly, here is short history of the beginnings of one of Utah's legendary mining boom towns. In 1871, the San Francisco Mining District was organized in San Francisco Mountains west and northwest of present-day Milford. In 1875, a rich ore body, mainly silver, was discovered on the east side of the range. A year later the **Horn Silver Mine** became the richest of them all and a small town developed around the previous camp. This mining camp was called **Frisco**, and by 1880 it was a full-sized mining boom town. More later.

Old 1875 Map: Black Rock Region, Stagecoach Stations & Utah's West Desert

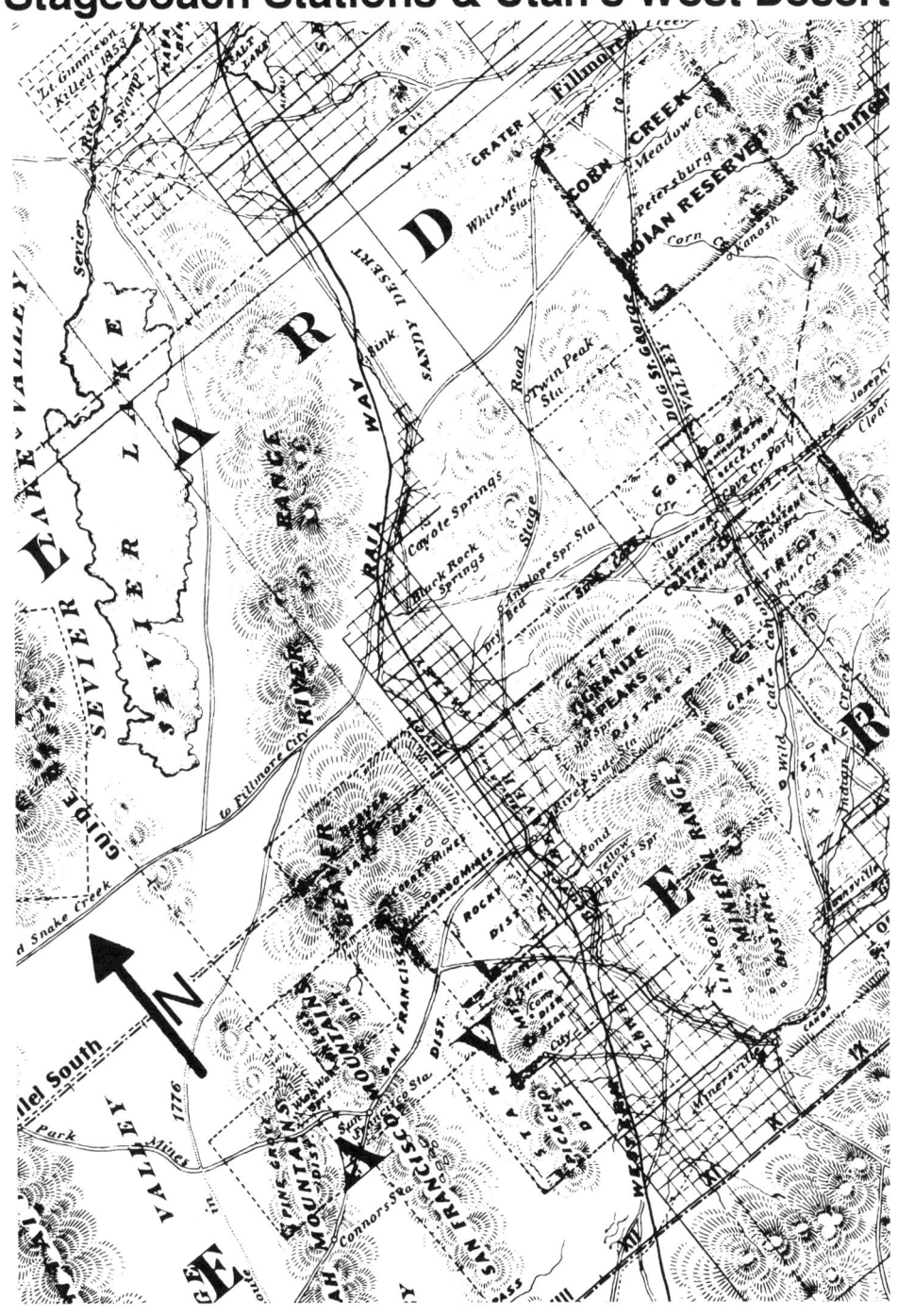

Chapter 3
History of the Black Region: From 1880 to about 1901

On May 10, 1869, the last rail was laid at Promontory Point, Utah, completing the first transcontinental railroad. Brigham Young and the Mormons had been involved with railroad building before the lines actually reached Utah, because they realized the value of greatly improved transportation of goods and services between their settlements. When Ogden was chosen as the terminal of the rails instead of Salt Lake City, little time was lost in organizing and building another line running south from Ogden. On January 10, 1870, the line to Salt Lake City was completed, then plans were begun to extend rails south through all the Wasatch Front communities. By September 1871, the main line running south reached Sandy, then the Point of the Mountain in August, 1872. The line was then extended to Lehi, American Fork and finally to Provo by November of 1873.

As enthusiasm increased and finances became available, still more extensions were planned. In 1871, the San Francisco Mining District was begun in the area west of what is today Milford. In 1875, a rich silver ore body was discovered, and in 1876, the **Horn Silver Mine** began operations. A small town grew up nearby and was called **Frisco**. Partly because of these big strikes, and the potential for a big mining boom in the **San Francisco Mountains**, money was easily raised and the railroad headed south for Frisco. This was to be the first leg of the railroad going to Southern California, and the newly discovered mining area was just an added bonus.

Again using gentile money and Mormon labor, the Utah Southern Railroad reached York near Santaquin in February, 1875. It's extension reached Chicken Creek in Juab County by June of 1879. Later that year the rails reached Mud Lake a few kms north of Clear Lake, then stopped for the winter; but the teams making the railroad grade were way out in front of the track layers. One of the best sources of information about building the railroad to Black Rock, Milford and Frisco comes from the diary of **Abraham A. Kimball**. He was a good Mormon, inside and out, who lived in Kanosh and had worked with teams laying a grade for the railroad in the area south of Deseret until late November, 1879, then headed south to Kanosh for the winter. Before winter fully set in, he made a quick trip to Black Rock to make plans for work in the spring. On **December 8, 1879,** he left Kanosh very early and:

About sun down we arrived at Black Rock Springs (Co-op Ranch) expecting to find the [railroad] Surveyors there but they had gone up the [Beaver] River. Webb was at the Ranch establishing a trading post for Bishop Callister to supply Rail Road teams so we obtained quarters for ourselves & horses, awful cold & windy.

December 10th *After breakfast we set out for Smiths Ranch some 6 miles [10 kms] distance, on arriving there the Surveyors had just set out to work so we found them all along the line. We found the Chief Jesse W. Fox at Lumroeaus Ranch or Riverside Station where we got some dinner & remained all day boarding with the Surveyors, received the promise of a job of grading [next spring].*

What this short statement tells us is that the main ranch at Black Rock Springs in December, 1879, was owned and operated by a cooperative of the LDS Church. They were also in the process of setting up a store for the first time. The need for building a store would have been the direct result of the coming of the railroad.

The next spring, Kimball returned to do grading work, but he began at Yellow Banks Stage Station about 3 kms north of present-day Milford. See the 1875 map on page 13. In his diary, Kimball seldom mentions where the track layers were, only where the graders were building up the railroad bed. Briefly jumping ahead, the first passenger train arrived at Milford on May 15, 1880, so we can assume the tracks were first laid to Clear Lake in

March, and to Black Rock sometime in **April, 1880**.

Before going further into the Black Rock story, a little more history of Frisco and Milford is in order. Kimball also helped finish the railroad grade right up to Frisco. He was like a private contractor of today and he ran a crew of men & teams with scrapers. He also had a few choice comments about the situation at Yellow Banks, gentile swearing, Milford and Frisco, that are worth mentioning. His last camp was very near Frisco. Parts of his diary went like this:

***Antelope Spring Sunday March 7th 1880** Arose early,... arriving at Yellow Banks 3 p.m. where our job was,.... spent afternoon in fitting up camp by tearing down an old log house & putting up the same, also putting up tent.*

***Yellow Banks March 8th** The boys arrived with hay & grain from the end of the track so after dinner the boys went up the river to shut off the water as it was ruining our job.... Some of the boys was inclined to profane the name of god so I proposed to them that the ones who done the swearing should do the praying which was agreed to. I was surprised to find that in one week's time the swearing was about done away with. So much so that I had to offer prayer occasionally myself....*

***Thursday April 8th 1880** ....Moved camp to **Milford** 2 1/2 miles [4 kms] to commence another job, worked hard all day moving, put up a good camp and was awful tired. Milford is a town consisting of one Quartz Mill, one Smelter & some 12 houses & one store & saloon & one barn and several camps of railroad [workers]....*

***Wednesday May 19th 1880** Went to Frisco which is a noted mining camp but of low grade society, mostly Irish [and] 5 to 8 hundred inhabitants.....*

***Sunday May 30th 1880** .....returned at dinner time, found cook & all gone from home so I shaped dinner for 5 of us, then went out to see the bears dance as some Italians came along with two trick bears, all went off nicely, good dancing.....*

***Sunday June 13th 1880** After breakfast washed & cleaned up & set out for the Bonanza Mine one of the greatest bodies of ore known..... Then hitched our team up and drove to Frisco where we called at the post office, also done a little trading as the stores were in full blast failing to observe the Sabbath day, being a mining camp composed of Jack Mormons, Jews & Gentiles.*

***Near Frisco June 17th** Commenced loading up to start home so after dinner the teams set out for Milford, the cook (Miss Prons) set out for the cars to ride down on them. On arriving I met J. W. Fox, Surveyor so he wished me to return to Frisco with him so we proceeded on train to my old camp & from thence by waggon to lay out the depot which was accomplished at the bottom end of Main St..... The engine had gone to Milford taking cook so the construction boss (Watson) said we could take a couple of flat cars down having to brake being heavy grade..... Making the trip in 37 minutes some 13 miles [21 kms] without aid of steam [engine].*

During this time and until about 1885, Frisco had many shops and houses, also a hotel, a butcher shop, a dance hall which served as a town meeting place and for church services, a school and a newspaper. Peak population was 6000. In 1884, there was a collapse of the main tunnel in the Horn Silver, but another one was dug. The really big boom at Frisco lasted until about 1885, then slowly faded. More will be said about Frisco later in this story, but it's important to know that this town and the Horn Silver Mine was the terminus of the Utah Southern Railroad extension for over 20 years. It was also the magnet for all of the earliest settlers who made Black Rock their home.

Now back to Black Rock's history. Courthouse abstract book records are often confusing. The dates shown are filing dates only, and many times don't give a clue as to when a person actually bought or moved onto the property; or if someone ever actually lived on the place! In the abstract book for Section 22, T24S, R10W, we see 160 acres being obtained by **James H. Hedges** on a Patent Deed in 1884, but the same land was sold to **William L. Raht** on November 26, 1881(?). Perhaps it was sold by Hedges before he completed his homestead requirements and actually got the deed? This same William L. Raht also homesteaded and obtained a Patent Deed to another quarter section in Section 22 in 1888.

Courthouse records indicate that Hedges, then Raht, got the land where the main Black Rock Ranch House is today, next to what is called the **Ranch House Spring**. He also got the land next to the **Big Spring**, just south of the main ranch house. The quarter section--160 acres--that Rappleye homesteaded in 1876(see last chapter) was just to the north of Hedges' and Raht's land. It extended west in a narrow strip for the length of the section(one mile), from what is the **Tie House** or **Farm House Spring** of today, and down to where the railroad depot would later be built. Eight months after Rappleye got his Patent Deed, he sold his land to the Millard County Co-op Stock Company for $350. This is believed to be what Kimball called the **Co-op Ranch** in his diary.

Because of increased business from miners, and especially the coming of the railroad, the Millard County Co-op apparently built a store there, perhaps near the Tie House Spring(?). In 1880, the Utah Southern Railroad Extension bought out the Co-op Ranch and they used the water from the Tie House Spring for their locomotives from1880 until sometime in the early 1900's. It's believed the water from the Tie House Spring went to the original water tank located between Walter James' store & hotel, and the shearing barns(which were built in about 1900 or 1901?). See the picture on page 26.

The railroad also bought the water rights to the Big Spring, perhaps in about 1905(?) when they completed the rail line from Los Angeles to Salt Lake. The Big Spring is where they got the majority of their water throughout the years. Water from the Big Spring was piped down to the newer tank, which was built near where the depot would later be constructed. See map on page 81. After 1880, whoever had the Ranch, got only the water the railroad didn't use. Jumping ahead in our story a little, later in time Walter James got the 160 acres, but not all the water. Much, much later, the Ranch eventually got all the water from both the Tie House and Big Springs.

For years, much of the drinking water for all the railroad sidings between Clear Lake and Frisco was shipped from Black Rock. The people who lived in Clear Lake remembered water coming from Black Rock was always the best. For about 75 years the railroad used a good deal of the water from the Tie House and Big Springs at Black Rock.

Many years later, and after her father Walter James died, **Benita James Burke**, wrote a history of Black Rock for the Daughters of the Utah Pioneers(DUP) book, *100 Years of History of Millard County*. She also wrote a little family history of **Walter James**, which has many more details of Black Rock's history than in the previously mentioned book. She obviously didn't have all the details or dates and probably didn't investigate courthouse records. However, she probably got the main dates and the leading characters right as the story of the **Black Rock Ranch** was handed down to her as family oral history. Here is the first part of the history of the Ranch by Benita James Burke:

At the time, there was lush pasture land adjacent to the Beaver River, as well as near the springs. The next owner of the ranch was James Hedges, father of Allen Hedges, now retired, but a well-known detective[or special agent] for the Union Pacific Railroad Company. In 1881, the property was sold by Mr. Hedges to William Raht, chemist and assayer for the Horn Silver Mine, Frisco, Utah. During the time of Raht's ownership the ranch was operated by his daughter and son-in-law, **Mr. and Mrs. John B. Travers.** *Later his youngest daughter and her husband,* **Mr. and Mrs. Willard Burbank** *managed the place. In 1910, Mr. Raht sold out to his [other] son-in-law,* **Walter James.**

Please note that date 1910. This is the date that appears in the book mentioned above. However, in another copy of the same story, the date is shown as **1901**. Going back to the Millard County abstract book, it shows Walter James' name appearing for the first time along with the date March 8. 1901. This seems likely the date they first signed a sales agreement, but it wasn't filed until later. Later, perhaps when the debt was paid off, there are filing dates on several pieces of land in Section 22 in the years 1904 and 1905. The date of the actual sale or agreement is always prior to the filing date, so it seems the March 8, 1901 date would be the correct one(?). The sale price appears to have been $7,000.

Before going on to the Walter James story, something should be said about the Raht Family, little as it may be, who owned the Ranch for about 20 years. Using tidbits of information from many sources, including obituaries in old newspapers, one letter by Clara Raht Schindler belonging to the Kaufmans, presently of Black Rock, and a genealogy sheet titled *The Raht Family Tree*, the original of which belongs to Elise McMillen Brougham of Wheat Ridge, Colorado, here is what we know of that side of the family.

The name William Lewis Raht appears in the abstract book in the Millard County Courthouse in several places. But according to the family group sheet his name was **Wilhelm Raht** and he was born April 18, 1834, in Wiesbaden, Germany. He came to America at about age 19 and apparently changed his name to William, perhaps the Americanized version of Wilhelm(?). William married a woman named **Sophia Florence Geisse**, who was born in Dillenburg, Germany, on February 2, 1836. They were married in Cleveland, Tennessee on June 15, 1859. William was employed in machine shops at Pierpont, New York before they were married, then later was in charge of some copper mines and smelters at Duckdown, Tennessee during the Civil War. During this time he was detailed by the Confederacy to keep some mines operating, but during November or December of 1863, he and his family, accompanied by a friend, ran the blockade to Cincinnati, Ohio. William eventually died December 29, 1914(?) in San Diego, California. Sophia died May 18, 1912, in Seattle, Washington.

The William Raht's had 5 children. The oldest was named **Wilhelmina Raht** who was born in 1860. She went by the more common American name, **Minnie**. More on her below. Next was **Carl Raht** who was born in 1861, and who died in 1929. His last address was in Salt Lake City, and he apparently never married. Then came **Helen Raht** who was born in 1864. Helen is the one who married **Walter James**, who was two years younger than her. This couple was destined to be the two most prominent people in the history of Black Rock. At one time the Raht family lived in Nashville, Tennessee, because one foto still exists of Helen Raht when she was there as a little girl about 6 years of age.

After Helen, the next child was **Clara Raht**, born in 1868. She eventually married **Robert Schindler**, and their last address was in Medford, Oregon. Throughout the years, and going through the old newspapers, nothing is mentioned of either Carl or Clara. Apparently neither of them stayed close to home and it seems they had nothing to do with

From the Black Rock Ranch looking west toward the railroad. Early 1900's.
(Elise M. Brougham collection)

the Black Rock Ranch.

The last of the family was **Elise Raht**, born in 1869. Elise later married **Willard Burbank**, whose family appears to have been among the earliest settlers in the little farming community known as Burbank, which was located south of Garrison near the Utah-Nevada state line. The Burbanks had two children; **Sidney Raht Burbank**, born in 1891; and **Margaret Burbank**, born in 1897. Margaret later married a **Bert Scott**.

Sidney and Margaret Burbank were close friends of the children of the Walter James family, and their names appear quite often in the old newspapers when the families would visit each other. Willard & Elise lived and worked at the Black Rock Ranch throughout the 1890's, and it was they who were running the ranch when Walter & Helen R. James bought the place in about 1901. No one knows for sure, but they likely stayed at the Ranch for several years after the James bought the place. Later it seems they lived in the settlement of Burbank for a time. Throughout the years there was close contact between the Burbanks and the James' at Black Rock.

When farming and ranching at Burbank was finally given up some time in the 1910's(?), Willard & Elise ended up in the Seattle, Washington area, where Willard died in 1931, and Elise in March, 1932.

According to the information above written by Benita James Burke, it was Helen Raht's oldest sister, Minnie who married **John B. Travers**. Apparently they were the ones living at and running the Black Rock Ranch in the 1880's, then some time in the 1890's, Willard & Elise Burbank ran it up until the time Walter & Helen bought the place.

No one is alive in the 1990's who knows anything about the situation at Black Rock during that time period, but the genealogy sheet on the Rahts gives us some clues. It appears that John B. Travers and Minnie Raht must have been married around 1880, because their first child **William R. Travers** was born in 1882. He later married a Clara Sue. William died in 1920 and Clara's last address was Provo, Utah. Then there was **Albert R. Travers**, born in 1884. No other information is available on him. Their 3rd child was **Minnie Travers**, born in 1887, but who died in 1919, apparently unmarried.

None of the three children above seems to have had anything to do with the Black Rock Ranch, except that they must have lived there as children. However, the last child of John & Minnie definitely had a long lasting connection. Their 4th child was **Jack Boyle Travers**, who was born in 1890. His mother also died that same year, very likely at childbirth(?). Baby Jack was taken in by his Aunt Helen Raht, who later married Walter James on January 14, 1892. Surviving family members still alive today will tell you that Walter James was well aware of little Jack's predicament, and agreed to raise him even before they were married. For all intent and purposes, Jack Travers was the first child of Walter and Helen R. James, although he always kept his father's name of Travers.

In this time period before 1901, there were other transactions and Raht got more land than his original 160 acres. Raht was a chemist and may or may not have ever lived there himself. It appears that he turned the Ranch over to his sons-in-law to run. Today there is no documentation on him except that he died in 1914, perhaps in California.

With the introduction of Walter James into this story, this is a good place to stop and go back in time and take a look into the James family. Benita James Burke continues with the story of the Thomas & Ann Phillips James family up to when Walter & Helen purchased the Black Rock Ranch in 1901:

Walter James was born May 27, 1866 in Baltimore, Maryland. His mother, Mrs. Ann Phillips James, left Baltimore that year for California where she planned to meet her husband, Thomas James, who had preceded her. The mother and baby traveled by boat from Baltimore to the Isthmus of Panama, which was crossed on the back of a mule, the little son being clasped tightly in his mother's arms. Another boat trip up the Pacific Coast to San Francisco was followed by a stagecoach trip to Port Wine, California, where the family remained for several years.

News reached them of greener pastures in Utah, hence, after a long hazardous trip the family settled in Silver City, Utah, [which is just south of Eureka], which was a lively mining town. Walter's father being an expert butcher, he realized there would be a livelihood from selling meat in a locality where hundreds of men were being employed and their boarding houses would consume large quantities of meat. As other towns sprang into prominence the family moved to them. Some other places they lived at were Silver Reef, [northeast of St. George], Kimberly, [northwest of Marysvale], and Pioche, Nevada; then Murray and Sandy near Salt Lake City, and at last **Frisco, Utah**, where tne family lived for the longest period of time. Some of the eleven James children were born and raised at Frisco.

[Here's a brief rundown on the all the children of Thomas and Ann James. Elisabeth was the first born but she only lived for 5 months. Next was Walter, and he was always considered the oldest in the family. Then Hannah, born in 1869, and Daniel in 1870. These two were born in Port Wine, California. Then while living in Northern Utah, John was born in 1874, Henrietta, or Retta, in 1875, and William, born in 1877, but he apparently died at or near birth. These 3 were born in West Jordan. The last 4 children were born in Frisco. They include, Thomas born in June, 1882, but who died in April of 1883. He is buried in the Frisco cemetery and his gravestone is still there. Next was Ernest, born in 1884, and finally the twins, Arthur Garfield and Albert Lincoln James. Albert was always known as Bert, and Authur was usually referred to as AG or Art. They were born on September 30, 1886. Thomas and Ann had 11 children, but raised only 8 to full maturity.]

Once in Frisco, the family immediately launched into the slaughter house business, and Walter's mother operated a hotel. Thomas James realized there was abundant forage for stock and the range was free. Cattle were purchased with the idea of raising cattle and thus having their own beef for the slaughter house and butcher shop. Walter assumed care of the cattle, and as was hoped for, the cattle would fatten on the range and could be brought direct to the slaughter house for butchering. A thriving business was built up.

One day when Walter was driving down Frisco's one street his eyes rested on a very young girl, who apparently was a newcomer to the town. She had two long beautiful golden braids hanging down her back. Walter made the remark to his companion, "That's the girl I hope to marry some day". The girl, [Helen Raht], now bears the name of Mrs. Walter James.

The severe winter of 1889 all but exterminated the cattle herd, though Walter, as reported by his brother Dan, made heroic efforts to save some of the stock. However, the 32° below zero temperatures with little variation for six weeks, took a heavy toll of all southern Utah cattle herds. Later many critters were found dead in a standing position under cedar trees where the animals had sought protection.

One instance Walter often related which will give some idea of the severity of the weather is as follows: Walter and Dan were endeavoring to move whatever cattle might be located. Dan was instructed to remain in a crude cabin and keep up a roaring fire while Walter made a search. When he returned to the cabin the horse was unsaddled, blanketed and fed before he entered the warm cabin. A short time afterward the horse lost most of his hair except where the saddle sat. Apparently the outer skin of the horse had frozen causing the hair to loosen.

Helen Raht, daughter of William L. Raht, and Walter James were married January 14, 1892 in Frisco where they lived for a short time. A homestead was filed upon at Black Rock, Utah, by the young couple and an old frame dance hall, owned by Henry Bowen, was moved from Frisco to Black Rock. It was a sorry looking sight to be used as a home for a bride.

The dance hall that was moved to Black Rock was placed on land in Section 15, not in Section 22 in which the Black Rock Ranch is located. It appears it was moved from Frisco in about 1892 some time, while either the John B. Travers, or more likely the Willard Burbank family, was living at and running the Ranch just to the east.

Now back to the combined story Benita James Burke wrote about Black Rock and Walter James. In places the two stories have been combined:

About this time what appeared to be a renumerative proposition was made to the young couple. They were to live in a mountain cabin in the vicinity of Kimberly, and Mr. James to have charge of the mine work and Mrs. James to cook for the men. Aside from

The Black Rock store & hotel, mid-1890's. This was the old Henry Bowen's Dance Hall from Frisco. This foto appears to include Helen Raht James, Jack Travers and the baby Benita James on the burro. Notice the Cellar to the right. (Kelsey collection)

the dull monotony of daily meals and of course no household conveniences, there was no diversion except to have a niche cut from the snow around the windows and see a bit of sunshine now and then. For six months Mrs. [Helen R.] James did not see a woman or child and knew she was virtually a prisoner. The snow being very deep and she knew nothing of using snowshoes as did the men who went to Joseph for food supplies. She often speaks of the cheery dispositions displayed by John James, Walter's younger brother who spent the winter with them at the mine. When spring came one of the owners left for parts unknown with whatever money had been made and Mr. and Mrs. James were a bit wiser and very short of money.

They returned to the desolate homestead at Black Rock and a few head of cattle on the range. After living at Black Rock for a while the young couple noted that quite a number of large flocks of sheep passed through Black Rock on their way to the winter range and that the flocks ranged to the south, north and east of Black Rock. Mr. James realized that the various camps would be in need of supplies, particularly hay and grain for their horses. At that time the men in sheep camps lived on a very meager diet consisting mostly of sour-dough bread, sorghum and mutton, but Mr. James had an idea that a mercantile business could be built up. In 1893, Mr. and Mrs. Walter James started a mercantile business about a mile [1 1/2 kms] west of the Ranch, next to the railroad.

He went by train to Salt Lake City and contacted several wholesale houses, though he had little to offer as security except a strong body and plenty of ambition. He was assured of goods being furnished so he returned home.

To illustrate just how little buying was done at first, Mr. James said a case of milk lasted a year. The men who were in charge of the camps made their purchases with utmost care and thought.

Little by little the business increased as the men realized that Mr. James made every effort to have in stock whatever they needed. Comfortable beds and wholesome home cooked meals were available and a real treat to men who had been doing their own cooking. It was not unusual for a customer to lay a one hundred dollar order on the counter, exclusive of oats. By bed time the order would be filled and standing on the counter. Of course there were no demands on the part of the customer such as "I do not want that brand", or "that size can please". He took what was furnished. The shepherds spent their evenings writing replies, and occasionally rolling dice to see who paid for the candy and nuts which they munched on during conversations that included news from their homes, range and weather conditions, etc. Mr. James had the first post office, something for which the shepherds were very thankful. [The first post office was set up at Black Rock on April 1, 1891. It's not known who the first post master was, but it may have been Walter James.]

Mr. and Mrs. James were always hospitable to their customers, though many times late at night when the sound of an approaching team could be heard, Mrs. James would be weary from a long working day, yet the driver found warm food and his team was cared for. Many an injured hand and foot was cared for, and a few "tummy aches", too.

The store had a small room on the south which served as a post office. The north end of the store had a partial partition. On all sides of this department were shelves containing work shoes and work clothing. The rafters in the main part of the store were generously perforated with hooks and nails from which hung pots, pans, skillets, coffee pots, spurs, halters, bridles and sheep & horse bells. In the middle of the room was a large, wood burning stove surrounded by benches which served as a lounging place for the men during their one evening in town. The next morning would find them perched on a heavily loaded wagon headed for the desert for another four or five weeks of isolation.

Mr. James purchased many tons of oats from John White and William Bond who operated farms in the vicinity of what is now called Reed. When they delivered the oats, Mr. James would say, "Weigh up the grain boys and bring in your figures". A check for the same was handed to him or perhaps they took some of their pay in groceries. It never occurred to anyone to check on the weights and when dealing with such men there was no need to doubt their word at any time. The above is a perfect demonstration of honor and trust that existed between many men in the old days. While there was little time for visiting in the busy life of Mrs. James, she valued the friendship of Mrs. Matty Armstrong, Mrs. John White and Mrs. William Bond--all three of these ladies were still living in the 1940's.

The mercantile business grew steadily until it became necessary for Mr. James to have an efficient bookkeeper and clerk. So the services of Mr. William Burbank, brother of Mrs. E. W. Clay--a grand old lady of ninety-four years--who resided in Snake Valley, was hired. Among the help hired by Mr. James to assist him in the store business from time to time were: the three Bellander brothers, William Travers, and the late Ernest Winkler--well known assistant regional forester of Ogden, a most efficient helper. The money earned at Black Rock by Mr. Winkler made possible the education that paved the way for the position he held in the Forestry office. John James, E. W. Clay and [adopted son] Jack Travers were willing and efficient helpers from time to time.

The business being in such able hands, gave Mr. James the opportunity to branch out so he engaged in buying and selling of sheep and eventually bought a herd for himself, which he operated for some time. Finally selling out and following the purchase of the late Mrs. Ketchum's holdings in Pine Valley which consisted of springs and range, Mr. James and Mr. E. W. Clay went into the sheep business on a larger scale. Later Mr. James bought Mr. Clay out and operated the flocks for himself.

It was at about this time, 1901, that Walter & Helen Raht James purchased the Black Rock Ranch. To review briefly, they set up a store in 1893, then gradually built it and a sheep business up in the 8 years before 1901. It was during this time period before 1901, that Helen had two of their three daughters. **Benita** was born on January 30, 1894 in a Salt Lake City hospital(perhaps Holy Cross?). She was named after one of the Italian nurses there named **Beniti**. Her name is officially spelled Beniti, but everyone always called here Benita or Benny. The next daughter was **Thekla**, who was born on April 30,

1898. And as previously mentioned, **Jack Travers** was born in 1890, and he was the oldest child raised by Walter & Helen R. James.

It's not known when **school** was first held at Black Rock, but it is known to have been in operation in the fall of 1899. Carl Neilson, a 50 year sheep herding veteran of the West Desert, tells a little about it, as well as a lot of other stories, in the next chapter, from 1901 to 1916. Briefly, he states the person teaching there in 1899 was **Mrs. Willard (Elise Raht) Burbank**, who was Helen Raht James' sister, and very likely Black Rock's first school teacher. The Burbanks were running the Ranch at the time and it's likely school was taught there. In Benita's history of Black Rock, she states: *Mr. and Mrs. Walter James were staunch supporters of the small school that was maintained for over forty years, but was closed during the first year of World War II [in the fall of 1942]. Miss Nellie Holbrook of Fillmore was one of the first teachers of the little school. There were other young women from Millard County who taught there. Also Walter's wife Helen Raht James and her sister, Mrs. Willard Burbank. The three daughters of Mr. and Mrs. Walter James received their early schooling at the little school.*

In later years it was Walter & Helen R. James who donated a small building to be used as Black Rock's school, so a good guess is that the original school would have been of their making. Jack Travers would have been of school age in about 1896 or 1897, and Benita by about 1899 or 1900. Earlier in life, Helen Raht and her two younger sisters, Clara and Elise, all had good educations at St. Mary's Academy in Salt Lake City. The Rahts were a well-educated family, which rubbed off onto their children and grandchildren, as we will see later in this story.

Not a lot is known about the **railroad** during this period from 1880 to 1901. There was no station or depot building, but at some point in time they had what was called a depot, or a place to buy a ticket, which was in an old railroad car on a side track. There were some passenger trains running from Salt Lake City to Milford and Frisco, but it's likely not many people were getting on or off at Black Rock. There just weren't that many people around at that time; and not that many sheep to be shipped in or out.

In the very beginning, when the railroad was being built, they apparently had a "Y" junction at Black Rock. This was a temporary system of side tracks extending west from the main line a ways, which allowed trains to turn around without the use of a roundhouse or turntable. Faint signs of that grade can still be seen there today.

They also had a major siding or side track there ever since the railroad went through Black Rock, because they owned and used some of the water from the Tie House and Big Springs all this time. This means there must have been some railway workers there to operate the water tank, the siding, maybe telegraph operators and probably section workers who maintained the rail line. They may have lived in railway cars placed on what they call a "house track".

There were also some freight trains which carried sheep & cattle, hides & wool, and consumer goods for Milford and Frisco, and of course ore from the mines. At this time it appears very little was shipped in or out of Black Rock. There were shipping corrals and a chute, and two big sheep shearing barns built by the railroad, but those may have come right at the end of this period, or the at the beginning of the next chapter. It's believed they were built in about 1900 or 1901, at about the same time Walter James bought the Ranch.

Thomas and Ann Phillips James, left. Perhaps 1870's or 1880's(?). Also, the twins Albert(Bert) and Arthur(AG) James in the early 1890's. (R. Bobbie James collection)

Walter James, in about the 1890's(R. Bobbie James foto), and Helen Raht James, 1896. (Elise M. Brougham collection)

Helen Raht (James), left, in about 1870 in Nashville, Tenn. (Elise M. Brougham collection), and Minnie Raht Travers in the 1880's. (Inez B. Travers Beers collection)

Clara Raht Schindler, Frisco, 1888, left, and Clara Raht Schindler holding Benita James in front of the James store & hotel, Black Rock, 1894. (Elise M. Brougham collection)

Benita James, upper left, then Sydney Burbank(upper right and far right). Lower left is Margaret Burbank, and Thekla James. Left foto from 1898 or 1899. Sydney's foto, about 1910. The Willard & Elise Raht Burbank children grew up at Black Rock in the 1890's and probably early 1900's.
(Elise M. Brougham collection)

Benita James (Burke) in baby carriage on south side of Black Rock store & hotel, 1894.
(Elise M. Brougham collection)

Jack Travers and his dog "Badger" at Black Rock, 1894. (Elise M. Brougham collection)

A very old, early-day water tank at Black Rock. Looking south from a point between the store & hotel and the shearing barns. (Elise M. Brougham collection)

Chapter 4
Black Rock from about 1901 to 1916

This chapter begins at the time when **Walter & Helen Raht James** bought the Black Rock Ranch, which is about one km east of where the townsite of Black Rock was located along the railroad tracks. This original transaction is thought to have been in March of 1901. At that time, the Ranch was officially owned by William L. Raht, but was being run by his son-in-law and daughter, **Willard & Elise Raht Burbank**. They had two children, Syney and Margaret. These two were about the same age as Jack Travers and Thekla James. For a time after the sale took place, the Burbanks stayed there and ran the Ranch, but sometime later apparently went west to the tiny settlement of Burbank, located next to Utah-Nevada state line south of Garrison and at the extreme south end of the Snake Valley. Without knowing a lot about the history of Burbank, it is assumed that some of Willard's relatives lived out there. It wasn't until 1915 that old newspapers are available which documents people's movements in the area, but by about 1915 or 1916 the Burbanks seem to have been living in the Seattle, Washington area. The Burbank post office ran from 1881 until 1919, indicating that community was being abandoned during this time period.

When the sale of the Ranch took place it's not certain whether or not the Walter James family moved up there, or continued to live down at the townsite. It's believed they stayed at their home which was in the store & hotel building, at least for a few years.

Continuing now with Benita James Burke's story of Walter James: *The mercantile business had continued to increase and also the number of sheep wintering in the valleys and hills adjacent to Black Rock increased. From conversations with various sheep owners Mr. James knew that a large shearing corral would be welcomed by the owners of various flocks. The sheep would thus be able to make the long trail to the lambing grounds in San Pete County minus their heavy and often wet fleece. The many pounds of wool would be right at a shipping point, all of which was to the sheep owner's advantage.*

Some time just after the turn of the century and apparently about the time he bought the Ranch, Walter James made several trips to Salt Lake City where he had interviews with the railroad officials. A bit hesitant to grasp the picture as Mr. James painted it, they at last did start action on two large shearing sheds equipped with corrals, shearing pens, chutes and a wool-sacking platform. At that time all the shearing was done by hand clippers and for several years the crew consisted of at least two hundred men. The railroad company was pleased with the extra freight business created by shipping the wool. One spring, a million pounds of wool was shipped to various points, but most of it was shipped to Boston, Massachusetts.

When the shearing business became a reality the railroad had need for a telegrapher and his telegraph machine, hence one more corner of the already crowded store [was used]. A small table served as a desk for the telegrapher and his telegraph machine. When the shearing season was ended, the telegraph office was dispensed with until the following spring. Having launched the sheep shearing business, Mr. James had prompted a project that was helpful and profitable to all concerned. To give help and advice was an outstanding part of Walter and Mrs. James' lives.

One of the original old time sheep herders in the country west of Black Rock was **Carl Nielson** from Fairview, Utah, in Sanpete County. In 1947, and near the end of his sheep herding days, he wrote a little story called *Home on the Range*. In it he tells about the early days at Black Rock and his sheep herding experiences. Much of his story fits in well in this time period from about 1901 through 1916. Here's part of his story:

During my 49 years experience in handling sheep on our western Utah desert of which Juab, Millard and Beaver counties are an important part, my operations have been about 90 percent in Millard and Beaver Counties. A great many changes have taken place in those 49 years of which I have spent at least part of every winter, and many times the entire winter, [in the West Desert].

My first trip out here was the fall of 1899 and my first visit to Black Rock was in November at that year. There I had the privilege of first meeting the families of Mr. and Mrs. Walter James, Mr. and Mrs. Willard Burbank and Mr. E. W. Clay of Burbank [near Garrison and the Utah-Nevada state line], Utah.

At the time Mr. and Mrs. Walter James operated a hotel and a mercantile establishment at Black Rock where they carried a general supply for sheepmen, namely;

Black Rock Ranch before 1908. The couple on the right may be the Burbanks. The house in the background burned down in about 1908. (Kaufman collection)

Black Rock Ranch in about 1906 or 1907. The little girls appear to be Margaret Burbank(?) and Thekla James(right). Ranch house is the original one which burned down in about 1908. (Kaufman collection)

hay, grain, food, and clothing. Mr. James was also in the sheep business that I know of as early as 1901 and up to a few years prior to his death on March 2, 1944. [His wife], Helen James was the finest cook and housekeeper I have ever known and her daughters are likewise today.

Mr. and Mrs. Willard Burbank at the time lived on the now James Ranch located immediately east of the Union Pacific Railroad Depot. Mrs. Burbank was then the Black Rock school teacher. Mr. Burbank helped Walter James in the store where the Black Rock Post Office was also located. Sheepmen came from as far south and west as Wah Wah Valley, Pine Valley and Hamblin Valley, and as far north and west as Snake Valley and the Cricket Mountains area, for supplies.

Mr. James built and rebuilt a dam across the Beaver River bed and stored the water from his ranch for the sheep during the dry part of the season when there was no snow. When there is snow on the ground the sheep get their moisture by eating snow and require no water. I have seen in the early days as many as 6 and 8 herds going to and from that watering place almost every hour of the day, traveling as far as 10 to 15 miles [16 to 24 kms] for feed.

At that time the largest sheep shearing corrals in the western states were located at Milford and Black Rock. A large percent of our central and southern Utah sheep were sheared at those two places.

The first man that I can remember operating the shearing corral at Black Rock was Andrew Morris of Beaver. Mr. Morris and his son Bill Morris, now a resident of Milford, operated a shearing corral at Newhouse later on for many years.

I'll give one illustration of shearing sheep at Black Rock. On April 16, 1905, they sheared three herds, a total of 9000 sheep in one day, and this was done by the old hand blade method. The sheep belonged to a N. S. Nielson of Mt. Pleasant, Utah, and I was herding one of the herds. Mr. Neilson then operated 6 herds in winter and from 10 to 15 herds in summer. There were about 75,000 head of sheep operated here from Mt. Pleasant, Utah. A few years later there were over 100,000 head of sheep owned by residents of Fountain Green also wintered in western Beaver and Millard counties. The average shearing season at Black Rock and Milford was from 20 to 30 days each spring season, [usually in April].

There's not a lot of information available for this time period from 1901 to about 1915. The earliest local newspapers available date from about 1915 onwards. Also, the Daughters of the Utah Pioneers(DUP) history books on Millard and Beaver Counties have very little information on Black Rock. No doubt the reason for this is the fact that the Raht and James families were non-Mormon. Also, the place was not settled by the LDS Church, as most other communities in Utah were, at least after the initial ranch was set up. As a result there was never an LDS ward or church house built, which meant it never received much attention from those who wrote the DUP history books. Those in Black Rock who wanted to go to an LDS church had to go to Reed which was located not far to the south. There were people living in Reed and nearby Malone, only in the decade or two up to approximately 1920, then most of those people left.

The Black Rock School

The school at Black Rock was operating at least as early as 1899, but no real records exist from this time period. Throughout its history, this was always a one-room school with one teacher teaching grades from one through eight only. Children over the 8th grade level had to go away to a boarding school, or the entire family had to move. Attending the school would have been **Benita, Thekla,** and **Helen(Babe)** the daughters of Walter & Helen R. James. Thekla and Babe were born in 1898 & 1903(some sources say 1902 or 1905?), and were a little younger than Benita who was born in 1894. There were also railway workers living down near the tracks, and undoubtedly some of those people had children attending school as well. There were also some new families moving into the area just to the south, the east and southeast of Black Rock after the turn of the century. This trend continued until the late 1910's, then families began to move away. Some of them also had school-aged children, some of whom may have gone to school in Black

Rock.

Another young person who would have been in school in about the first half of this time period was **Jack Travers**, the adopted son of Walter & Helen R. James. Jack was born in 1890, and his mother died shortly thereafter. He would have likely been at home and in school there until about 1904 or 1905--if the school would have been even close to

The James girls. Benita above, then Thekla, and baby Helen(Babe), about 1904.
(Elise M. Brougham collection)

Benita James south of the old haystack, which was in between the Cottage and the Big House. If she is about 10 years old, the time would be 1904 or 1905. (Kaufman collection)

normal--which it wasn't much of the time. In fact, during some years school was not held at all due to lack of students.

It appears the school was located up at the Black Rock Ranch until 1923-24. Elise Raht Burbank, sister to Helen R. James, may have been the first school teacher. She probably taught until Walter James bought the ranch in 1901, and perhaps afterwards for several years(?). Whenever the Burbanks moved away, it's believed Helen R. James became the next school teacher. It's not known how long she may have taught, but at some point later, a woman by the name of Ella Brunson Day was also the teacher. In the February 12, 1915 issue of the *Millard County Progress(MCP)* out of Fillmore, it mentions that Ella died, and that she had been a school teacher at Black Rock. A list of known school teachers is on page 54, but that list is very incomplete.

Also in the 10/17/1913 issue of the *MCP*, it mentions that for the school year 1913-14, the teacher was a Miss Ames. From old newspaper accounts we know the enrollment for that year was 20 students. Also, for the school year 1915-16, the scheduled teacher was to have been a C.W. Taylor, but something happened and Mamie Sawyer from Hinckley ended up being the teacher that year. The number of students that year was only 13. For the school year 1916-17, Lavina Hunter was the teacher.

It's not known where these teachers may have lived, but since the school at that time appears to have been at the Ranch, then the school teachers may have also boarded there. If not, then they likely stayed in the store & hotel building which had been the James' home for some time, and was located down at the railroad tracks and townsite.

The Railroad

There were big changes in the railroad during this time period. From the time the railroad started south from Juab, which is Nephi today, the company was called the Utah Southern Extension Railroad. In 1889, there was a merger between several railway companies which created the Oregon Short Line & Utah Northern Railway. Most people just called it the Oregon Short Line.

Throughout the years there was talk of extending the line all the way to Los Angeles, but there were all kinds of law suits, squabbling and delays. Finally on March 20, 1901, a new company was formed in California. It was called the San Pedro, Los Angeles & Salt Lake Railroad Company. There were still delays, but on the north end there was activity along the Oregon Short Line which slowly started laying tracks south out of Milford. Finally on May 1, 1905, the new line was completed forming one rail line from Utah to the coast. From that time on, rail traffic increased through this part of the country.

The first station at Black Rock was actually a converted railroad car, as shown in the foto on the cover and on page 59. It's not certain when they first had this depot, but they must have had one after the shearing barns & corrals were built in about 1900 or 1901(?). The attached box car in the rear of the picture was where the railway agent(station manager) and his family lived. Hamp Burke, the fellow who later married Benita James, jokingly said they may have had to burn it down because of bed bugs and/or cockroaches!

Because the depot was in an old railroad car, indicates there wasn't a lot of passenger or freight traffic coming or going through Black Rock, at least early on. In the very beginning of this time period, about the only people who may have used the station were sheepmen and their camp suppliers. The shearing sheds or barns and loading chutes seem to have been built in about 1900 or 1901, but there is still no definite date on exactly when. Before they were built, passenger traffic must have been almost nothing, but afterwards, Black Rock must have been a much busier place, especially during winter, and even more busy in April, which was the normal shearing month. People from the Kanosh region and Cove Fort, as well as a few miners and farmers to the east and southeast of Black Rock came there to board trains for Salt Lake City or California

In 1915 and 1916, there appeared in the *Millard County Progress(MCP)* out of Fillmore, many short news clips titled simply Black Rock. Papers don't exist before then, and later, Helen R. James must have been sending the news down to Milford and the *Beaver County News(BCN)* and *Milford News(MN)* instead of to Fillmore. From the *MCP* we find several news clippings indicating that for some time up to November, 1915, W.D. Livingston, a British citizen, was the agent or station manager at Black Rock. At that time he retired from the Salt Lake Route and was made a US citizen. He was replaced by A.J. Sieber, who brought with him a wife and one young child. He was the agent for many years.

Every once in a while somebody would lose livestock on the railroad. One such incident occurred in February of 1916. The 2/18/1916 issue of the *MCP* mentioned this in the Black Rock news, which was written by Helen R. James:

Theodore Olsen of Mt. Pleasant had the misfortune to have ten valuable bucks killed as he was crossing the R.R. tracks at this place. [Train] No. 19 came swinging around the curve just north of Black Rock with such terrific speed that it was impossible for Mr. Olsen to get all the sheep off the track before the train crashed into them and ground them to bits.

When asked if there was a cemetery or anyone buried at Black Rock, Hamp Burke

An old San Pedro, Los Angeles & Salt Lake Railroad steam locomotive some time between 1905 and 1915. (Kelsey collection)

Home and mercantile business of Walter & Helen R. James, south side. Railroad freight house on the right. About 1908. (Kelsey collection)

replied: *No cemetery, but there was one guy buried at Black Rock. That was before my time and it was way up northwest of the Ranch and northeast of the depot. There was one lone grave. It seemed like about one mile from the depot. It was just before you get to the bench. There was some boards there and a marked grave. It was supposed to be a guy that laid down in front of the train.*

Others people mentioned a similar story, but there was never anything found in the newspapers, so this apparent suicide may well have taken place before about 1915(?).

Dry Farming and Mining

For the years 1915-16, there were many news items indicating that people were coming to Black Rock by train, then going out to dry farms to the south, southeast and east. Some were south of Antelope Spring, where the old stagecoach station used to be, and others were just east of Antelope Point, which is at the north end of the Mineral Range, all of which were south and east of Black Rock. There could have been more than a dozen dry farms in the area east and south of Black Rock. Those areas to the south were known as Malone and Reed. These were busy farming communities up until about 1920 or so, then people slowly realized they couldn't make it farming without irrigation. Then they slowly moved away. But while they were there, many were coming and going via the Black Rock Station. More on dry farming, the Beaver Bottoms and the Rocky Ford Dam in the next chapter.

Here are some names of people who had homesteaded 160 acres in the region. E.R. Niles and family lived at Antelope Spring Stage Station. They must have rented or leased that land, because his name never appears in the county abstract books showing land ownership. His was the only place around to have a permanent water supply. They were there for many years and had close contact with the James'.

Frifeld & Foley had a farm out around Twin Peaks. Lester Alluisi was a name that popped up a lot. He had spent 3 years on his land south of Antelope Spring and finally got his Patent Deed late in 1915. There were L.E. Hodgson, F.B. McCrosky, and a Fouts and Johnson who had farms out around Antelope Point. Before 1916, these last 4 people were considering drilling wells so they could at least have water for livestock. Other names were E.R. Ludwig, O.S. Taylor, James Curfew, R.C. Main, H.E. Fairfield, M.W. Bayer, Harry Calahan, Al Dutton and J.W. Burtner, just to name a few. From news

Walter James' rock cabin at the Black Rock Mine, near West Spring, in the Beaver Lake Mountains Mining District southwest of Black Rock. (Kelsey collection)

reports, it appeared most of these people were absentee owners, coming only in the spring or fall to plant or harvest, then returning to the Midwest or California.

One farmer who homesteaded and stayed in the region for the rest of his life, along with his family, was **Horace Allbright Stahl**. Horace was born in 1858; his wife Rachel Wesley Mitchell, usually called **Wessie,** was born in 1864. They had two children, **John**, born in 1903, and **Helen Annette**, born in 1902. Wessie had 3 other children by a previous marriage. One was **Ina Mae Stanfield**, who later married a **Milliken** fellow. The Stahl family had lived on a 40 acre farm in New Cambria, Kansas until coming to Utah in 1911. They brought with them 2 teams (of horses), 2 milk cows, farming implements, and their household goods in a box car on the railroad. The mother and 2 children came on a passenger train.

They settled on 320 acres in Section 17, T25S, R9W. Their dry farm was 2-3 kms southwest of Antelope Spring. They lived there for several years only to find out it was too dry to even dry farm. But they did see a big increase in the number of cattle in their herd. Their one boy, John Stahl, tried to go to school at Black Rock, which was about 13 kms away. But that didn't work out. The thing that kept the family going was that Horace Stahl worked part time for Walter James for many years. In October of 1915, he made a business trip with Walter to Southern California, as well as many other trips closer to home. He also did some of the farm work there at the Black Rock Ranch. He was selected for jury duty in 1916. More on this family in the next chapter.

In the vicinity of Black Rock were two mining areas. One was to the southwest of Black Rock about 30 kms. This was the **Beaver Lake Mining District** and **Mountains**. Walter James had a mine out there called the **Black Rock Mine**. His brother John was a partner and helped do some work out there before the turn of the century. In 1915-16, there were many news items in the local paper about the place. Apparently some of the people going that way got off the train at Black Rock, but it was much closer to Milford, only about 16-18 kms to the northwest. Walter never did get rich off that one, but he had a rock cabin there at one time.

The other mining area that was starting to boom in the 1915-16 period was at the north end of the Mineral Range at a place they called **Antelope Point.** That region was called the **Galena Mining District**. Those mines or claims were located about 15 kms southeast of Black Rock and on the west side of the point in Sections 22 & 23, T25S, R9W. Walter James had claims there early on, but so did a lot of other people. The first ore shipped out of the **Antelope Star Mine** was in December of 1915. The mine was worked off and on for years, and it seems Walter was always trying to show the place to interested investors.

The Entire James Family History

As we shall see, the history of Black Rock is also the history of the James', so a little should be said of all members of the **Thomas** and **Ann James family**. Thomas ran a butcher shop, and Ann ran a boarding house for many years at Frisco. Thomas also did some prospecting. He and some of his boys and some friends found silver and gold in the Beaver Lake Mountains, so eventually he sold his butcher shop, and invested $50,000 of his own money into the venture. Others matched that amount. They worked the mine they called the Annie Laurie, until the money ran out. They never did find any rich ore, but Ann keep them afloat with her work in the boarding house or hotel back in Frisco.

Then Thomas' health began to fail. Earlier in life he had had measles, and had lost the sight in one eye, but then the other eye began to fail as well. He applied for a veteran's pension on September 18, 1893 while at Frisco. The family stayed in Frisco until sometime after 1897, then moved to a house at 1095 3rd Avenue, in Salt Lake City. It was a large home and Ann once again made it into a boarding house. Thomas soon had two strokes; the 2nd of which killed him on December 22, 1902, at the age of 67. Ann ran the boarding house, which catered mostly to the extended James family members going to school or working in Salt Lake. She died April 22, 1917. Both are buried in the Mount Olivet Cemetery in Salt Lake, at about 1400 East, 1300 South.

After Walter, the next to the oldest child was **Hannah James**. She met **John P.**

Rossiter in Frisco and they were married on July 2, 1888, the first recorded marriage in the Beaver County record books. According to Anna Mae James Robison, the youngest daughter of John James, Rossiter was a mining engineer and they immediately moved to Butte, Montana. They lived there the rest of their lives. They had a daughter named **Agnes M. Rossiter**, born in 1889. Agnes became a home economics teacher who never married. Hannah also adopted a boy named **Lester**, but no one knows a lot about him. He lived his entire life in Butte(?). They all died in Butte, Montana. John Rossiter died in 1934, Hannah in 1953 at 84 years of age. Agnes died in 1956, at age 67. All three are buried in the Mount Olivet Cemetery in Salt Lake.

Next was **Daniel James**. Not much is known about his earlier years, but he mostly worked as a butcher along side his father in Frisco. While there, Dan met a girl named **Belle Sherwood**, who worked for Ann at the boarding house. They were married in April, 1901. He was 30 years old at the time, she 19. They moved to Milford where they bought a home and lived for the rest of their lives. They eventually had four children; **Glen, Leona, Wanda, and Tom.**

According to Tom's wife **Ruth (Bobbie) James** of Milford, Dan did lots of jobs throughout his life just to make a living. One job he did for years and years, was out at Black Rock during the shearing season which was during April of each year. Most of the time, Dan and Belle ran the boarding house, which was where the sheep shearers and other workers ate. Throughout the years all their children must have worked out there, but Bobbie only remembered Wanda and Tom being there during the 1930's. During that time, Dan, Belle and Wanda cooked and served food, and Tom wrangled sheep in the corrals. During the other 11 months, Dan did some butcher work and caught wild horses and sold them, along with other odd jobs. Bobbie James thinks that Dan and Belle worked at Black Rock every year at the shearing corrals until about 1938. The shearing at Black Rock started in about 1900(?). More on shearing later. Dan died in 1949, while Belle died on Valentine's Day, February 14, 1965. Both are buried in Milford.

The next child was **John James**, and he, like Dan, was a minor player in the history of Black Rock, but mostly after this period of 1901-1916. John worked at Frisco, mostly in the mines. In 1886, he injured his arm using a circular saw and had to be sent by train to

A tunnel and tailings pile in the background, and vertical shaft near cedar tree. Both are part of the Antelope Star mining area at Antelope Point southeast of Black Rock(1995 foto).

St. Marks Hospital in Salt Lake City. For the most part he recovered, but while there he met a nurse from Beaver named **Sarah Slaughter**. They eventually got married on October 6, 1897. While still living and working out of Frisco and/or the immediate area, they had two of their three children; **Evelyn** was born July 28, 1898, while **Theron** was born February 19, 1900.

John P. James and Sarah S. James. (Anna Mae James Robison collection)

AG(Arthur) & Velora S. James, and Christy Ann McLeod right. About mid-1910's.
(Beryl G. Sorensen collection)

Agnes M. Rossiter, left, AG James, Christy Ann McLeod. The boy is Lester Rossiter, the adopted son of John & Hannah James Rossiter. (R. Bobbie James collection)
AG(Arthur) James in the 1910's(?). (R. Bobbie James collection)

From the flagpole, looking south at the old barn and haystack, with the Big House in the background. The Kaufmans took the barn out in about 1960. (Kaufman collection)

After John was hurt, he learned to be a telegrapher, but he also went into the grocery business with Sarah's brother in Frisco. In this same time period, John had invested money in a pumice mine in Nevada. Slowly Frisco faded and people moved out. In about 1906, the family moved to Salt Lake City and paid $5,000 cash for a house at 462 C Street in the Avenues. The money came from the pumice mine. John again went into the grocery business, but during this time he always had contact with his brother Walter at Black Rock. Those two seemed to have had something going on all the time in the way of mining, mostly out in the Beaver Lake Mountains. John's family lived in Salt Lake throughout this time period. More on him in the next chapter.

After John came **Henrietta James**. Most members of the family called her **Retta**. While living at Frisco, she met a fellow named **Angus McLeod**, who worked in a bar. He had TB early on. They were married sometime in the mid-1890's, and had their only child **Christy** in 1898. Because of TB, Angus had to leave Frisco for warmer climes, so they moved to Arizona, where he died in 1903 at age 35. Retta and Christy then moved back to Salt Lake City and lived with her mother Ann James in the big house there on the Avenues. Retta, who never had anything to do with Black Rock, helped with the boarding house business. Christy eventually went to the University of Utah, and later taught school at West Junior High. After Ann James died, Retta apparently inherited the house and the grocery store building which was always rented out to someone else. Retta lived there until she died in 1948 at age 73. Christy never did marry and she died young at age 60 in 1958. All three of the McLeods are buried in the Mount Olivet Cemetery in Salt Lake City.

Next down the line was **Ernest James**. Being one of the younger ones, he had grown up, at least in his late teen years, in Salt Lake City. He never had a connection with Black Rock and must have been considered the "city slicker" of the family. Ernest became an accountant, and eventually met **Pearl Mae Crane**, who was also an accountant. They married June 3, 1908. They never owned a home of their own. Mae had one miscarriage which frightened Ernest so much that they never again tried to have children. They lived the rest of their lives in Salt Lake City. Ernest died on March 29, 1966 at the age of 82. Mae died on July 14, 1978. They are buried in Salt Lake in the City Cemetery.

The un-identical twins, **Authur(AG)** and **Albert(Bert)**, were the last of the James children. Little is known about **Bert** in his early life. He probably moved to Salt Lake City with his parents, Thomas and Ann, but not for long. He seems to have stayed pretty close to Frisco, then Milford and Black Rock. He basically lived his entire adult life in the Milford and Black Rock area. During this time period of 1901-1916, it's been said that he, along with older brother Dan, always helped out during the shearing season out at Black Rock. He did some shearing early on, then probably after this time period, was generally the sheep wrangling foreman around the shearing corrals. He had a girl friend before the war, and later was sent overseas during World War I. More about Bert's connection with Black Rock in the next chapter.

AG and his wife are probably the second most important couple in the history of Black Rock. Little is known about AG in his early life. He was at Frisco with the rest of the James family until some time in the late 1890's, then he surely went to Salt Lake City with his parents and spent some time there, but he appears to have returned to the country he knew and liked best--the Milford, Frisco and Black Rock area. There he likely was involved with mining and/or jobs with cattle or sheep with his older brother Walter. In 1912 he was married to a girl named **Velora Styler**.

Later in life, and after AG had died, Velora, with help from her daughter Dorothy, wrote a little story of their family history. They titled it, **The Life Story of Velora, Arthur, Dorothy, Al, Larry, Ralph, Ramona, Marshall and Brian.** Below is the part of that story up to 1916, with some editing:

Velora Styler was born in Oasis, Utah, on June 17, 1890, as was her twin sister Elnora. Velora's parents were John and Almira Styler. At that time there were five children in the family under the age of five.

Velora went to school in Oasis through the 8th grade [about 14 years old and 1904] and worked for many neighbors washing, cleaning, and cooking for $1 a week and did many chores at home on the farm....

When Velora was 13 years old [1903], she got a job cooking for the Railroad Co. and lived on the outfit cars on the Union Pacific Railroad from Salt Lake to Caliente, Nevada and at out-of-the-way places. This job paid her $5 a week. While in Lynndyl she became acquainted with the owners of the hotel there and when her job ended with the Railroad Co. she got a job cooking at the Lynndyl Hotel.....

Once her father John Styler had a contract to build a canal and Velora and her sister Nell cooked for the workers on that job. When the job ended her sister Bell was working in Black Rock for Mrs. Walter James and wrote Velora to come there and work in her place because she had a job in Caliente, Nevada, that paid more. Velora was glad to get the job, so she went to Black Rock and cooked for sheepmen there. Her salary was $5 a week. It was while she was working there that she met Arthur James. He often came to Black Rock to visit his brother Walter.

Velora's older sister Hilda was working for the Ryans on their cattle ranch in Caliente, Nevada, and decided to go back to school so Velora went there to work in her place for the Ryans for $40 a month.....

Arthur made many trips to Caliente to see Velora and finally persuaded her to marry him. They were married in Salt Lake at the home of Arthur's mother Ann Phillips James, by Dr. Goshen, a very prominent and popular minister of the Congregational Church, on January 3, 1912.

Arthur and Velora went by train to Los Angeles, California on their honeymoon. When they returned to Salt Lake they lived at his mother's house at 1083 3rd Avenue. Arthur was working at Continental Oil Company as a bookkeeper. His father had passed away in December, 1902 and his mother had her widowed daughter Retta [Henrietta] James McLeod and her daughter Christy living there as did her son Ernest and his wife Mae, and Walter's daughter Beniti [Benita]. Mae and Ernest both worked and Christy and Beniti were going to the University of Utah. Arthur's mother and Retta were not well so Velora became the cook, maid and laundry woman for all of them.

Arthur and Velora were paying board and Velora was doing all the work. After some time and much persuading Velora finally got Arthur to rent an apartment and they moved into their own home. After they were settled, Velora took a dressmaking course in her spare time.

During these 2 years, Arthur and Velora had been buying sheep and running them with his brother Walter's sheep in Black Rock. Arthur decided they could get out on their own in the sheep business so they bought a sheep wagon and team of horses, and other supplies and went to live in the sheep wagon. They spent winters on the desert at Abraham and Black Rock and the summers in the mountains at Pine Valley, Kimberly Mountain and Mountain Home. Most of the time they were more than 50 miles [80 kms] from a store, post office, doctor or any other human beings and had to go by wagon or horseback to get to civilization and pick up supplies. They spent 3 years living this way, and enjoying it, but wanted to be with other people again.

It was then [about December 1, 1916] they bought the General Merchandise Store, Hotel and Post Office from Arthur's brother Walter and his wife Helen Raht James.

The rest of Velora's story will be in the next chapter under AG & Velora's lives.

Now back to the **Walter & Helen R. James** family. Walter & Helen's story has pretty much been told above, so here's what is known about the James children. First, **Jack Travers.** He surely stayed there in Black Rock as a child being cared for by his adaptive parents until about 1904 or 1905(?). That's when he would have gotten out of the little Black Rock school, presuming for the moment there was a legitimate school there at the time. Had he finished the 8th grade there, then he must have gone elsewhere to high school, but no one seems to know anything about that. Two guesses would be; Wasatch Academy in Mt. Pleasant, or one of the private schools in Salt Lake City. Perhaps Rowland Hall(?).

He definitely did go to high school some where, because he later went to the University of Utah for one year. That was in 1913-14. It's likely he did not graduate from the U. of Utah, but he was a member of the **football team** the one year he was there, as we see in the picture. This information comes from the yearbook collection at the U. of Utah library. Jack's obituary states he also went to the University of Montana. If so, it was before 1915, because that's the first year any of the local newspapers are available, and they mention nothing about his college or football career. Newspaper clippings tell where he was after about 1915, but not much else. By 1915, Jack was delivering supplies to sheep men for Walter James in the Mtn. Home area of the West Desert, and apparently was working at, or just visiting, Park City as well.

Because Walter James was into mining, and spending time in Park City himself, this may have been the place where Jack Travers met his future wife, **Frances Treweek.** Their story is told in the next chapter.

Benita James must have started school in about 1900, finishing the 8th grade in about 1908 or 1909(?). Then it must have been to Salt Lake to high school, but no one knows where. After that her obituary states she was at the University of Utah during the school year of 1913-14. The U. of Utah yearbook for that year confirms this. After that, news clippings indicate she and her sister Thekla had both been in Salt Lake going to school at Westminster College during the school years 1914-15, and 1915-16. It's not for certain, but they likely stayed in the home of their grandmother, Ann Phillips James, which was up on the Avenues.

Toward the end of this time period, Benita was also driving a car and doing some traveling around on business trips with her father. She was definitely a liberated woman.

Thekla James was the 2nd daughter in the Walter James family. She would have been of school age in about 1903, and been out of the 8th grade in about 1911. She went to high school some place unknown, then in 1914-15, and in 1915-16 she was at Westminster College with Benita.

Helen or **Babe James** was the last daughter of Walter & Helen R. James. She was born on May 8, and in either 1902, as shown on the Raht family genealogy sheet; or 1903, as her daughters believe; or in 1905, as she told her family. Later in life she married a fellow younger than her and because of that, her daughters think she lied about her age. We know she graduated from East High in Salt Lake in 1920, so take your pick on the year she was born. Babe would have gotten out of the Black Rock school in the mid-teens some time, and then went to Salt Lake City to high school. One newspaper report indicated she may have spent a year at Rowland Hall High School, but that's not confirmed.

This chapter ends with Walter James selling the store & hotel to his younger brother AG & Velora Styler James in December of 1916.

Walter James and his last buggy, early 1910's(?). (R. Bobbie James collection)

Jack Travers. The football picture is from the fall of 1913 at the University of Utah. The one on the left was likely taken sometime in the 1910's. (Elise M. Brougham collection)

Walter James, left, and brother Dan James, right. (R. Bobbie James collection)

A receipt from Walter James' store dated December, 1902. The person buying is John J. (Jack) Watson, who operated the little sheepherder store & boarding house at Ibex, west of the Sevier Lake in the West Desert. This receipt is proof the shearing barns were there in 1902. Below is a postal cancellation mark for the Black Rock Post Office.

Sheep wagon & tent, a typical sheep camp of the 1910's and 1920's. (Kelsey collection)

Walter James on a horse in winter(Jim Travers collection), and trucks leaving the Black Rock Ranch with hay for starving sheep in the West Desert during February, 1949.
(Carl Neilson foto, Kelsey collection)

Walter James' pond at the Black Rock Ranch. (Jim Travers collection)

Chapter 5
Black Rock from about 1917 to 1944

The reason for making a new chapter here is because by 1916-17, Walter James had more than he could handle. His store & hotel were doing well, at least in the winter and spring seasons. He had sheep & cattle of his own, had interest in several mines, and he had a large ranch to look after. Business was good. So to reduce the burden, he sold his store & hotel business to one of his youngest brothers, **Arthur Garfield James**. Everyone referred to him simply as **AG** or **Art**. Thus began a new era in the history of Black Rock.

When several of the descendants of the Thomas and Ann James family got together to do a history of the family and Black Rock, they did it many years after several of the leading characters had died. In Benita James Burke's writing on Black Rock and her father Walter James, she stated that the sale of the business to AG took place in 1912. However, there is an article in December 8, 1916 issue of *The Progress*, the Fillmore newspaper at the time, that goes like this: *A. G. James and wife now have charge of the Mercantile business of which Walter James was proprietor so many years.* This date right at the end of 1916 is also confirmed by Dorothy James Leonard in her little story of the her father and mother. Near the end of this chapter we will return to the AG & Velora James family story.

Store & Hotel, and The Ranch
It's during this time period that we have a few people still alive who lived and worked at Black Rock, and can remember the place. Two of the people who worked there were sisters from Meadow. They are **Della** and **Mae Labrum**. Della was born in 1907, Mae in 1909. Della began working at Black Rock at age 16, in 1923. Mae graduated from high school, then worked there for the first time in 1927 at age 18. Della worked up at the Ranch for Walter & Helen, and Mae worked for AG & Velora at the store & hotel. Della eventually married a sheep man named Madsen who is now dead. Mae never married and passed away in 1995. These two ladies were interviewed together several times in 1994 and 1995 at their home in Meadow. The following is a summery of both of their experiences at Black Rock, which ranges from 1923 until well into the 1930's. Remember, when the discussion is about Walter James at the Ranch, or boarding house, it's normally Della who is doing the talking. When discussing the store & hotel, Mae was doing most of the story telling. It was these two gals who drew the floor plan of the store, hotel and post office. See the floor plan on page 48.

AG had the hotel, store and post office, all in one building. There was a lot of different girls from Meadow and this part of the county that went down there to work. Ellen and Luzene Pearson were two. Luzene Pearson Nelson now lives over in Ephraim. At the hotel we were busy all winter.

The **hired girls' bedroom** was off the **kitchen**, to the east. In the **entrance room** they kept their coats and coal buckets, then there was a doorway from there into the **Cellar** & storage room which was made out of black rocks. [That's the part that's still standing today]. Then there was a doorway from the kitchen to the entrance room. You entered the post office from the **store** and there was no outside entrance. James used to just walk back into the post office and hand the mail to people over the store counter. There was another bedroom west of the **dining room** where a Mr. Jenson used to stay, but his days was before our time. He was a big shot from over in Sanpete. When we were there, his son-in-law Stanley Gill, was out there taking Jenson's place.

The **bathroom** and **toilet** was like a hallway, just about, because there was so many doors into it. There was a door from the **Jenson bedroom**, but not a doorway to the outside. I think the reason they made that open space on the outside was so they could get to their plumbing, because there was a sink on the west wall of the kitchen, then the

The Black Rock store & hotel, and post office. One of these girls married Lester Alluisi, an early-day race car driver & mechanic, and settler at Malone in the 1910's. (Kaufman collection)

Another foto of the Black Rock store & hotel. (Kaufman collection)

toilet was in the northwest corner of the bathroom, and the tub in the northeast corner.

AG and his wife slept on the **sleeping porch** which was on the west side of the house. They called it a sleeping porch, but it was just a big bedroom. It was a nice room. Sometimes Ralph, the James' son, slept in that little bedroom in between the bathroom and the sleeping porch. I remember he slept in there when he had pneumonia once. Then there were two other **bedrooms** south of the sleeping porch and **Ralph's bedroom**, and they were rented out. I remember Velora James' dad was in one of those when I was down there. The only time he rented those two bedrooms downstairs was when the upstairs was full.

There wasn't any pool hall when we were there, but they occasionally had dances on the **glassed-in porch** which was on the south side of the hotel. There was a window between the **parlor** and the south porch, so someone could play the piano in the parlor, and you could hear them pounding that piano all over the house! They had dances maybe on someone's birthday, but no specific days of the week. There was this one old fellow, he played the accordion. I think his name was Freeman. Then there was another old feller who used to play the piano for dances. They kept the piano in the parlor. We also had a big graphanola. There was chairs out there and it was glassed-in. They had a heaterola there too. You'd be surprised at the number of people who would drop in to that place for dancing. There were all those section hands from the railroad who had wives, and there were several women up at the Walter James' Ranch. Also, there was the telegraph operator, and she was single at that time. So there were enough women to go around.

I [Mae] really didn't have much to do with the store and post office. Usually in the winter time AG was there to take care of his own business. He took care of the store and post office. And all we girls had to do was the cooking and the cleaning and the washing for the hotel. We also cooked for AG when his wife wasn't there. When she was there she was the main cook. She was there most of the time. Then in the spring, when it was house-cleaning time, we had to paint all of those rooms.

In winter time, the upstairs rooms, which was the main **hotel** part, were often full, because the sheepmen were out there with their sheep in the winter time. They'd come in there to get supplies from the store. They would normally stay in the hotel one night before going back out to the desert. It would be the camp tenders who would come in to get supplies. Each sheep herd had one herder and a camp mover. In the long hall upstairs there was a register, a grate, and that was directly above the heaterola down in the dining room. So the only heat they had upstairs was what escaped from the stove downstairs. I don't know how those guys stood the cold!

The sheepmen would get supplies like canned goods, overalls, or some clothes. Then after the sheepmen started using trucks, I think they found out it was cheaper for them to haul all their supplies out to the desert, than to buy them there at Black Rock. But when we were there they all had wagons, and before you'd start to cook supper, you'd go out and look around the hills to see how many sheep wagons were coming in for the night.

There wasn't anything going on out there at Black Rock in the summer time. They just drove the sheep out from Sanpete County or wherever in the fall, and trailed 'em back in the spring. I never did see any of 'em being unloaded from the railroad, but they did ship some sheep out of Black Rock. After the shearing, they loaded some from the loading chutes on the west side of the tracks. Nowadays they pretty much truck 'em around.

AG had a Buick in the **garage**. There was an old outhouse out north of the old Malone school house, but they had an indoor toilet in the house and running water in the bathroom and the kitchen sink.

The old **Malone school house** was there when I got there. There was several little towns south of Black Rock. They was Reed and Malone. When I first went out there, there was still some houses left, but you know how people vandalize those old places. I remember this one place was built with cobble rock, and how attractive it was. A lot of those people came from the east. The James' had moved that old school from Malone, because they didn't have school at Malone anymore. They just kept the supplies for the store in there. The perishables like milk and that kind of stuff was kept in the basement of that old school. I think it was still there the last time I worked at Black Rock.

There was two houses south of the hotel and west of the railroad tracks and loading chutes & pens. They were made of railroad ties. They were the two **tie houses**, and I think the Roger's family lived in one of those. Dalles worked at the hotel and store for AG. This is the husband of Rose Rogers, the school teacher. She was teaching when I [Mae] was out there, which was in the late 1920's.

I don't remember them raising a garden down there, or having fresh vegetables. I do remember Mrs. James cooking cabbage though. She'd cook it all day until it was as brown as this table. She'd fill that big pressure cooker and cook it and cook it. I remember Dallas Rogers milking once. Also Cocky Robison, that's what we called him. He usually hired some one to do the milking out in the barn.

They had only two girls working there, especially at house cleaning time, and they slept in the **utility room**. They had about a 3/4's bed when Ellen Pearson and I worked there. We both slept in the same bed.

It was just a one-room **school** house at Black Rock. It was smaller than the one at Clear Lake. Rose Rogers taught school out there for years, [2 years only] and she used to walk to school every day. The Nays had kids, and Rose Rogers had kids, and some of those section people had kids. Rose taught from first grade up to the 8th grade. Ralph James went to school during the years I was there.

The **boarding house** was a place that they opened up during the shearing season. The boarding house was north of the depot, east of the tracks, and south of the shearing corrals. It was just north of the road going up to the Ranch. There wasn't any rooms there for shearers to sleep in, but the cooks did have a room or two for themselves. Just the cooks slept there. The shearers ate there, but they didn't sleep there. Seems to me the shearers stayed in a railroad car, at least some of them. I didn't know too much about them, only to feed 'em.

They had 2 cooks most of the time, and then usually 2 girls to wait on the tables. We had two great big long tables and we served the food family style. We had to wait tables, then wash dishes--and that was before paper plates! The cooks would cut the meat all up in slices,. The boarding house belonged to Walter, but the meat came from down at AG's store. Walter and AG must have run it together. But then one year I remember Dan James run it.

Sometimes during the shearing times, they'd have dances at the boarding house. We'd move the tables back against the walls, scrub the floor and have a dance. Everybody from far and near would come to the dances. Sheepmen, railroaders, ranch workers. It was funny what a big crowd we'd get.

The boarding house is where they fed the **sheep shearers** in the spring of the year. The sheepmen would have their sheep out on the West Desert during the winter, then they'd come in to the shearing corral at Black Rock. There were fellows from all over the country there shearing, some of them were even from Canada. Some of those crews would go from place to place around the country. As I recall the shearing was done in about April. I don't know how many sheep were sheared, but each herd would have more than a thousand head. And they would shear for several weeks. Some of the shearers stayed in the hotel but some may have had tents too. Now some of them had railroad cars and they stayed in them. And they would start in the south and move on the railroad; after they sheared here, they'd move north to Jericho or Vernon or some other place.

Concerning the building next to the hotel which they labeled the **Malone School. Deon Gillen** of Oasis, who is a son of one of Velora's sisters, went to school in Black Rock in the school year 1923-24. Their school house in Oasis had burned down, and they needed extra students in Black Rock, so they could get a teacher and have a school maintained. He had this to say about when they moved that Malone school house up to Black Rock:

I was there when they moved that Malone school house. It came from Malone, which was about 5 miles [8 kms] south of Black Rock. It was at another little town where the dry

Black Rock Store, Hotel & Post Office Floor Plan--1930's

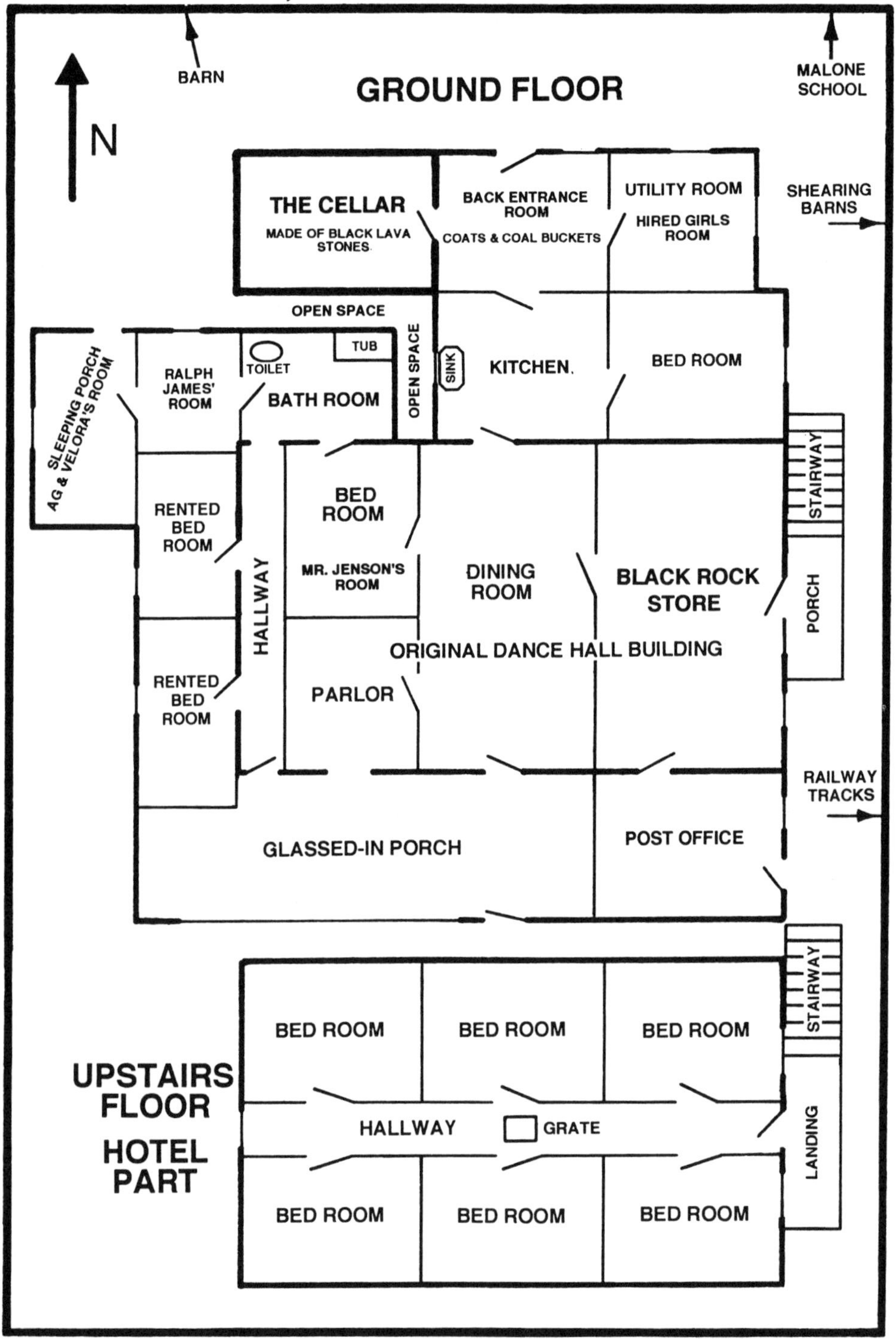

GROUND FLOOR

N

BARN
MALONE SCHOOL
SHEARING BARNS
RAILWAY TRACKS

THE CELLAR — MADE OF BLACK LAVA STONES

BACK ENTRANCE ROOM — COATS & COAL BUCKETS

UTILITY ROOM — HIRED GIRLS ROOM

OPEN SPACE

SLEEPING PORCH — AG & VELORA'S ROOM

RALPH JAMES' ROOM

TOILET / TUB

BATH ROOM

OPEN SPACE

SINK / KITCHEN

BED ROOM

RENTED BED ROOM

BED ROOM

MR. JENSON'S ROOM

DINING ROOM

BLACK ROCK STORE

STAIRWAY

PORCH

HALLWAY

RENTED BED ROOM

PARLOR

ORIGINAL DANCE HALL BUILDING

GLASSED-IN PORCH

POST OFFICE

UPSTAIRS FLOOR — HOTEL PART

| BED ROOM | BED ROOM | BED ROOM |

HALLWAY — GRATE

| BED ROOM | BED ROOM | BED ROOM |

STAIRWAY / LANDING

48

farmers lived. It was a pretty good-sized school house, and all the books and everything was in it. I'm not a 100% sure it was at Black Rock in the summer of 1924, because we used to go down to Black Rock every summer just to stay awhile. Us kids would usually go down and stay a week or so, to visit Aunt Velora. So I was there when that Malone school house was moved up to Black Rock, but I can't remember exactly what year it was. It had to have been moved there sometime in the 1920's. When they brought it there, they jacked it up in the air then poured the cement, then sat it right down on the foundation. AG used that to store stuff in it, including the basement part. I know Uncle Arthur used to store a lot of dynamite and stuff like that down there. He had a big old steel door to it and a good padlock on it to keep people out.

Concerning what happened to the boarding house, shearers and the shearing pens, here are a few comments by **Hamp Burke**, the man who eventually married **Benita James**. Hamp lived at Black Rock from 1929 through the end of 1960. His comments about the shearing were about conditions in the 1930's and early 1940's. He was 83 and 84 years old when interviewed:

*At the **boarding house** where the shearers ate, I'd say they probably ran 5 or 6 people there to cook the meals and serve the food and wash dishes. Food was served family style. The girls would put the food out on the tables in great big bowls and they'd serve themselves.*

At one time the boarding house had to be moved a little to the east and south so they could build that drainage canal. You wouldn't see any foundations there today; it was all blocked up. That building was later moved up to the Ranch, and we used it for a shop, but I don't know what Kaufman used it for. It was located west and a little bit north of the Big House. It's there with the corrals and hay stacks.

*They had **two shearing sheds** all together and they could put 100 sheep in each shed. Later on they had the electric machinery and they had one bunch of clippers on one side and another bunch on the other. There was never electric lines running out there, so they used a generator. They had a great big Diesel engine running the generator.*

We generally had around 50 or 60 head of sheep around the Ranch, and I had it fixed up so we could shear about 10 sheep at a time. They weren't electric in the early days, they were run off a great big pulley. The shears just hung down on the pulley and the shearers operated them by hand. Later on they had electric clippers, like they have today. There was one guy named Tom Larry, he come there in the spring of the year and he stayed and sheared sheep until fall, then he came back and worked for AG. He worked the next year then left. He could shear a 100 head of sheep a day with hand clippers.

In the old days, and when they were at their peak out there, there would be at least 100 men to a shearing crew. There were shearers, then there were wranglers, as they called 'em. Then some would take the wool and tromp it. A good stomper would get 350 pounds [160 kgs] into a big bag. If they couldn't do that, then they'd get somebody else. They'd put a great big pole underneath it, lift it up, then sew it, and roll it out of the way. They were round, just like a gunny sack. Then they shipped the wool out on the railroad, ever bit of it.

The shearing crews started in California and they moved north by train, to Montana and elsewhere. When I first came there in 1929, they were doing lots of shearin', and they lived in tents right around the shearin' pens and boarding house, and lots of 'em had old automobiles. Sometimes they'd go off and leave their cars; wouldn't run.

It seems to me one of those shearing barns burned down, and the rest of 'em they tore down for the material that was in 'em. The equipment that was in those shearing barns and pens was Walter James'. So we salvaged that and sold it all but 15 or 20 drops, that's what we called 'em, that we kept to shear with ourselves. Some of the material we used up at the Ranch. This was after World War II, maybe in the late 1940's. [It's believed the shearing sheds or barns were torn down in about 1949].

Now let's go back to Della Labrum Madsen's story about the Black Rock Ranch itself. She worked there for the first time in 1923:

At the Ranch they ran sheep and cattle, and it was a good-sized ranch. There were several springs all along that black ridge behind the Ranch. On maps one of those springs

From inside the shipping corrals looking northeast at the freight house, left, and shearing barns across the railroad tracks. (Elise M. Brougham collection)

The Big House and pond at the Black Rock Ranch sometime in the 1910's. (Kaufman collection)

The Big House at the Black Rock Ranch in winter. (Kaufman collection)

is called Tie House Spring. The railroad got their water from there. It was good water. They raised some alfalfa and they had some grain but I don't know what kind. They of course had a big garden, and then they had a bunch of apple trees. There was also some plum trees over to the south at the Stahl's place. They had chickens, and they had geese, and turkeys. And lots of cats and dogs!

That Stahl's family lived on the Black Rock Ranch, but to the south a ways across a field and there was a spring over there too. It was maybe a block south of where the main Ranch house was. Earlier, they lived up at Antelope Spring, then they moved down there to Black Rock. The house where the Stahls lived wasn't very far to the south, because when Mrs. Walter James would go someplace, Mrs. Stahl would come over and stay with me so I wouldn't be alone. Then later on they moved to Milford.

In my day, the only thing I can remember about Antelope Spring was a pond of water and a watering trough. I guess there was some kind of old tumbled down cabin there too. It was on the main road out to Black Rock. When we went out there, we passed right by Antelope Spring. In the old days they had a stage station there.

I [Della] worked there off and on for years, until I got married in 1947. I was 39 years old. I did house work at the Ranch. I cooked for everybody, including the ranch hands. They had a separate place to sleep, but they ate with the family. They didn't have too many workers there, but more at times. In the summer they'd have 3 or 4 men; hired hands. They'd put up the hay and do stuff like that, and they had sheep that they ran out to the southeast.

When I was there, Hamp and Benita lived in the house to the north **[Cottage]**. Then there was the **Big House** [the main ranch house where Walter and Helen James lived]. Then just where you turn into the property, out to the north, was the **Tie House**. When I was there Shirl Nay lived in that house, he was the farmer.

In 1994, Hampton Burke was the only member of either James family still alive, but he passed away on August 8 that year. Here's more of his story, the first part of which is told by his sister Emma Burke Hair, plus a few of his own recollections on when he first arrived at the Black Rock Ranch and what his job was:

[Emma Burke Hair's story: My father worked on some mines for Walter James once in awhile. So he was out at Black Rock at times. My father's name was Thomas James Burke. He would go into Walter's mines occasionally and do the yearly assessment work. One place he used to work was in a mine over around Circleville.

Later on, Hamp went to Milford with my father who was working at a garage at the time and Mr. James came in wanting to hire some help. So Hampton went out there with him then. That's how he met Walter James, through my father.]

I [Hamp[came from Beaver to Black Rock when I was 18 years old. That was in 1929, just at the beginning of The Depression. My mother was a Mormon, my father non-Mormon. To start with, I was just a ranch hand at the Walter James or Black Rock Ranch **[the James' called it The Tall Trees Ranch]**. The Walter James family lived there in the Big House. The workers used to stay in that other house just to the north of the Big House. We ran sheep and cattle. He raised alfalfa and then would change over into grain, like they have to. His cows were mixed, white face mostly. That's what they originated from. When we finally sold out, we had 350 head of cows and calves.

When I got there, he had one farmer working there, and then later I became the farmer. That was all the hired hands he had. When I first went there, I trucked groceries and hay to the sheepmen. The sheep run east over around Marysvale in the summer time, and they wintered out west.

The Black Rock School

The school at Black Rock was located due east of the depot and the operator's houses, and just south of the present county road running east to the Ranch and beyond to Cove Fort. It was about 125 meters east of the tracks. See the list of known school teachers on page 54, for the number of students and names of teachers for some of the years. It also shows the number of people living in the Black Rock voting precinct. That must have included anybody who lived out at Malone, or in the area of Antelope Spring.

Most of the people who taught school at Black Rock were women, and they usually taught just one year before they were married. One exception was **Rose Davies Rogers**.

The Big House at the Black Rock Ranch. (Elise M. Brougham collection)

She has since passed away, but two of her daughters are still alive and well in 1996. They are Frances Rogers Green of Alta Loma, California, and Christine Rogers Mathews of Cedar City. Frances is the oldest of the two and she remembered more. Most of the following is her story about the Rogers family and the school at Black Rock:

My mother had taught in Black Rock before she was married, and she married Dad in 1919 right after World War I. She may have taught in the 1917-1918 school year. Her name was **Rose Davies** then and she was from Fillmore.

Dad, or **Dalles Rogers**, was from Kanosh. Before my father went into the service in World War I, he taught school one year in Delta, and a year in Scipio. And a year after they were married they both taught in Kanosh. Then my mother didn't teach again until after we were all born, which was when I was 5 years old. At the time they went to Black Rock, Ted was about 7, I was 5, Jake was 4, and Christine about 2 years old.

When they went to Black Rock, I think they had a choice as to who would teach. Either one could have taught. My dad didn't like to teach in the lower grades--he always taught shop class in junior high or high school--so she taught and he had this opportunity to work for Arthur James.

There were 2 or 3 homes there near the James' hotel and we lived in one of those **tie houses**. They were built of railroad ties. They were unfinished on the outside, but were plastered on the inside. It was a four-room house we lived in, and I remember it being warm and cozy in the winter time. That house belonged to Arthur James, and I think it was rent-free which was part of the deal for coming to Black Rock to open the school.

At the time we were there, the school year of **1928-29**, they had to have **8 children** before they could have a school. There was Ralph James, AG's & Velora's boy, then there were several families of railroad workers. I don't remember Dorothy James, she may have gone someplace else the year we were there. And they made up about 7 children, and then my older brother Ted was there. But by the time we got ourselves moved out there, one of the railroad families had moved away and had taken one child away. I was 5 years old, so they said I could go, so I was the 8th child. This happened just a week or so into the school year. Even though I was 14 months younger than Ted, we just stayed in the same grade and eventually graduated from high school together.

On the left, R.R. agent Andy Anderson, then Rose & Christine, Ted, Frances & Jake Rogers in 1928-29. Dalles & Rose Davies Rogers. (Christine R. Mathews collection)

Black Rock School Teachers, 1899-1942
Number of Students & Population of BR

School Year	# of Students	Voting & Precinct Population	Teacher's Name
1899-1900	Unknown	61	Elise Raht Burbank
1900-1901	Unknown		Helen Raht James
1901-1902	Unknown		Unknown
1902-1903	Unknown		Unknown
1903-1904	Unknown		Unknown
1904-1905	Unknown		Unknown
1905-1906	Unknown		Unknown
1906-1907	Unknown		Unknown
1907-1908	Unknown		Unknown
1908-1909	Unknown		Unknown
1909-1910	Unknown	52	?Ella Brunson Day?
1910-1911	Unknown		Unknown
1911-1912	Unknown		Unknown
1912-1913	20		Unknown
1913-1914	13		Miss Ames
1914-1915	Unknown		Unknown
1915-1916	Unknown		Mamie Sawyer
1916-1917	Unknown		Lavina Hunter
1917-1918	Unknown		Rose Davies (Rogers)
1918-1919	Unknown		Unknown
1919-1920	Unknown	41	Unknown
1920-1921	Unknown		?Nellie Holbrook?
1921-1922	No School Was Held?		No School
1922-1923	No School Was Held?		No School
1923-1924	Unknown		Unknown
1924-1925	Unknown		Unknown
1925-1926	Unknown		Unknown
1926-1927	Unknown		Miss Barnes
1927-1928	Unknown		Unknown
1928-1929	8		Rose Davies Rogers
1929-1930	Unknown	72	Unknown
1930-1931	15		Mrs. William Holt
1931-1932	11		Miss Wright
1932-1933	17		La Preal Utley Wilson
1933-1934	17		La Preal Utley Wilson
1934-1935	20		La Vell Wright
1935-1936	13		Bernice Miller Smith
1936-1937	15		Josephine Hunt
1837-1938	13		Mrs. Hazel Trimble
1938-1939	16		Lettie Stevens
1939-1940	16	46	?Lettie Stevens?
1940-1941	19		Lettie Stevens
1941-1942	13		Unknown
Fall of 1942			Mrs. Jack Geist

School Closed at Christmas Time 1942--Insuficient Number of Students

My father used to get up early in the mornings in winter time and go over and build a fire in the school house, so it was warm when we would get there. And the boys would go over near the railroad buildings with a bucket and get water for us to drink during the day. Everyone brought their own cups.

*As I recall, the **pot-bellied stove** was on one side of the classroom and the windows were on the other side. The entrance was at the one end, then the black board and teacher's desk was at the other end.*

*I know my father did do some **carpentry work** on the Cottage for Walter James up at the Ranch. I think he may have done that before we moved out there in 1928. He may have worked on it so that Merrill Miller and Thekla could live in it. Dad also did some carpentry work at the hotel building.*

We left Black Rock in the spring of 1929 right after school was out, then the next school year, my mother and father both taught in Lynndyl.

There aren't many former teachers still alive today, but one was **La Preal Utley Wilson** who was born in 1906 in Flowell, just west of Fillmore. In 1995, she lived north of Richfield a short distance. La Preal was interviewed when she was 88 years old. Here's what she remembered about the school:

I graduated from high school in Fillmore, then went on a mission, then I went to the B.Y. Academy to school for 2 years. We just had to go for 2 years to be a teacher then. Then I taught school in Black Rock for 2 years, my first two years of teaching. That was in 1932-33, and 1933-34. Then I taught school in Sutherland in the fall of 1934, quit at Christmas time, then I was married to Keith Wilson who was a sheep herder around Black Rock when I was there. That was in January of 1935. Then I didn't teach school anymore. In those days they wouldn't let you teach school if you were married.

I stayed at the hotel there in Black Rock, downstairs. I stayed in a room by the kitchen, and with the hired girl that worked there. I think her name was Hannah Swenson, from Mt. Pleasant. She worked there the first year I was there. Then the next year, I had a room back in the back, but I always stayed downstairs. They had the rooms upstairs for people who came for just one night.

The picture [on page 57] is of the north side of the school and the school faced north. On one side of the entrance inside there was a place for wood and coal. That was on the left as you entered. The coats were on the right side. Then there was a second door to get into the main school itself. It was quite a big room, maybe 20 feet [6 meters] long. It was longer than it was wide. There was windows on two sides [the south side]. There was an organ and an old pot bellied stove in there. The stove was on the north side of the room. I taught school and did the janitor work. I built the fire in the mornings, and swept the floors and dusted. I think I had about 8 or 10 students, it wasn't very many. Some grades only had one person in, but I taught all grades one through 8. They sat on benches and had a little desk in front of them, and a place for books. They were just regular school desks. When I was there no one knew how to play the organ. There was a playground outside but there was no swings or anything like that. Nothing for children to play on. And they had one outhouse, for both boys and girls. Each school year lasted about 9 months.

La Preal also remembered a little about 2 of her students, **Ralph James**, the son of AG & Velora James, and **Walter James (Wally) Miller**, the son of Thekla James and her husband Merrill Miller. Also, La Preal knew a little about the Wasatch Academy:

When I was at Black Rock, Ralph, AG's son was still there, but their daughter Dorothy was gone up to Mt. Pleasant going to the boarding school. They had two high schools in Mt. Pleasant, one was the public school, and the other was a church school, and a boarding school. They stayed there at the Wasatch Academy. Dorothy only came back to Black Rock for a visit once or twice. I taught Ralph the first year I was at Black Rock, then he went up to Mt. Pleasant the second year. They boarded there, and worked a little for their board, or some of their board, anyway. I think everyone who stayed there had certain chores to do. Ralph was a brilliant boy.

Another boy I taught was Walter Miller. He was the son of Thekla James and Merrill Miller. He was in the 1st and 2nd grades when I was there. He was on crutches much of

Foto on the left shows at least 4 Nay boys, with Merrill being the tallest. Wally Miller is on crutches. At the school between 1932 & 1934 (La Preal U. Wilson foto). On the right are school children on the James' pond, believed to be in the winter of 1933(?), but maybe in the late 1920's(?).
(Elise M. Brougham collection)

Teacher and students in front of Black Rock School, in about 1924 or 1925. Dorothy James is 3rd child from the left, and just left of the teacher. (Kelsey collection)

North side of Black Rock School showing entrance, 1933 or 1934. (La Preal U. Wilson foto)

the time. He had something wrong with his foot.

Here's a brief story of the Black Rock school building. It was originally located up at the Ranch. School was likely taught in the Big House there at the Ranch in the beginning, then Walter James built a small one-roomed building specifically for the school. We think it was then moved down near the depot during the 1923-24 school year. It stayed there until it was closed. Next is a short piece from the Black Rock section of the *Milford News* for February 25, 1943, which tells us when the school was actually closed:

Mr. and Mrs. Jack Geist and children are moving to Milford, where Mr. Geist will be employed as third trick operator. The Geists have been here several months and during that time Mrs. Geist taught school until it was closed because of an insufficient number of children to justify continuance.

It appears from this that Mrs. Geist taught during the fall of 1942 and possibly up until Christmas time or a little later. Also, Benita James Burke has stated in her writing that the school was open for more than 40 years and that it closed down the first year of World War II. These sources point directly to the fall of 1942 as the time when the Black Rock School closed its door forever.

The Railroad

During this time period, the railroad continued to grow and be an important part of Black Rock. In 1916, the name San Pedro was removed, making it the **Los Angeles & Salt Lake Railroad**. However, it was always known locally as the **Salt Lake Route**. Even though this route went by various names, it seems to have always belonged to the Union Pacific Railroad system.

The reason the railroad became interested in this site in the beginning was the good spring water available. They of course needed water to run their steam engines, so early on they bought the water rights to the Tie House and Big Springs located due west of the depot about one km. For most of the history of Black Rock, the Ranch got what ever water the railroad didn't use.

Black Rock was really in the middle of nowhere, so passenger traffic was never very high. Occasionally someone from Kanosh or Cove Fort would come to get on or off a train. During the early 1900's and up to about 1920, there were dry farmers who settled just to the south of Black Rock at Malone. They used this station often but primarily it was a jumping off point for sheep men, mostly herd owners or camp suppliers, who had flocks in the desert to the west. Like the store, hotel and post office, the busy season was in winter and spring.

The Black Rock Station was used mostly for shipping freight. According to Hamp Burke, at one time they used to ship sulfur from the Sulphurdale area which was to the east. Interstate Highway 15 runs through that little valley today just south of Cove Fort. Throughout the time from the 1910's to 1930's, some ore from the Antelope Star Mine about 15 kms southeast of Black Rock was shipped from the depot. In the early 1920's there was some activity in Walter James' Black Rock Mine to the southwest, but no ore from that place was ever shipped out of Black Rock. And of course there were miners & prospectors coming and going too.

Starting in December, 1925, oil exploration began about 13 kms southeast of Black Rock, and that got everybody excited. It was promoted by Walter James, who was about as influential as anybody around. His influence with Union Pacific is surely the reason a new and bigger depot was built. More on the oil well later, but below is part of an article which appeared in the Milford *Beaver County News* for September 24, 1926 concerning the new depot. It has been modified down from the original text.

The union station recently completed at Black Rock, located on the main line of the Union Pacific railroad 21 miles[34 kms] north of Milford, and within the oil field territory where drillers are at work at this time, is now ready for occupancy.

This union station is known as a combination passenger and freight station, measuring 20x110 feet [6x30 meters], of frame and stucco construction and designed after the mission type of the old Spanish building.

Waiting room and office section measures 20x18 feet [6x5 meters] and 13x18 feet [4x5 meters] with concrete floor. In the waiting room, a beautiful fountain has been installed and the famous water of Black Rock is available to the patrons of the Union Pacific system.

The freight house section measures 18x30 feet [5x9 meters], and has two large massive doors at the south end which open to the outside. The living quarters consist of bedroom, livingroom, bathroom, hall, kitchenette and breakfast room and three closets.

The United States weather bureau equipment will be located at the north end of the union station. New equipment has been furnished and will be installed for service at an early date.

This new station replaced the earlier one which was in an old railroad passenger car, and which sat on a side track. Hamp Burke describes the new station and how it worked:

*The station was there when I first arrived in 1929. The Black Rock Station was exactly like the Clear Lake Station except for the south end. The difference on the south end was that this station had great big sliding doors. This one was also stuccoed and painted yellow. Black Rock was mainly a freight depot. Other than that the two stations were exactly alike. The old station, it burned down; or it was carried away by cockroaches! There used to be 3 people there to take care of the depot; a station manager or agent, and 2 telegraph operators. The **agent** lived in the north end of the depot itself, and the **operators** lived just east of the station in some houses. Then down to the south a ways was where the section hands stayed. There was **2 bunkhouses** there.*

Throughout this time period, there were always several families of railroaders living there, and it seems they supplied most of the children for the school. However, few stayed for very long, and the turnover rate was extremely high. Because of this, there was always a little distance between those working at the Ranch or store, and the railroaders.

Many of the section hands were Mexicans, Japanese or other nationalities, some of whom weren't US citizens. Occasionally there were blacks. Many others were young men from nearby towns.

The old Black Rock Depot which was used before September, 1926. Shearing barns are to the left and in the background. (Kelsey collection)

Black Rock Depot after 1926. Section foreman's house is to the left. (Kelsey collection)

Dry Farming, Beaver Bottoms, Mining and the Walter James Oil Wells

As this chapter begins in 1917, there were several families living east and southeast of Black Rock, and east of **Malone**. They moved there and tried homesteading in the early 1910's and were attempting to make a go at **dry farming**. The main crop they tried raising was winter wheat, but most people had some sheep and cattle. However without water they couldn't do much. During the late 1910's, these same people were moving away and abandoning the land they had homesteaded. This must have been one of the last places in the US that homesteading was allowed.

As things turned out, dry farming was a flop. It really was a little too dry even for dry farming. Most of the people who attempted it were absentee owners who lived elsewhere. Many were from the Midwest or California. Two families who homesteaded about due south of Antelope Spring and southeast of Black Rock, and who stayed around a long time were the Stahls and Kaminskas. More on them later. Lester Alluisi was another man who was there a long time.

The **Beaver Bottoms** was another farming area closely linked to Black Rock during the late 1800's and up through the 1910's to about 1920. It is located west of the Milford-Delta road(Highway 257), the railway line, and west of the abandoned townsites of Malone and Reed. The Bottoms was a sandy region southwest of Black Rock where the Beaver River used to sink into the ground and die. During spring runoff this river ran into the Beaver Bottoms, but was normally all soaked up. Seldom did it flow past Black Rock on its way north toward Clear Lake, or its final destination which was the Sevier Lake. Very rarely did it reach the Sevier Lake in recorded history.

Some time just after about 1900, and after Walter James bought the Black Rock Ranch, he made a dam across the Beaver River channel just north of the store & hotel, but seldom was he successful at getting any water stored there. What water he got from the Beaver River surely came during the spring floods. He likely stored some of the runoff water from the Black Rock Springs as well. His goal was to have another waterhole for sheep, so they would have more water during the shearing season.

In the early days before the Minersville Reservoir(known early on as the Rocky Ford Dam) was built in 1914, the Beaver Bottoms had lots of water, mainly just below the surface. What surface water they had was mostly in the spring of the year during the annual flood of the Beaver River. The grass was up to a horses belly, or higher. For years people would go out and cut wild grass hay anytime they wanted. Later they used sub-irrigation to grow alfalfa and alfalfa seed. It was also a good winter range for cattle and sheep.

The most successful farmer or rancher in that area was Dan Smithson, of the **Smithson Ranch**, who settled in the southern part of the Beaver Bottoms. At one time he built a small earthen dam, called Five Mile Dam, across the Beaver River and would store some water for his ranch, but he was about the only one who had any kind of a reliable source of water. Others who tried to settle and farm downstream from him had to drill wells for irrigation water, but they never got much.

In 1914, a group of people known as the **settlers**, apparently those who lived mostly in Reed and the Beaver Bottoms(maybe some from Malone?), went to court to get the excess or runoff water from the Minersville Reservoir upstream. They had used and depended on the spring runoff for years. But the Beaver River water had been used for years and years for irrigation by the people of Minersville and other areas upstream too. It's a long, long story, but in 1914 the case was first filed. It took 10 years to go through the court system, then it was retried, and finally in 1931, the case was finally settled. The **farmers** of Minersville and the Beaver Irrigation Company won. There was to be no more spring runoff water flowing into the Beaver Bottoms.

At one point there was a compromise put forward for the settlers. They would swap their Beaver Bottoms land, for land and water south of Milford and west of Minersville. That apparently never took place. Gradually the settlers of Reed, the Beaver Bottoms and Malone abandoned their homes and moved away. By about 1920 most people were gone. At one time there was a school in Malone, but some time around 1924, or shortly thereafter, this school was moved up to Black Rock and set on a cement foundation immediately north of AG James' store & hotel. That building was always referred to as the Malone School, even as it sat there in Black Rock until 1945. More on its demise in the next chapter.

The town and ranch at Black Rock were out in the middle of the valley and a few kms from any mountains or **mining areas**. However, Walter James was heavily involved in a mine or mines in the Antelope Point area southeast of Black Rock and Antelope Spring. In the Milford *Beaver County News* for 2/23/1917, it was reported there were 9 different companies operating in the Antelope group and AG James had his hotel full almost every night. His store was doing well too. He used his old car to deliver groceries to the miners.

The main mine Walter was involved with was the Antelope Star. It began at about the beginning of this time period, but really got going in about 1921. According to news items in the Milford newspaper, he wasn't doing much mining himself, but was hiring men to work for him. Walter was mostly a promoter, and he had some officials from the big mines in northern Utah come down periodically to check things out, hoping they would find something they liked and invest in the project.

The Walter James family was always hosting guests throughout the history of Black Rock. They even had a few "big wigs". *The Progress* newspaper out of Fillmore for December 8, 1916, reported the biggest wig of all:

Ernest Woolley of Salt Lake City accompanied by Gov. Wm. Spry and six prominent business men visited the Antelope Star Mine on Sunday last. They were much pleased with the appearance of the mine, after which Governor Spry and Mr. Woolley were entertained at dinner at the home of Mr. and Mrs. Walter James.

There were all kinds of mining people coming and going via the depot at Black Rock throughout the years up to the mid-1920's or so.

Walter was also involved with his mine in the Beaver Lake Mountains southwest of Black Rock. That was his and John James' Black Rock Mine. He even had a mine in the Cricket Mountains and in the Big Sage Valley almost due north of Black Rock. That old mine is located west of today's Continental Lime Plant on Highway 257.

In 1925, there was also lots of work being done on a claim on the east side of Antelope

Plowing scene on someone's dry farm at Malone in the 1910's. (Kaufman collection)

Point called the East Antelope Mine. But this didn't have anything to do with the James'. Occasionally there was ore being shipped, but nobody at or near Black Rock ever made a big strike. What little mining there was seems to have been because of the promotion efforts done by Walter James.

Being a big-time promoter, Walter James got involved with **oil exploration** beginning in about 1924 and 1925. The only real source here are newspaper clippings from Milford's *Beaver County News* (before 1926 and after 1956) or the *Milford News* (1926 to 1955). Same paper, different names. The first news item noticed was in the April 3, 1925 paper. Walter James went to Cheyenne, Wyoming, and consulted with petroleum geologists about a geologic report stating the valley southeast of Black Rock was actually an anticline that ran north-south. There is often oil in such geologic structures. From that point on, there were almost weekly reports on the plans, promotion and drilling of that well for the next three years.

The best single source for information on the whole history comes from the *Milford News* for **October 16, 1941**. That feature was reviewing the history of oil exploration in the region and also outlining plans for what was happening at that time which was to be the second period of exploration. Here then are the most important parts of that article:

History of the Black Rock vicinity as a potential oil reservoir dates back nearly 20 years and is closely linked with drilling operations of the Beaver Valley Oil company. Petroleum possibilities there probably were first recognized by Herman T. Kaminska, a homesteader who had once been an oil driller in Texas but is now living in Ogden. Mr. Kaminska even attempted to put down a prospect hole himself, but lacked the necessary finances.

It was during 1924 that attention of Walter James, prominent stockman of Black Rock, was first called to the structure. Mr. James stated that oil was out of his line, but efforts to interest him continued, and in March 1925 he hired the late A.G. Burritt, consulting geologist of Salt Lake City, to examine and report upon the potentialities of the Black Rock area.

Mr. Burritt spent several days [there] in his first study of the region. Early in April [1925] he submitted to Mr. James a short report in which, after reviewing geological conditions and pronouncing them favorable for oil accumulation, he said:

"In the Black Rock district, an east-west flexure trends across the valley and there is some evidence of a north-south fold. At the crossing of these two folds (there is) a structural high. There is hydrostatic pressure from east and west Why should this structural high not be a favorable gathering place? Evidence to date suggests that it is. Further evidence of a petroliferous condition was found in a well drilled near Fillmore, the log of which shows a number of sands containing good showings of oil. I believe the Black Rock district is well worth a test well".

As a result of Mr. Burritt's visit and report, the Beaver Valley Oil company was incorporated, with Mr. James, president, in charge of both financing and field operations. A well site was spotted in Section 20, township 25 south, range 9 west. Drilling there was commenced in April, 1926, and continued intermittently for over three years-- intermittently,--because four months each winter were excluded on account of cold weather, a delay which will not be necessary with modern equipment.

The well was sent to a total depth of 3492 feet [1064 meters]. Strong showings of gas with some oil were passed through at various depths, as shown on the company's log. The drill had entered an important strata known in many other regions. In a comprehensive report upon the entire region, dated March 3, 1932, Mr. Burritt reviewed the fate of the well as follows:

"To assist possible theories that may explain a mysterious occurrence which wrecked the well at that time, I will state here that Mr. James informs me the well was left unguarded for perhaps 24 hours about August 10, 1929, the only time that had occurred in more than three years. Fresh water, to replace the salt water was being run into the hole, and advantage was taken of the opportunity to give the men a needed rest. It proved an unwise move; for in the interim a piece of case-hardened steel was dropped into the hole-- perhaps more than one.

To review the first drilling, it was December of 1925 the drilling rig arrived at Black Rock

Perhaps the opening ceremonies for the drilling of the Walter James Oil Well, in April of 1926. South of Antelope Spring. (Kaufman collection)

The Beaver Valley Oil Company Office south of Antelope Spring and near(?) the Walter James Well. (Kaufman collection)

and was hauled to the drill site by teams and a large traction tractor. At the site, men were building a structure around the proposed well site to allow for winter work. **Herman Kaminska** was in charge of drilling to begin with, but was joined later by a Mr. Engle and a professional drilling crew from Texas.

In early April, 1926, Walter James was hospitalized in Salt Lake City and missed the opening ceremonies. He had cancer of the stomach and part of it was removed. Merrill Miller, his son-in-law, was there acting in his behalf. The well was called the Walter James Well No. 1, and it was spudded in during the week preceding April 23. Drilling was fast at first, but the deeper they got, the more breakdowns and problems they had. News reports indicated they were always waiting for more pipe!

After the first well was stopped by sabotage or accident in August, 1929, they started a new well about 1 1/2 kms southwest of the first one. It appears the first was in Section 17, contrary to what's stated above, the second in Section 20, T25S, R9W. They referred to this one simply as Well No. 2. Things apparently didn't go well, or the money ran out, because the last report on that well was on April 6, 1930 at a depth of 730 feet [222 meters].

There were no other news reports about oil exploration again until the above stated article in October, 1941. In that news item it reported that a new outfit called the Oil Exploration company would drill again in Section 17 near the original Walter James Well No. 1. The new company was being set up and ran by C. Ed Lewis. By that date, they had already drilled a well and found water at only 10 meters. That water was to be used for the camp and for drilling a new test oil well. They apparently had no success in finding oil, because there were no more news items in the local paper.

The Walter James Family

This chapter will end on March 2, 1944 upon the death of Walter James, but first a brief look at various other individuals who were important in the history of Black Rock.

Helen Raht James, Walter's wife, was well educated for her time and seemed to like civic involvement, at least in her younger years. She was a member of the Eastern Star, a civic club which held meetings in Milford. She and her daughters were constantly going to town(Milford) for meetings as well as everyday shopping. In her younger days she was a real go-getter, but with age, she made fewer trips to town. She, as well as Walter and her daughters were also always going out to Burbank and Garrison on the Utah-Nevada line to visit relatives and friends. Some time during the 1910's(?), Helen's sister, Elise Raht Burbank and husband Willard, moved to Seattle, Washington, then members of the James family were constantly going up there. At one time Helen even sailed to Europe for 2 months on the S. S. Champlain.

Much of this information comes from news items listed under *Black Rock* in the local newspaper. All these news items about Black Rock were sent in to the Milford paper, but prior to about 1916, they were sent to the Fillmore paper, *The Progress*. For at least half a century Helen was the one doing this. Only after she moved into Babe's home in Denver in about 1947 or 1948, did someone else do it. Thanks to her efforts, we have a written record of at least part of Black Rock's history.

Throughout the years Helen always had a teenage girl or young woman living and working there at the Big House, which was the main ranch house. The girls usually worked in the summer months when school was out. Dawn Kelly Anderson from Oasis was one. Some of her comments are seen in the CCC camp part later in this chapter. Also, Della Labrum (Madsen) worked there from 1923 on, and for many years. Once, Della went with Benita to California on a vacation for a month or so. In the late 1930's Della had a beauty shop in Milford, but she was always mentioned by Helen in the news items.

It seems that everyone got along fine with Helen, except for little boys! **Jack Stahl**, now of Washington near St. George, and the son of John Stahl, remembers going back out to Black Rock to visit and remembers the James' women a little different than most-- partly because he was so young:

After Grandma and Granddad [Wessie & Horace Stahl] had moved to Milford, we'd go

Back row, L to R, Benita and Thela James, then Helen Raht James, Helen (Babe) and Walter James, sometime in the mid or late 1910's. (Elise M. Brougham collection)

down there to visit, and boy I'd go in their house and I wouldn't even dare move. If you'd even breathe wrong why that old woman would snarl at ya, and I was scared to death of her! I liked Walter James, but I didn't like Helen. She was a snobby, snotty old gal.

Benita and Thekla kinda ran things at the Ranch. When Thekla told Merrill to squat, he squatted! They inherited ways from their mother. They all seemed to be domineering women, or at least they seemed that way to me. But old Walter James, he was a good natured old guy.

Benita James was the oldest child of Walter & Helen. Her name is often spelled Beniti, but pronounced with the "A". Benita was at Black Rock for this entire time period, but she did go away to school during the 1910's. Some time in the early 1980's, she was interviewed by Gladys Whittaker of Milford. In that tape she mentioned a little about her college days:

I went to several schools, and I was willing to do it, and mother said she'd do anything to keep me in school. I went to Westminster and the University of Utah in Salt Lake, and one in Colorado Springs. But I didn't graduate from college.

News clippings indicate she and Thekla had both been in Salt Lake going to school at Westminster during the school years 1914-15, and 1915-16. Benita also spent the winter of 1918-19 in Salt Lake, presumably at the U. of Utah(?). That seems to have been the last year she was away from home at Black Rock.

After her school days Benita was constantly going on business trips with her father Walter. Some have said she was Walter's right-hand man because she helped a lot with rounding up cattle and was in the saddle quite often. Her mother however prevented her from doing all that much work with the men. Sometimes they went by train to such places as Nevada, California, and Salt Lake. On shorter trips they went by car, and it seems Benita was the one doing most of the driving. The family often motored to Burbank and Garrison in the West Desert. Other trips were to the Marysvale area where the family had a cabin in the mountains and a herd of sheep during the summer months. The shopping place for people of Black Rock was always Milford, since it was the closest real town, but it was in Beaver County. There were also trips to Fillmore for business, since they lived in Millard County, but it was at least twice as far as driving to Milford.

For fun trips in the late 1910's and 1920's, Benita would often drive members of the family and friends to places like the warm springs west of Meadow, or to the Roosevelt Hot Springs northeast of Milford. That popular place was maybe 10-15 kms south of the mines at Antelope Point, and up against the west side of the Mineral Mountains.

The most important thing Benita did during this time period was get married. But it wasn't the kind of marriage you'd expect from a 42 year old woman. She ran away with a young fellow named **Hampton Burke**, who was 24 years old at the time. **Hamp** was the ranch hand who was working for Walter James there at the Black Rock Ranch. He had been there since 1929. According to Donetta Hardy of Delta, they drove to Ely via the Black Rock-Crystal Peak Road running due west from Black Rock and were married there.

They were married on January 23, 1936, by James E. Huntley, a pastor of the First Methodist Church in Ely. This was exactly one week before her 42nd birthday, which was January 30, 1894. Hamp was born May 18, 1911, so he would have been lacking about 4 months of his 25th birthday.

Years later Benita became good friends with Floyd & Donetta Hardy, the couple who worked for the railroad and lived at Black Rock in 1946 and 1947. After these two gals knew each other well, Benita told Donetta about the time she and Hamp got married. Here's what Donetta Hardy remember as of 1995:

Benita and Hamp went to Ely, Nevada, to be married in 1936. Afterwards, they came back and picked up the mail at the Black Rock post office and found out that Babe had TB. So instead of telling her folks that they were married, they didn't say a thing just then. Benita got ready and went to New Mexico and picked up Babe and brought her back to Black Rock. It wasn't until after she returned from that trip, that they told Benita's folks they were married. Later they sent Babe to a sanitarium in Los Angeles.

The first time most people in the Beaver County knew of their marriage was when the Milford paper came out on July 7, 1936. That's when Helen R. James, who was the one writing the Black Rock news item for the paper, first referred to them as a couple, Mr. and Mrs. Hampton Burke.

Some people have jokingly stated that Hamp moved from the bunkhouse into the Big House. Actually it was the **Cottage** they moved into which is just north of the old bunkhouse and the main house, which is usually referred to as the Big House. Between her marriage and Walter's death in 1944, there doesn't seem to be have been much change in the lives of either Hamp or Benita. They both continued to live and work right there at the Ranch.

One more thing Donetta Hardy remembered about Benita. She was not a real good cook. All her life, she had gone with her father on business trips, and had done some wrangling of cows to some extent as well. That left Helen, Thekla, or Babe, or one of the hired girls there at the Ranch to do the cooking.

Thekla James was the second of the three girls of Walter & Helen R. James. She went to college with Benita during the school years of 1914-15, and 1915-16 at Westminster College in Salt Lake City. She was also in Salt Lake during the 1918-1919 school year, but at which college is unknown. It's not certain if she graduated on not(?), but 1919 seems to have been the last time she attended school or lived away from home.

Thekla, like Benita, did a lot of traveling. She went to California every year or two, and to Seattle where there were family members on her mother's side. But she didn't travel around with her father like Benita did. She perhaps spent a little more time attending social events like the Eastern Star club in Milford along with her mother.

The big event in Thekla's life was her marriage to **Merrill Miller** of Milford. They were married June 16, 1924, in Beaver. According to one-line news items in the local newspaper they had been attending social functions together for a year or two before their marriage. Merrill was the son of a William Miller of Milford. William was the owner and operator of a grocery store there before the family moved to Beaver later on.

News items about Black Rock were scarce during the 1920's for some reason, but it seems that Merrill and Thekla lived in Milford and helped Merrill's father in the grocery business. This lasted about 4 years, then Merrill went to work for Walter James and the couple moved into the Cottage at the Black Rock Ranch.

On October 4, 1926, their one and only child, **Walter James Miller**, was born. He was named after his grandfather, but to save confusion, they usually referred to him as **Wally**.

Merrill & Thekla lived and worked at the ranch until about July, 1933, then Merrill joined the Civilian Conservation Corps(CCC's). He was stationed at the Beaver Canyon CCC camp east of Beaver(8/3/1933-*MN*). He was classed as a Local Experienced Man(LEM) and a foreman for the **Forest Service**. This began his very long career with the Forest Service which lasted 20 years over a span of 35 years. In the meantime, Thekla and Wally stayed at the Ranch at Black Rock.

Not long after Merrill joined the CCC's, Wally injured his foot on the farm and had to be hospitalized. **Nola Miller**, the woman who would later marry Wally, remembered what happened: *Walt had just barely turned 7 years old in the fall of 1933, and he was sitting on one of those old hay rakes with long tines, and the rake caught his leg and one tine went right through it. From that he got ostiomylitus, an affliction of the bone. They used to confuse it with bone cancer years ago.*

He was taken to L.D.S. Hospital in Salt Lake City at the end of October, 1933. He was home for the holidays in Black Rock, but spent the better part of the winter of 1933-34 in the hospital. Throughout his life, Wally had relapses of ostiomylitus every few years.

Merrill's CCC group was moved from high in Beaver Canyon to another camp site near Fillmore for the winter of 1933-34. By June, Wally was undergoing his last treatment at the hospital in Salt Lake. Everybody who examined Wally had no idea what the problem was--a complete mystery to everyone at that time.

By July, 1934, Merrill was at a new camp in Oak Creek Canyon east of Oak City, which is located east of Delta. He and his group planted all those big ponderosa pine trees up near the head of the canyon near the campground. Then it was back to Fillmore in August, and to Kanosh by November of 1934. At this same time, the fall of 1934, H.L. Hall who was doing work on Taylor Grazing projects, had just completed drilling the well located just west of the store & hotel at Black Rock. It has always been known as the Black Rock Well, but it has brackish water.

Hamp & Benita J. Burke, and Merrill & Thekla J. Miller, right. Black Rock Ranch 1930's.
(Donnetta Hardy collection)

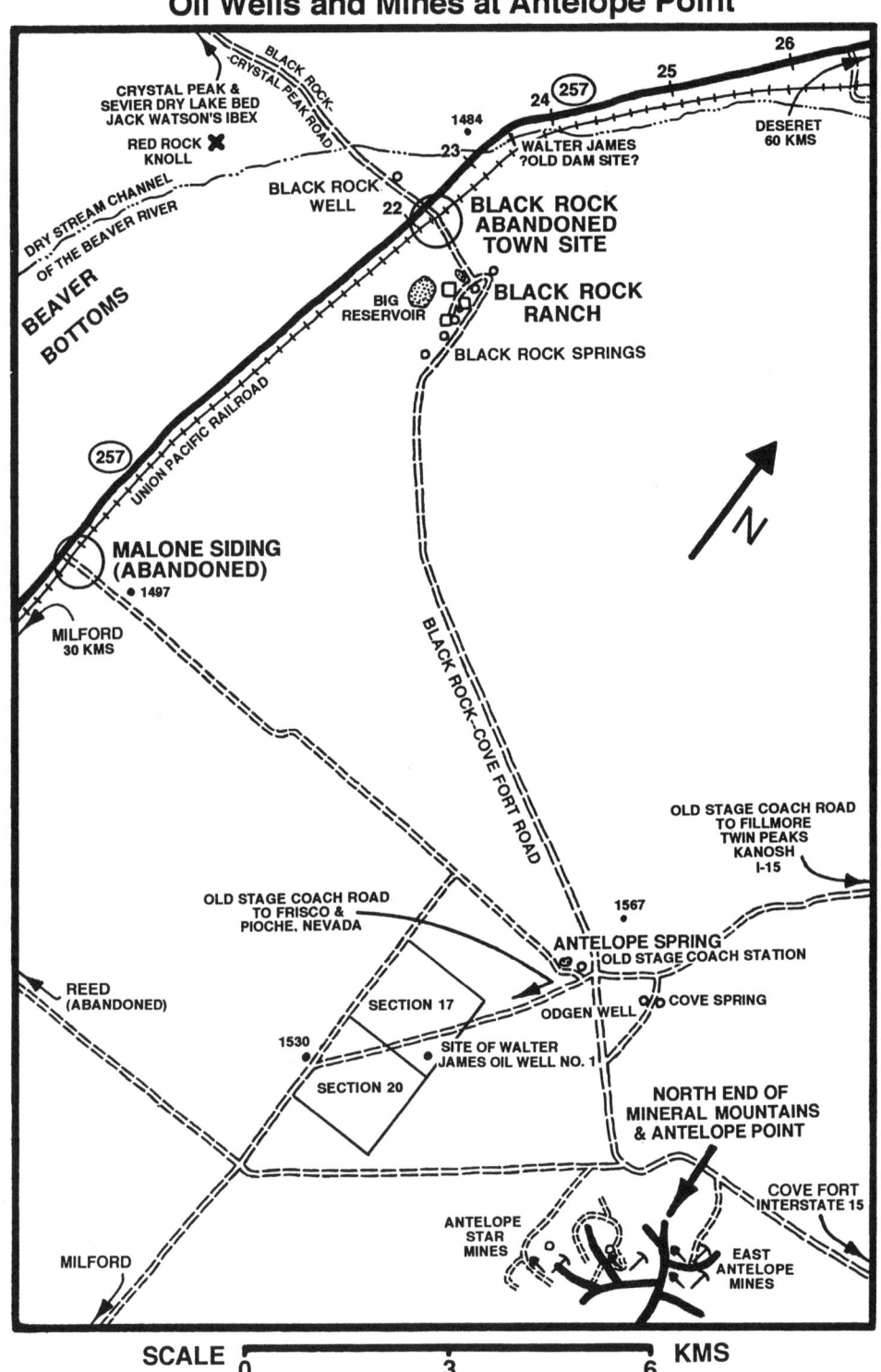

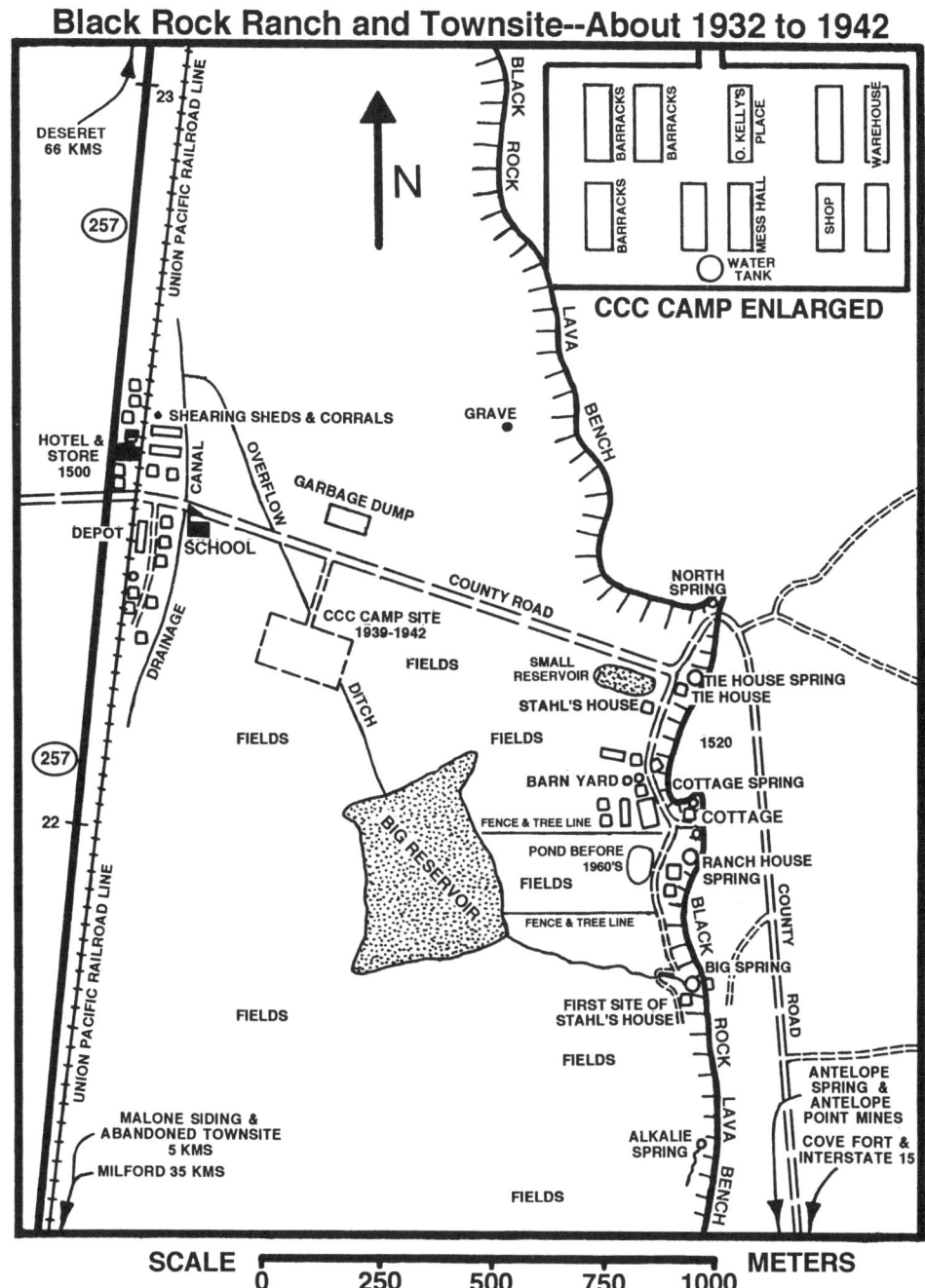

Black Rock Ranch and Townsite--About 1932 to 1942

During the summer of 1935, Merrill was transferred to the Mirror Lake CCC Camp. This time they had quarters for married people and apparently Thekla and Wally spent the summer there with him. By October, Merrill was sent to Salt Lake, and his family spent the winter there. By summer, they were living in Bountiful. They rented a home there, and that's where they spent the next few years with Merrill working for the Forest Service in Salt Lake City. While there, one of his jobs was to return to the Black Rock area in February, 1937, and run a bulldozer out in the desert clearing snow off roads so sheepmen could get supplies to their sheep camps. Merrill, Thekla and Wally remained in Bountiful throughout the rest of this period while Merrill worked for the Forest Service.

The third child of Walter and Helen James was the girl named **Helen.** In the family, and to save confusion, she was usually called **Babe.** As this time period begins, Babe is at home in Black Rock. In a short piece in the Milford newspaper (8/31/1917--*BCN*) it states Thekla and Babe are going to Seattle where they will attend school. That would be for the 1917-18 school year, and they would have stayed with their mother's sister Elise Raht Burbank. It's not certain whether they stayed there the whole year or not. We do know that all 3 daughters spent the 1918-1919 school year in Salt Lake, then Babe went to East High School the next year and graduated in the spring of 1920.

Her next school was Colorado College in Colorado Springs, Colorado. How she got out there is a mystery. News from the local newspaper is sparse in the 1920's, but it seems Babe graduated from Colorado College in the field of nursing. By the summer of 1926, she was in California taking special classes in nursing, then spent the next couple of years at home in Black Rock. In the school year of 1928-29, she was in Southern California, perhaps in Santa Monica, and either in school or working(?). By January, 1931, she was enrolled at the University of California at Berkeley.

For part of 1932 and 1933, she was a nurse in Eddy County, New Mexico, then she attended summer school at the UCGA in Los Angeles. Then in Alamagordo, N.M., she worked in the public health department as a school and county nurse. By May of 1934, an article appeared in the *Alamagordo News*, and in the Milford paper, part of which went like this:

Miss Helen James, county health nurse, has been signally honored, in that she has been requested to prepare an article on Public Health Work in New Mexico, which will be published next fall in the official organ of the Public Health Nursing Association..... Dr. Earp, head of the state health department, has also requested Miss James to prepare a

Hamp Burke, left(Rosalie K. C. Burke foto?), and Benita J. Burke, next to the Wash House in August, 1942. (Dawn Kelly Anderson collection)

paper on health work in Otero County, to be presented at the convention of health workers to be held in Las Vegas in July.

During the summer of 1935, Helen instructed Red Cross classes at the Agricultural College in Fort Collins, Colorado. Everything was going so well for Babe, then an article in the 3/12/1936 issue of the *Milford News* states: *Benita James has returned home after spending several weeks in New Mexico and southern California. Miss James was called to New Mexico because of the illness of her sister Helen, who has been employed as a public health nurse for Otarion county for the past three years..... Miss Helen is convalescing in Barlow's Sanitarium, Los Angeles, and hopes to soon return to her home for an indefinite time.*

Apparently she contracted TB from a patient and spent 6 months in the Barlow's Sanitarium.

After Babe regained health, she spent the first 6 months of 1937 at Columbia University in New York, then returned to New Mexico as regional health consultant. The next big event for Babe was marriage. The 2/10/1938 issue of the *Milford News* ran the announcement:

*Mr. and Mrs. Walter James announce the marriage of their daughter Helen to **William N. McMillen** of Amarillo, Texas. The ceremony..... was at Borger, Texas,... The bride, a graduate of the U. of California, is regional consultant in the public health nursing for the state of New Mexico. Mr. McMillen received his education at Northwestern University, Evanston, Illinois. He is with Bovaird Oil Well Supply and Equipment Company, Borger, Texas.*

The next big event for Babe and William (Mac) McMillen was their first child, a girl, who was born June 11, 1941, in Amarillo, Texas. Her name was **Sophia Ann**. Some time in the fall of 1941, William was called into the Navy. By January of 1942, Lieutenant McMillen was in command of a ship near Philadelphia, then was stationed at Wilmington, North Carolina by April. It was a minesweeper, and Babe was there with him part of the time. During the summer of 1942, Helen and Sophia were back home at Black Rock where they stayed for the rest of the war, while William was in foreign waters.

Merrill & Thekla J. Miller, and son Walter James (Wally) Miller(left). Helen R. and Walter James, holding the baby Sophia McMillen, and Wally Miller. Black Rock Ranch, Christmas, 1941.
(Elise M. Brougham collection)

The oldest child raised by the Walter James family was **Jack Boyle Travers**, the son of Helen Raht's sister, Minnie. They reared him from infancy, and he was just part of the family, although he always kept his father's name. At the beginning of this time period of 1917 to 1944, Jack was at the Ranch working for his adoptive father Walter James. He was sometimes herding cattle, or rounding up sheep, either way out to the west in the Pine Valley or Mtn. Home area of the West Desert. Sometimes he and Walter would go to the Marysvale area on business. As far as the sheep business is concerned, Jack was the camp mover or camp supplier, not the sheep herder.

Babe James at the Ranch in about 1920(?). (Elise M. Brougham collection)

Babe James in an old "flivver" or stripped down car, in the late 1910's or early 1920's. (Jim Travers collection).

Jack also spent lots of time in Salt Lake and Park City. Some time during his trips to northern Utah, he met a young lady named **Frances Treweek**. She was from Salt Lake City, but her father, Nicholas Treweek, was a well-to-do mining man who had large investments in Park City. Nicholas was born and raised in Wales, but migrated to western America and was deeply involved in mining at the corporate level in Nevada, Idaho and Utah. Locally, he organized the Alliance Mining Company of Park City, as is told in the book, *Men who made good in Nevada, 1905-1906*. Frances was born in 1897, and was from a wealthy and well-educated family. **Jack & Frances** were married on **June 28, 1917** in Salt Lake City.

It's not certain where they lived for the next three years or so, but it appears from one-line news items in the local paper they lived in Salt Lake City most of the time. Jack made many short trips back to Black Rock on occasions. By February of 1921(2/23/1921--*BCN*), Walter had **Frank Andre**, a carpenter, build a new bungalow there at the ranch for Mr. and Mrs. Jack Travers. For several years Jack & Frances lived at the Ranch in Black Rock, but commuted back and forth to Salt Lake often.

A bit earlier, in 1918 in Salt Lake, they had their first son named **Jack Travers Jr.** In 1920, they had another son named **Walter James (Jim) Travers**. At this time Jack was working for his adoptive father in the sheep business. Jim Travers' birth certificate also states his father's occupation as *"sheepman"*. By late 1921, Jack and his family were spending lots of time in the West Desert at Mtn. Home, just northeast of Indian Peak.

By the summer of 1928, and probably 2 or 3 years before that, Jack and his family were living in Ely, Nevada, and he was working for the Adams McGill Livestock Company. It was about this time, or perhaps a bit earlier, that Jack and Frances split up and/or had a divorce. Frances took the two boys to Caliente and got on a train for Los Angeles. What happened to her and Jack Jr. and Jim will be told in the last chapter.

Continuing now with Jack's story. In January, 1931, Jack had just spent time at the Ranch for Christmas, then returned to Casseon, Colorado, according to the Milford newspaper. But according to Inez Bertoldi Travers Beers, he must have been in Oak City, which is south of Steamboat Springs. He was somehow involved in the sheep business there for a while. Another news clip mentions he took a trip to Steamboat Springs with Merrill Miller, this time on official business.

In the early summer of 1933, Jack began working for the very first CCC camp built in the West Desert, and one of the first in Utah. The camp was located in the Wah Wah Springs area. He was the fence foreman at first, but a year and a half later he supervised the construction of the Old Dutchman Reservoir, 8 kms northwest of Newhouse.

At this time he was living at the CCC camp but occasionally returned home to Black Rock on weekends. Jack's 2nd son, Jim Travers, spent the summer of 1933 at the Black Rock Ranch, then returned to Los Angles to attend school. Jack stayed in Black Rock and probably with the CCC's until sometime in 1936, then moved to Montello, Nevada, which is located in the extreme northeast corner of the state, not far east of Wells. He returned to Black Rock for the Christmas holidays in 1936, as did both of his sons, Jack Jr. and Jim. The boys were living in Hollywood at that time.

It was in Montello he met and married a young gal named **Inez Bertoldi**. She was still alive in 1996, and has told about their marriage and their first years of life in Craig, Colorado:

*I met Jack in Montello, Nevada. At that time he was superintendent or head foreman for the **Utah Construction Company** which had about 10 or 12 ranches from Montello north going to the Idaho line. They owned sheep and cattle and different ranches at that time. Each place he went to to check on the foreman and stock, was at a ranch. Each ranch had houses and we stayed in them. The main ranch was just outside of Montello, and that's where I met Jack. That was at the Gamble Ranch. I was visiting with my cousin, one of the Daz family; they had a business down there.*

I didn't know him too long before we got married, seems like it was maybe 6 months or so. I was from Ogden. When we got married he came to Ogden and picked me up and we flew to Reno. We bought our marriage license in Reno, and we were married on December 30, 1939. I was born in 1914, and we were married when I was about 26.

From the left, Jack Travers, Benita James, 3 unidentified men with Hamp Burke behind, then Walter James, Wally Miller, Helen R. James, Thekla & Merril Miller. This was about 1933-34, and when Jack and Merrill were in the Triple C's. (Jim Travers collection).

Walter James, left, and Jack Travers, at the old Black Rock Depot sometime before 1926(Elise M. Brougham collection). Jack Travers & Jack Jr. in the mountains near Marysvale, 1920. (Jim Travers collection).

On the left, Jack Jr. & Jim Travers in about 1923-24. Jim, Frances Treweek, and Jack Travers Jr. at the Black Rock Ranch in about 1921. (Jim Travers collection).

Camping in the mountains near Marysvale. Frances & Jack Travers and their little boys, Jack Jr. and Jim. (Jim Travers collection)

James' sheep cabin in the mountains near Marysvale. (Jim Travers collection).

From the left, Wally Miller, Helen R. James, Merrill Miller, Benita J. Burke, Inez B. Travers, Jack Travers, Thekla J. Miller holding Sophia McMillen, Walter James and Margaret Burbank, at the Black Rock Ranch, Christmas, 1941. (Elise M. Brougham collection)

When we met he was divorced, and the kids were with his ex-wife in California. We spent about 3 years at Montello, and then he had this offer from Ralph Pitchforth here in Craig, Colorado. Ralph was a friend of his, and he wanted Jack to come here and take over this sheep outfit. They had 10,000 breeding ewes up here, and Jack had a lot of experience with cattle and sheep at Black Rock, and then with the Utah Construction Company job in Montello. So we came up here to Craig in about 1943, and he was involved with quite a big sheep operation. He ran sheep east to the Utah border in the winter time, on the winter range; and then up above Craig to the southeast in the summers, up on the summer range in the mountains. The ranch itself was up in the mountains on William's Fork about 40 miles [65 kms] southeast of Craig and we lived there in the summer time, then in winter time we lived in Craig. Throughout the year he just went back and forth to check on the herders and everyone, and the sheep.

The rest of the story of Jack & Inez Travers, his ex-wife and two boys will be told in the next two chapters.

The AG James Family

Probably the second most important family ever to have lived at Black Rock was that of **Authur** and **Velora James**, and their two children, **Dorothy** and **Ralph**. AG & Velora took over the little store, hotel and post office at Black Rock in December of 1916, and lived there for about 24 years, almost to the end of this time period from 1917 to 1944. One description of the store, hotel and post office has already been discussed earlier in this chapter, but below is this family's own story of their lives and their little business.

At the beginning of this period business was very good. There were lots of sheep & sheepmen in the country beginning in October or November of each year, and lasting through the shearing season which was always in April. After that, the sheep & sheepmen left for summer pastures high in the mountains from the Marysvale area northward to the Soldier Summit country. In the late fall or early winter they made the return trip to the West Desert often times passing through Black Rock.

In all these early years the sheep were herded all the way between summer and winter pastures and it might have taken them a month to make the trip. At first they had sheep

Jack Travers and 2nd wife Inez Bertoldi Travers. (Inez B. Travers Beers collection)

camps, or wagons, pulled by teams of horses, which followed the sheep herds; then later on in the late 1920's, small trucks and cars began to be used to pull the sheep camps. Also, small pickups began to be used to deliver supplies to the sheep herders in the desert. The use of these small trucks by the people who took supplies out to the sheep camps made it much easier and faster than with supply wagons pulled by teams. It also allowed camp movers to buy supplies at lower prices in the larger towns then take them to the camps, thus bypassing the little stores at places like Black Rock, Clear Lake, Newhouse and Jack Watson's Ibex.

Business was good for the store & hotel up to about the late 1920's, then there was a slow decline. The number of sheep in Utah reached a peak of just under 3 million in 1900 and 1901, then again in 1931, then the numbers slowly decreased to about 440,000 in 1994. There was also The Great Depression which began in about 1930. So as the 1930's progressed AG & Velora were the economic casualties of fewer sheep and The Depression. Up to this time the sheepmen would buy much of their winter supplies from AG's store on credit, then would pay off each year's debt in the spring after the sheep were sheared and the wool sold. When things started going downhill, the sheepmen couldn't get good prices for wool, and they started hurting. This meant they had a hard time paying their debts, including what they owed AG. That's when AG & Velora began to look elsewhere to make their livelihood.

But first their children and their life at Black Rock. Next is the second part of the life story of AG or Arthur and Velora James and their children. It was compiled, probably in the 1960's, by Dorothy James Leonard during the last years Velora was alive. Occasionally newspaper reports have been added for confirmation of dates, and there has been some editing. Also, there is some duplication here of what other people have already said about Black Rock:

At the beginning of 1917, the little store at Black Rock was a supply depot for the sheep and cattle men in the area when they were in the West Desert on the winter range. Shearing of the sheep was done in Black Rock in the spring and they had a dipping vat to dip the sheep in to get rid of the ticks.

The Union Pacific Railroad had a station there. Originally it was made of two old Pullman cars, and it was a water stop for all the trains. It was once one of the busiest stations along the Salt Lake Route which ran from Salt Lake to Los Angeles. Everything at Black Rock was shipped in and out by rail. Hay, grain, coal, groceries, clothing, hardware and other things came into Black Rock; while sheep, cattle, wool, and hides were shipped out.

The residents of Black Rock at the end of 1916 were the railroad agent [station manager], two telegraph operators, a few section hands, and the Walter James family-- Walter and his wife Helen, and their three daughters Benita, Thekla and Helen [Babe].

*When Arthur and Velora bought the store and hotel, Walter and Helen moved up to where Helen Raht James' parents old ranch was which was adjacent to the Black Rock Springs. Those springs were the source of water for the residents of the town and the railroad water tank. The Walter James' had two or three men working for them and Arthur and Velora had two or three employees. Thirty **(30)** permanent residents would be the maximum population from September to April or May in those early years.*

During the winter months, Velora served three meals a day to from 15 to 50 hungry sheepmen, cattlemen, trappers, prospectors, railroaders, and traveling salesmen. The salesmen traveled by train with catalogues rather than sample cases until more reasonable automobiles and passable roads were built.

In the spring at shearing time, Arthur hired shearers, wool trompers, sack rollers and wranglers. He also opened the boarding house and hired two cooks, and three or four girls to assist with the cooking & serving food and wash dishes. Two rooms were partitioned off at one end of the boarding house for the cooks and their helpers to sleep in. The shearing corral workers usually pitched tents between the corrals and the boarding house.

Usually there were a few fellows who could play guitars, harmonicas, fiddles, saws, wash boards, tubs or other contraptions to make music to dance to. If they got tired they would wind up using the victorola [grafanola?] to furnish the music. Corn meal was sprinkled on the floor to make it slick enough to dance on. The few ladies in town danced every dance and usually had to have two or three dances before they got to dance with all the men there. On Saturday night if they were not working on Sunday, they danced all night and the women cooked breakfast for everyone before they went home to sleep.

There were a number of scattered farms in a 20 mile [32 km] radius of Black Rock. These people were known as **dry farmers** because they depended on rain to water their crops. They dug or drilled wells for their drinking water and for their stock. The water was pumped by wind mill. These dry farmers came by buggy or wagon to buy groceries and other supplies from Arthur's general merchandise store.

The years from 1918 to 1924 were very dry years, with little rain and hot winds all summer and not enough snow in the winter. One by one the dry farmers were forced to leave from lack of water and crop failures. When they were ready to leave they would come and say good bye to Arthur and Velora and that they were leaving things behind that the James' might be able to use.

When the McCroskys left during one winter [early 1920's], they told Arthur they had left some building supplies they might be able to use. So Arthur and Velora put chains on the little Dodge truck they had and went to the McCrosky farm to get the things. There had been a snow storm and strong winds a few days before and Arthur and Velora were carrying a sheet of plaster board outside. Arthur was backing out the door and Velora was on the other end. Suddenly Arthur dropped his end and Velora yelled, "What's the matter with you, are you too weak to carry your end?" Then she heard a wee small voice answer, "I'm down here in the well."

They hadn't noticed the well because the snow had been blown and drifted into it. Luckily Arthur wasn't hurt and Velora found a rope in the truck which Arthur tied around himself under his arms and Velora tied the other end to the truck and pulled him out of the well. At that time Arthur weighed 250 pounds[114 kgs]. All their lives they laughed many times about this experience as well as about other accidents that turned out humorous instead of disastrous.

Many people called Arthur "Cupie" because of his large stomach and Cupie shape. But he had a good sense of humor and was a good sport. He was teased and kidded about every phou pau he ever made. Everyone liked him because of his pleasant, laughing personality. However, if his temper flared he would fight a giant, and he could cool down just as fast as he became angry and was always apologetic for his hot temper.

Velora was good at dishing out the kidding and teasing but couldn't take much herself. She had a keen sense of humor as long as she didn't have to laugh at herself.

There was never any electricity in Black Rock so everyone used coal oil [kerosene] lamps and lanterns for light. Wood and coal were the only fuel for heat and cooking. They hauled all the wood from the mountains. Gasoline engines were used to operate pumps and washing machines. There were no telephones in Black Rock except at the depot, and they were for railroad use only, so any emergency communication was sent and received by telegraph.

Arthur built an ice house and during the winter when the ice on the ponds was 14 inches [35 cms] or more thick, he and the hired man would cut it into blocks about 24 inches [65 cms] square. This they did with saws, then they hauled it to the ice house and packed it in saw dust until the ice house was filled. They used the ice in refrigerator-like ice boxes to keep meat, milk, butter and other food cool when the weather was warm in summer.

In those days, Arthur would do his own butchering of calves, beef, pigs, chickens, turkeys; and he made sausage, head cheese, smoked or salted ham, bacon, and corned beef. These they ate themselves or were sold in the store or used in the boarding house during the shearing season.

Velora bottled hundreds of quarts of fresh fruit, jam, jelly, vegetables, pickles and meat for use in the following winter. She baked all the bread, cakes, pies, cookies, puddings, doughnuts, biscuits, muffins, etc. She also made ice cream, cheese, cottage cheese and churned butter. She was one of the best cooks in the country. At different times, Velora's sisters Nell, Velva, and Nora worked for her in Black Rock.

Arthur hired his brothers **John, Dan** and his twin brother **Bert [Albert]** when ever he could. Bert and Dan lived there two thirds of the time, and were not very ambitious, to put it mildly. John was a good bookkeeper and helped with the accounts in the store and was bookkeeper at shearing time.

John's wife **Sara Slaughter James** worked there too, as did Dan's wife **Bell Sherwood James** and their two daughters **Wanda** and **Leona**, who helped cook for the shearers in the boarding house. They were all ambitious and pleasant to be around.

Six months before they bought the store & hotel, and on June 23, 1916, Arthur and Velora had their first child **Dorothy James.** She was born at L.D.S. Hospital in Salt Lake City. That fall when they hired help for the winter, they hired an extra girl to help look after their lively, but mischievous child and iron her clothes, which she changed every five minutes it seemed!

When World War I broke out, Arthur's' twin brother Bert went to Fort Lewis, Washington. Arthur didn't know he had to register since communications were so poor, and had to go to Salt Lake to see the governor about his error, but he was exempt because he operated the post office and had a wife and child.

The flu epidemic hit Black Rock as well as every place else [during the winter of 1919 & 1920], and many robust men died in Black Rock and many were nursed back to health by Velora and her twin sister Nora, who was a trained nurse and a good one. [The H. A. Stahl family lost two girls at this time, but more on them later in the Stahl family story].

Dorothy came down with the flu and developed pneumonia and was as ill as any child can get and still live. Nora was there to help nurse and care for her. The doctor came from Milford over barely passable roads and spent many hours working with Dorothy to pull her through. When the epidemic was at its worst and all the beds were occupied by ill men, Arthur and Velora hired a nurse at their own expense to help care for the many sick patients.

When the war was over Arthur built many bridges over the washes in the roads and dragged out the wagon wheel ruts in the roads between Milford and Black Rock, and the road from Black Rock east to Cove Fort.

He bought a Model T Ford touring car with isinglass curtains to be put up when ever it rained or snowed. When they went any place in winter time, they heated bricks or rocks in their stove and put them in the car to keep their feet warm. Everybody was so bundled up in sweaters, coats, mittens, stocking caps made of wool, and overshoes, it was difficult to even move.

Arthur was a poor driver and was always having car trouble or running out of gas. Velora said she pushed him up every hill in the county for years before Arthur learned how to drive, and until automobiles were better made. Even then, Arthur never was a good driver.

On September 23, 1920, a son, **Ralph James** was born in Salt Lake City. He was a big baby and weighed 10 1/4 pounds [4.5 kg] at birth. He ended up as good, as Dorothy was mischievous!

When Ralph was two years old [1922], he had pneumonia and they almost lost him. The doctor came from Milford nearly every day and Arthur and Velora nursed him around the clock. For weeks it was doubtful he would pull through.

Arthur loved to fish and hunt and bagged a deer for everyone in the hunting party every year, but seldom if ever caught a fish.

Dorothy and Ralph had many pets. Every spring France Brotherson, a good friend and sheep man who worked for the F.C. Jensons for many years, would give them a small shepherd puppy, then a year later would take back the year-old dog to help with the sheep. But there were three dogs they kept until they died. They were a large English sheep dog they called Rags; a pup given to them by Velva, which was half fox terrier and half English bull. They named him Beans and he looked like a greyhound. The third dog was a white toy poodle called Sport. They also had cats, horses, lambs, goats, chickens, turkeys, guinea hens, an owl, a crow, as well as horned toads, lizards and any thing else they could find.

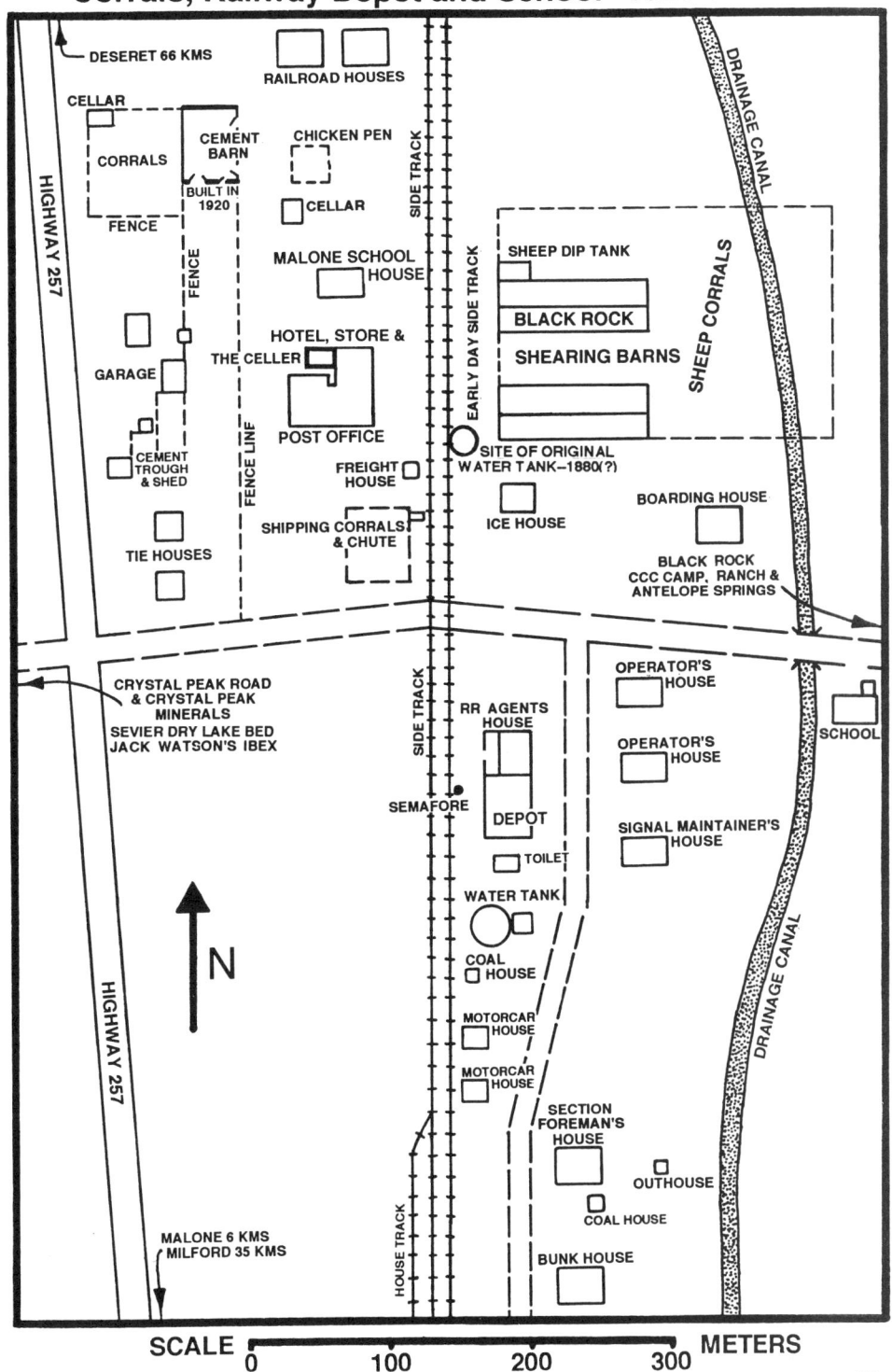

Black Rock Townsite--Store & Hotel, Shearing Barns & Corrals, Railway Depot and School--1925 to 1945

AG James and 1928 Buick, mid-1930's(?). (Kelsey collection)

AG & Velora James' store & hotel, mid or late 1930's(Kelsey collection); and Dorothy and Ralph James in 1920 or 1921. (Beryl G. Sorensen collection)

One horse was willed to Dorothy by Helen Stahl who lived at Antelope Springs 8 miles [13 kms] east of Black Rock. [Later they lived at Walter's ranch just south of the Big House]. That horse was named Trixie, and was half shetland, very old, and spoiled. She had to be led from the barn to wherever you wanted to go, but you could ride her home and into the barn where she ate and drank most of the time.

During the summer of 1925, Arthur, Velora, Dorothy and Ralph went to Yellowstone National Park, then on to Butte, Montana, to see Arthur's sister Hannah James Rossiter and her husband John and daughter Agnas, as well as their adopted son Lester. They had a tent and other camping gear tied all over the outside of their Jewitt touring car, which they owned at that time.

Arthur always dreamed of finding a rich mine and took Dorothy prospecting with him. She always went with him to round up cattle and watch the branding and marking of the calves.

Ralph was a studious, brilliant child and spent his time reading, making radios, experimenting with his chemistry set, and was an excellent violinist. At the age of 12 he traveled all over the state giving concerts at schools and was written up in all the papers. They called him a child prodigy.

[One article about Ralph appeared in the Milford News for August 6, 1931. The AG James' put on a musical with Ralph at the violin, Professor Meyers at the piano, and accompanied by a Miss Thompson. Ralph is mentioned again in the Milford News on August 20, 1931. At that time he had been practicing only 9 months. That article mentions that Carlos Meyers of Reno, the well-known violinist and teacher, was his instructor.]

Ralph's violin teacher was a man about 55 years old who came to Black Rock one winter as a hobo and asked for work chopping wood and doing chores. Arthur hired him and learned this man's name was **Karl Meyers**. Velora had bought a player piano years before and Mr. Meyers sat down to the piano and played like the best concert pianist.

Ralph showed interest in the piano and learned to play and write music. A bond of friendship grew between Ralph and Mr. Meyers and they spent many hours together playing the piano. Mr. Meyers suggested that Ralph should have a violin so Velora bought a violin for Ralph and Mr. Meyers gave him lessons. He was exceptionally gifted and Mr. Meyers was so proud of Ralph and his musical talent, but when shearing was over in the spring and every building was full of wood, he announced that he was leaving. Ralph was broken hearted when he left, but kept practicing on the violin and writing music.

After the weather got cold one day the next fall, Mr. Meyers came back to Black Rock and went on as if he had never been away, chopping wood, doing chores, playing the piano and giving Ralph lessons. Mr. Meyers was reluctant to talk about his past, but said he was born in Austria and lived in Germany. When spring came again he left, but returned again in the fall. He was a sensitive, temperamental, artistic, neat, clean, little man with light brown hair, light skin and blue eyes that really danced when he was playing the piano to accompany Ralph on the violin.

The last time he left Black Rock he had gone on a drunken binge. It was the only time he had ever had any liquor when he was in Black Rock, and he seemed so ashamed and remorseful even though no one said a thing about it. Everyone went on as if nothing had happened but he left a short time later and never returned to Black Rock. He was truly missed by Ralph and after playing with other accompanists and not being satisfied with their playing, Ralph put his violin away and never played again after he left high school.

For about 15 years it seems, Velora spent the month of February in the hospital in Salt Lake. She had 13 sinus operations and 7 abdominal operations and always bounced back to go back to Black Rock and the usual hard work.

In 1922, and when Dorothy was 6 years old and should have been starting school, Arthur and Velora tried to get the Millard County Superintendent of Schools to start a school in Black Rock. They learned they had to have at least 15 pupils to get a teacher from the county and maintain a school. So Arthur began hiring men with large families to work for him. [Walter James hired a Mr. Nay who had a large family, to work at the ranch at about this time]. He built houses for them to live in rent free [probably the tie houses?].

And he tried to get section men working for the railroad with school-age children to move there. When Dorothy was 8 years old, he finally had enough students to get a school started. [That was the 1923-24 school year]. The first lady teacher roomed at the hotel and was a general nuisance, doing her laundry, ironing, and puttering around. Velora once said she'd rather have ten men around than one woman, but tolerated her in order to have a school in Black Rock.

The school house was one room about 18 feet long by 15 feet wide[6x5 meters]. There was a water tap outside for water, and a "Chick Sales"[?] outhouse in one corner of the yard. All 8 grades were in one room. The school house was a mile [1 1/2 kms] from where most of the students lived. They walked or rode horses through the snow, mud and slush. They took their lunches with them, usually packed in 5 pound lard buckets. [Deon Gillen, who went to school that year in Black Rock, said the school house was located up at the ranch at first, then it was moved down to near the railroad tracks some time during the school year.]

Most of the shopping the family or other people at Black Rock did, meant looking through all the catalogs--Sears & Roebuck, Montgomery Ward, Butler Brothers, Fort Dearborn, Bellis Hess and others. [Buying meant] sending orders in, receiving the merchandise and maybe returning part of it and reordering several times before they found satisfactory fit, style, and quality merchandise.

When Dorothy was through the 3rd grade [in 1927(?) at age about 11(?)], the teacher advised Velora to send her away to school. She was spoiled, unruly, and had never been a good student, so she was sent to a boarding school for girls in Salt Lake. The place was **Rowland Hall,** an Episcopal school where the wealthy Protestant people in Salt Lake sent their girls as day students; and others that lived in isolated areas sent their girls as boarding students. Dorothy went there for 2 years, but was miserable and homesick all the time.

The next year, 1929, Velora took Ralph and Dorothy to Los Angeles. She rented an apartment at 91st & Normandy and Dorothy went to a new school that had just been built, Bret Harte Junior High School on 92nd & Hoover Street. Ralph went to Manchester Avenue School on Manchester & Hoover Street. These are now in what is called the Watts area, but in 1929 this was a new section of Los Angeles and integrated at that time. There were Mexicans, Negroes, Japanese, Chinese, Italians, Germans, and people from every other nationality and religion living together in the area and going to the same schools. Ralph and Dorothy both liked school there and had many friends of all nationalities.

Velora wasn't kept busy enough taking care of an apartment and cooking for 3 people so she enrolled at the Marinello Beauty School to take a beauty course. She studied hard and proved to be a very good student. She received 98% on the California State Board Examination. While Velora was busy at school, Ralph and Dorothy were supposed to clean house and wash dishes and all the normal chores that need to be done around the house. But as children, they would fight and argue over who did what. One night Dorothy got mad and broke a plate over Ralph's head. Later that night Ralph wrote a letter to his father Arthur saying, "Dear Dad: Dorothy broke a plate over my head. Your son, Ralph".

Later that fall of 1929, Arthur went to Los Angeles to spend Christmas and any other time he could, but it was the beginning of the Depression. It had hit the sheepmen and Arthur's business hard. Normally, he gave credit for everything the sheepmen needed from fall until they sold their wool and lambs in the spring. When they paid their bills, Arthur was able to pay all his bills too. He carried the sheepmen until his money and credit was depleted and finally had to close the store. [This is believed to be later in about 1941?].

Some time later, Velora, Ralph and Dorothy went back to Black Rock, and Velora still rented rooms and served meals to anyone that came there. She had a few railroad employees and the school teacher as steady boarders and got enough money from them to keep food on the table.

They sent Dorothy to another boarding school in spite of her rebellion and threat to gas herself. **Wasatch Academy** is a co-educational Presbyterian mission school in Mount

Pleasant, Utah, a small friendly town in the Wasatch Mountains in Sanpete County. Many of the sheepmen who came to Black Rock and the West Desert lived there and the surrounding towns. Most of the residents of these towns are of Scandinavian decent and with such names as Jensen, Johansen, Johnson, Christiansen, Munson, Madsen, Brotherson, Nelson, Neilson, Larson, Peterson, and Jorgensen make up most of the population and the majority belong to the Mormon Church.

In fact there are few small towns in the state of Utah with any church except the Mormon Church. Milford is one of the exceptions, with a population of 1500, there are 7 different denominational churches there. Mt. Pleasant has one Presbyterian church where the students at the Academy are asked to attend.

Dorothy loved the school and her teachers and made friends there, so when Ralph was to start the 8th grade, Velora insisted that he go to Wasatch in spite of his objections and threat to come home with the first sheep man to came back to Black Rock. [This was for the 1933-34 school year. He could have stayed at Black Rock for one more year of school there, but apparently didn't.] This was Ralph's first experience living away from home, and he was homesick and not too happy for a while, but he did very well in school and was well-liked by the teachers and students.

Dorothy and Ralph both took an active part in school activities and held offices in their classes and clubs. They both got jobs at school to help pay their way as money was still scarce.

When Dorothy graduated from Wasatch Academy in the spring of 1935, she went to Logan, Utah, with two teachers from the Academy--Miss Frink and Miss Barbee--to go to summer school and try to get a job so she could go to Utah State the next year. With their help she got a job working for the Presbyterian Minister, Reverend Keonig, his wife and three children. Mrs. Keonig wasn't well and needed help with the cooking, house work, washing, ironing and caring for the children, so Dorothy worked for them for her board and room and went to Utah State Agricultural College one year.

After that first year, Dorothy got a job in Roy, Utah, working for the Varneys. They owned a canning factory and paid $.25 an hour, but they had Dorothy keep their large house clean, cook three meals a day, wash, iron, etc., for her board and room, then work in the factory at night for the $.25 an hour. Dorothy had borrowed money from the school for books and charged a few clothes and was trying to get her bills paid up. About the time all her bills were paid, Velora wrote saying she had bought a tea room in Ventura, California and wanted Dorothy to go there with her. So Dorothy left and returned to Black Rock, then went on to Ventura. Arthur refused to leave Black Rock even though he couldn't make a living there. [This was in the fall of 1937]. He still hoped he'd find a gold mine or the sheepmen would get on their feet and pay some of the money they owed him.

[Deon Gillen of Oasis worked there at about this time. Here's a story he remembered: In about 1936, I went down there for about one year and worked on the railroad. And I stayed with AG then. We lived in the hotel. They said I could stay there if I did the chores, so I'd go out and get the cows, and milk 'em. AG didn't have any hay, so the cows just ran out in the flat, and all over. And I'd have to get on a horse and go out and find 'em in the mornings, and milk 'em, and then get to work in time. One morning I hunted for 'em until it was time to go to work and when I finally went, there they were, both of 'em, over by the water tank. The train had hit both of 'em, and they were dead, right by the water tank. They had come in for water.

Deon also mentions that the most of the store & hotel building had carbide gas lighting, similar to what they had in the Clear Lake Hotel down the tracks aways to the north: *They had been using **carbide gas** for lights when I was there. Out in the back of the hotel AG had a tank for the carbide. It seems to me it was about 4 feet [one meter] across, a metal tank, and it was down in the ground. To make carbide gas, you had to turn a valve and that let a little water down in there on the carbide crystals and that would form the gas. Then pressure would build up and it would go into these metal lines and into each lamp in the hotel. The carbide would come in small metal cans and he'd have to clean that out every once in a while. He'd get that sluge out of there, from the spent carbide. The hotel rooms and most of his house used carbide for lights. In some rooms they had to use* kerosene lamps. Me and another fellow had a room up there in the top of the hotel and we had carbide lights then.]

So Velora, Ralph and Dorothy went to Ventura to operate the tea room. The people Velora bought the tea room from had many cats in the old two story house and when they took the cats, they left all their fleas behind, and they nearly ate everyone alive, especially Ralph. The business wasn't as good as they hoped it would be, so Dorothy got a job working in a ladies ready-to-wear store and during the Christmas rush [1937] had a very sore throat, but didn't feel she could stay home when they were so busy and she needed the money. Christmas Eve she came home very ill and went to bed and was in bed three months with acute arthritis. A little later Velora sold the tea room and Ralph decided he would rather return to Wasatch Academy to school.

Velora waited on Dorothy until she was able to get around, then they both went to Santa Barbara where they got work at the El Encanto Hotel. It was a winter resort for wealthy eastern people. When the season was over [spring 1938?], they went to San Francisco. Dorothy got a job waiting on tables at the Women's Athletic Club and Velora got a job in the linen room at the Canterbury Hotel. Dorothy didn't like her job and as soon as she could find another job quit and went to work in a soda fountain. This job only paid $14 a week, for working 7 days a week during the Depression, but her employer was very nice and she could get three meals a day and her uniforms furnished.

While Ralph was at Wasatch Academy, the school sent a telegram saying he was gravely ill with pneumonia and they would keep Dorothy and Velora informed as to his condition. They kept their suit cases packed in case he should get worse, but he started to improve, much to their relief.

Ralph graduated from Wasatch Academy in May, 1938. For that, Dorothy and Velora went by train to Salt Lake, then by bus to Mr. Pleasant for the ceremony. Authur came from Black Rock. When the graduation was over, Velora went with Arthur to Oasis to visit with relatives. Ralph stayed at Wasatch to work for a while and Dorothy hurried back to San Francisco because her fiancee **Albert Leonard** had called and wanted her to come back.

Ralph went to San Francisco in September, 1938, and entered the University of California at Berkeley. He worked in Al's Cigar stand on Market Street early mornings and on Saturday and Sunday, and at the Canterbury Hotel running the elevator evenings. He had decided years before that he wanted to be a chemist. He studied hard and made excellent grades while working and commuting from San Francisco to Berkeley every day. It was tiring and time consuming, but he never complained.

Here's the story of how Al and Dorothy got married. Al thought he wanted to move to St. Paul, Minnesota, where he was born so they went there on their honeymoon. They first went by train from San Francisco to Ventura and got Dorothy's trunk that was stored there, then went on to Las Vegas. They arrived at 5:30 am, **July 29, 1939,** ate breakfast, then went to the county courthouse to get married. They went to see Boulder Dam and took the train that evening for Black Rock to see Arthur. The train arrived in Black Rock about 3 am and Arthur was there to meet them. After a few days they went on to St. Paul and had their honeymoon.

Al had forgotten how hot and humid it was in St. Paul in the summer and after a few days decided to return to Black Rock[fall of 1939]. He thought maybe they could open a business in Black Rock because they were starting to put up a CCC camp there. So they remodeled the store, built a beer bar, bought a jute box to take in nickels and dimes, and served sandwiches. Their only problem was money. Al made a deal with the carpenters building the CCC camp to give them three meals a day if they would do the remodeling of the store. Soon Dorothy was cooking three meals a day for eight carpenters, the school teacher and a few railroad men. [Deon Gillen also remembers Al Leonard tried to put in a Kolar plant, which is a small electric generating system, for lighting in the beer joint].

Arthur bought lambs and sheep and butchered them so they had meat to eat but had more mutton than they wanted. Dorothy realized she was pregnant when she couldn't stand the smell of food cooking and had to go vomit a dozen times while cooking each meal.

It was about this time [spring of 1940], Al received a telegram that his mother was very ill in Portland, Oregon, so Al left to go see her, and on his way stopped to see Velora and Ralph in San Francisco and persuaded Velora to go back to Black Rock with him to help Dorothy through her pregnancy. So Ralph found a place in Berkeley to get board and room and Velora packed her things and went back to Black Rock.

The whole family, except Ralph, was in Black Rock during the summer of 1940, then Dorothy's baby son **Larry Leonard** *was born September 21, 1940, in the Cedar City Hospital. Just before the birth, Al's mother died and he returned to Oregon, and Velora went with Dorothy to Cedar City.*

The business in their little bar at Black Rock wasn't very good, so they stayed in Black Rock until Larry was about 9 months old, until about May of 1941, then Al & Dorothy and Arthur & Velora had to look some place else to make a living. So they went north a ways to Delta, and bought a bakery and soda fountain.

For AG and his family, **May of 1941** appears to be the last time any of them lived in Black Rock. Deon Gillen of Oasis remembered a little about their place in Delta:

The James' moved from Black Rock up to Delta and started a bakery. It was located right next to the pool hall on the north side of the road there. It was east of Billy Van's [dance hall] and where Baker's drugstore used to be. I married my wife in 1941, and I met her up at their place in Delta one night, a few months before we were married. The James' and Leonards were here until about 1942 or 1943, then they moved down to Las Vegas.

No one seems to know how long they stayed in Las Vegas, but they apparently bought or ran a hamburger stand or restaurant. All four of them were there together when Walter James died on March 2, 1944, which will be the end of this chapter.

John, Dan and Albert(Bert) James

For the most part, the lives of Walter James' three brothers John, Dan and Albert(Bert) have been discussed in earlier parts of this chapter, but here is a brief summery of their lives during the time period from 1917 to 1944. Besides Walter and Arthur(AG), these

Dorothy James and Al Leonard. (Beryl G. Sorensen collection)

AG & Velora James. (Beryl G. Sorensen collection)

three brothers, and to a limited extent their families, are the only members of Thomas & Ann Phillips James family who ever had much to do with Black Rock.

Of the three, **John James** was the oldest. John and **Sarah Slaughter James**, had moved to Salt Lake in 1906. From then on John worked in the grocery business, and did some work as a telegrapher. They had 2 children; **Theron** was born in 1898 and **Evelyn**, born 1900. Then much later, on February 28, 1919, they had a baby girl, while living in Salt Lake. This last child was **Anna Mae James (Robison)**. She was born 19 years after Evelyn, putting her in a different generation.

The family stayed in Salt Lake until about 1927. Anna Mae, who was still alive in 1996, picks up the story from the time she was in the 3rd grade:

When I was in the beginning of the 3rd grade, my mother and I moved down to Milford to be with Dad That was in about 1927. Then we lived around Milford until I was finished with the 8th grade, or when I was 14 years old. Then we moved back to our home in Salt Lake in 1932 or 1933.

Part of the 5 years we were in the Milford area, we lived up at the Maud S Mine, where my father was employed. That was southwest of Milford. There was a big cabin there and we lived in it all the time for one year, and Dad drove me back and forth to school. We also lived in 2 different places in Milford.

Finally the family moved back to Salt Lake, because they lost their life savings and my mother and father didn't have a steady job. But we owned this house up here and my mother took in 2 of her nieces as boarders for 2 years. Then after that she had 2 nurses from the hospital staying there. So she helped keep the family alive. I used to sleep on the living room couch, so the boarders could use the bedrooms. Then we had another nephew with us and he slept on the dining room couch.

One time Wanda, Dan's daughter, brought John up on the train with ruptured appendix. But he still didn't want to go to the hospital, but he finally went, and he was in the hospital for 6 weeks. This was in about 1933 or 1934.

Then John went back to Milford and worked at different jobs, but he always went back and forth. He was always in Salt Lake for the holidays. It was during this time, the 1930's, that he was keeping record books at the Ranch and store for Walter and Arthur at Black Rock. My mother used to always go down to Black Rock and help cook during the shearing season. I think Dad stopped going back down to Milford and Black Rock after Arthur moved to California in the 1940's, and when Walter died in 1944.

But father was always doing some kind of work. Later, he was injured in the eye, but he didn't go to the doctor. This was in the early 1940's, '41 or '42? His retina was detached, but he didn't get it fixed, so he developed a tumor or growth in there. Finally they had to take his eye out.

John James died in 1948, his wife Sarah died in 1952. Both are buried in the Mount Olivet Cemetery in Salt Lake City.

The next brother was **Dan James**. All during this time period he lived in Milford with his wife **Belle** and family. He did odd jobs such as mining or butchering, but he spent quite a lot of time at Black Rock helping AG and Walter. He and his wife were always there during the shearing season helping out, as well as some of their children, Glenn, Leona, Wanda and Tom. AG seems to have been the organizer of the shearing operation until about 1939, then it was run by someone else other than a James family member. This must have spelled the end of the Dan James family dealings with Black Rock.

Dan & Belle James had 4 children. **Glenn** was the oldest, he worked on the railroad for a while, but he died in 1929 from a batch of bad home-made booze. **Leona** married in 1924 and moved to Salt Lake City. She had three children. **Wanda** married and had 3 husbands altogether, a Mr. MaChan, James Peter Holm, and then Marian M. Treet. She died in 1984 in Milford. And **Tom** James who was born in 1908, married **Ruth (Bobbie) Stewart** in February, 1933. Tom died in 1984. Bobbie James is still living in Milford as of 1996 and is the one who has supplied most of this information.

Dan James died August 13, 1949; Belle Sherwood James died in 1965. Both are buried in Milford.

The last brother having anything to do with Black Rock was **Albert(Bert) James**. He was AG's un-identical twin brother. During the late 1910's he was apparently drafted into the military and sent to Fort Lewis, Washington. No information is available on whether or not he went overseas(?). Bert never got married and so he was footloose all those years.

According to Dorothy James' story above, Bert spent a lot of time out at Black Rock working mostly for AG there at the store & hotel. He surely helped Walter out up at the ranch at times too, but nobody mentions that. Most of his time spent at Black Rock was in the spring of the year, especially April, when the shearing season was in full swing. According to Dorothy's story, it was AG who organized the shearing at Black Rock and the one who hired all the help.

The end of Bert's life is told in the last chapter.

Last Days of Sheep Shearing

This is a good time to discuss the shearing of sheep at the end of the 1930's and early 1940's at Black Rock. Some people have stated that as long as Walter James was alive, and that was up to March 2, 1944, the other James brothers were always there helping out and in charge of the shearing. However, in the late 1930's, AG was looking for a new way to make a living and stay alive. His wife and kids were going to and from California, but for the most part AG stayed there at Black Rock most of this time. He was there in 1939, at least in July, when Dorothy and Al were married, but a news clip from the April 6, 1939 *Milford News*, states: *Royal Buchanan of Gunnison was in town [Black Rock] recently making preparations to operate the Black Rock shearing corral*. From this it's not certain whether Royal was just taking Bert's place in the shearing barns and corral, or if he was doing AG's and Bert's jobs together and running the entire operation(?).

During the 1940 shearing season, AG, Dorothy and Al Leonard were there at Black Rock running a beer joint and the hotel or boarding house. Surely AG was involved with the shearing that year too. In the April 24, 1941 *Milford News*, one news item states: *Sheep shearing has started at the Black Rock corral. The plant and cook house are being operated by Royal Buchanan of Gunnison*. It seems that neither John, Dan nor Bert were involved that year, but AG may have had a hand in organizing it. In the spring of 1942, one news item suggested that Royal Buchanan would again be in charge of the shearing operation. This was the first year AG was nowhere to be found, at least in Black Rock country. It's not certain who took over the shearing operation after that, but there were sheep being sheared there through about 1949, when the shearing sheds or barns were torn down.

Here's a little something on **Royal Buchanan**, who appears to be at least a minor character in the late history of Black Rock. It comes from his only child, Dortha Buchanan Jensen of Gunnison:

Dad ran shearing crews all over Utah, including Black Rock. He also used to take crews up into Idaho, Montana and Wyoming. For years he had his own shearing machinery, and his own camp, and my mother was the cook. She took girls out there to help her with the cooking, while Dad ran the machinery and the crew. For several years my husband worked with my dad too.

When I was younger, before I was married, I used to go with my mother and dad, but I didn't do any work. I was the only child, and this was when I was in my early teen's.

Dad started the feed store when I was in high school, and I graduated in 1936. It was called Buchanan Feed Store, in Gunnison. With the store, he fed turkeys and other livestock, but he did the shearing crew thing on the side, just in the spring of the year. Then my husband usually took care of things here in Gunnison while my dad was away. Dad never did run sheep himself, but he started shearing sheep when he was only 18 or 19 years old. Royal was born in 1890, and died in 1962.

Other Important Residents

Perhaps the most important people ever to live at Black Rock, other than the two James families, were **Horace A. Stahl** and his wife **Rachel Wesley (Wessie) Mitchell**. They brought 3 children to Utah in 1911; son **John** and daughter **Helen Annette Stahl**, and Wessie's daughter by a previous marriage **Ina Mae Stanfield**. They had settled on a 320 acre homestead about 2-3 kms south of Antelope Spring, and southwest of Black Rock.

Almost immediately, Horace began working for Walter James at the Black Rock Ranch, but it was only part time. He of course was trying to make a living at dry farming, but that never panned out. He did a lot of traveling around for Walter going out on business trips to various places, but he was getting a little older at that time, having been born on May 11, 1858.

John Stahl, who was born in 1903, also worked for Walter James, beginning probably in the late 1910's or around 1920. He started out sheep herding in the desert west of Black Rock, and doing some farm work. John worked for Walter for a time after he was married in 1925. He married **Gladys Elizabeth Robinson** of Fillmore. Their first child **Jack Stahl**, was born September 14, 1927. By December, 1927, they moved into the bungalow or Cottage at the Black Rock Ranch, and John was working for Walter James full time.

During the winter of 1919-20, the Stahl family suffered a great tragedy from the deaths of their two daughters. That was the winter immediately after World War I, and the soldiers who were returning from Europe brought with them the flu. It spread like wildfire throughout the country. Ina Mae had married a James Milliken, who may have also worked for Walter James. She got the flu and died on December 24, 1919. She was buried on Christmas Day. Helen Annette Stahl got it a little later, and died on February 4, 1920. They are both buried in the Milford Cemetery next to their father and mother. All four of them were living on their dry farm at the time.

At some point in time, the family moved into Black Rock and lived in a house about one city block south of the Big House. It was located just west of the most southerly of all the springs at the Ranch. They call that the Big Spring, or sometimes the Railroad Spring. Exactly when they made this move is unclear, but they were at their homestead in February of 1921, and at the Ranch by the summer of 1923. That was the year Della Labrum first worked for Walter & Helen R. James, and she thinks they were at the Ranch

Sheep shearing with pulley & drop system. The location of this foto is not known, but the shearing system is the same as that used at Black Rock for nearly 50 years.
(Utah State Historical Society sheep collection)

that year. Everyone always referred to that house as the **Stahl's house**, even after the Stahls moved into Milford, and the house was moved up north of the Big House and corrals.

The old homestead south of Antelope Spring was abandoned, but later Walter James bought it and that's where he was drilling for oil during the period from 1926 to 1929. No oil was struck so that land was worthless.

John Stahl had quite an experience during the summer of 1928. In the July 20, 1928 Milford News, it states:

JOHN STAHL STRUCK BY LIGHTNING BOLT
HORSE KILLED AND FELL UPON RIDER Last Sunday morning John Stahl was struck by lightning while riding horseback. Mr. Stahl was rendered unconscious and the horse was killed. After Mr. Stahl had become conscious he had considerable difficulty in extricating himself from under the weight of the horse. One leg was painfully injured but he apparently sustained no burns, although he has considerable internal pains. Doctor H.C. Hunter was summoned and at the present writing Mr. Stahl is improving.

According to **Walter James (Jim) Travers**(son of Jack Travers) who was just a boy of 8 and once lived there at Black Rock with his parents, told this writer that John was very near the Big Spring and likely up on the bench just south of the Big House when the lightning hit and he was pinned under the horse. He was in a little gully, and the storm water was rising fast. He was having a hell of a time getting out from under the horse but then someone came along and helped him before he drowned. Jim thinks it may have been Babe James who found John(?). The lightning had gone down his leg and into his boot and evidently left some scars. The horse died because he was connected to the wet ground; John lived because he wasn't touching the ground.

A little later John took his family east to Sulphurdale, not far south of Cove Fort, and worked there for a year or two in a sulfur mine. He was there in the summer of 1930. By the summer of 1931, John had bought a farm out on the flats south of Milford and was living there. He also ran a few head of cows out on the desert.

Now back at the Ranch. Horace & Wessie were getting older by the minute, and with their two daughters gone since 1920, and their son having moved to Milford, they decided to call it quits at the farm. A short piece in the *Milford News* for November 17, 1932, tells what they did next: *Mr. and Mrs. John Stahl, Sr. [actually Horace Stahl] of Blackrock, have moved to Milford for the winter and are located in Mrs. Dan Ferguson's home on Main street.*

It wasn't for just the winter, it turned out to be for the rest of their lives. They lived at several different homes in Milford throughout their last years. They rented at first, then bought a little place which has since burned down. They returned to Black Rock often to visit their old friends Walter and AG James and their families, and the James' often visited them in Milford. These families were very close.

Finally, Horace Allbright Stahl died on September 14, 1944, at the age of 86. He died just 7 months after Walter James passed away. Wessie Stahl died on March 13, 1957, in a Provo rest home at the age of 93. They are buried in the Stahl family plot at the Milford Cemetery, but as of 1996, Wessie still didn't have a grave stone!

In 1938, John's wife Gladys died after they had 3 children. Then he had a number of different women come to take care of the kids. He ended up marrying one of the babysitters, **Dorothy Sly** of Milford. They had two more kids, making 5 in all for John. In about 1953, John Stahl's family moved to Idaho and much later he died in Weiser. John's daughter Sylvia Stahl Hulyn is living in Council, Idaho, while the oldest son Jack Stahl is still alive and living as a widower in Washington, Utah. Jack is the one who made the statement: *Milford is a great place to be FROM!*

Another important family that lived in the Black Rock region was that of **Herman T. Kaminska**. Not a lot is known about Herman or the family by people living in the mid-1990's. Most people remember him as the oil well driller, but not much else. The only real source for this information comes from the local Milford newspaper. The single best paper was the January 23, 1936 issue which reported on the funeral of one of the boys in the family. More on him below.

The Kaminska family was originally from Beatrice, Nebraska, then they moved to Texas. From there they came to Utah in about 1904(32 years prior to the 1936 report) and settled near Black Rock. They apparently had a homestead at or near Malone, which was just down the railroad tracks 7 or 8 kms south of Black Rock. Malone wasn't really a town, but rather a cluster of scattered dry farms and a railroad side track.

The earliest newspaper article about the family was in the November 19, 1919 *Milford Times* under the *Malone Notes*. It stated that Mr. Kaminska was drilling a well on his farm and was down 50 feet or about 15 meters. He expected to hit good water at 125 meters. While in Texas, Herman apparently had some experience with oil wells, and evidently had a drilling rig of his own, because he drilled many water wells in the region.

Also mentioned, Mrs. Kaminska was going to live in Mr. Johnson's home for the winter so her two boys, Cecil and Leonard, could attend school there at Malone. Evidently the Malone School was in bad shape, perhaps it hadn't been used for a year or two and the broken windows and lights were being replaced. That year would have been the 1919-20 school year, and may have been the last year the school house was used(?). Some time in the mid-1920's, this same Malone School was moved to Black Rock and sat next to AG James' store & hotel until 1945.

In the Kaminska family were three boys; Raymond was the oldest, born in 1898. Then there was Cecil and Leonard. These two were younger and the ones in school in 1919-20. They would have been in some grade less than the 8th, as that school ran grades from one to 8 only.

Horace & Wessie Stahl at their home at Black Rock(left), and Wessie, John and Jack (baby) Stahl. (Jack Stahl collection)

After the late 1910's and early 1920's, the dry farmers of Malone and all over that region, were beginning the move away because of the water situation. Discussed earlier was the fact that because of the building of the Minersville Reservoir in 1914, that dam, known as the Rock Ford Dam, prevented spring flood waters of the Beaver River from flowing down to the Beaver Bottoms which was just west of Malone. Prior to that time, farmers were growing good crops of wild hay and alfalfa. There was very little if any surface water to be found, but they used the sub-irrigation method and grew good crops for many seasons Slowly over the years the water table lowered, leaving the dry farmers high and drier than ever.

But the Kaminskas hung in there. In January, 1922, Herman started working for Walter James at his ranch. He must have been doing farm work and maybe running a few cattle. Then late in the year of 1925, Herman was in charge of drilling a well for Walter James. The story of the oil well south of Antelope Spring has been told earlier in this chapter. The two wells they worked on lasted from 1926 until 1931. All those years Kaminska was working for Walter James.

In 1935, **Raymond Kaminska** took his wife, the former Valerie Appegate from Parowan, and 2 young sons, and moved to Southern California. About a year later Raymond had a terrible accident while working in the Rosslyn Hotel in Los Angeles. He fell into a boiler he was repairing and was scalded by hot water and steam. That occurred on January 4, 1936, and he died 5 days later. The funeral and burial took place in Parowan about two weeks later.

Valerie stayed in Parowan near her parents, but Herman Kaminska moved to the Ogden area in about 1940(?).

Another important family was the **Nays**. They consisted of **Shirl Nay** and his wife, a former **Miss Thompson**, and children **Susie, Clinton, Merrill, Arden,** and **Harvey**.

Shirl Nay was hired by Walter James to come and work on his Black Rock Ranch as a farmer. The Nays had a large family with school-age children and they lived in the **Tie**

House which was located just north of the main ranch buildings, and immediately west and downhill from the **Tie House Spring**. It used to sit inside the circle of trees, right where you turn right, or south, to enter the area of the Black Rock Ranch. That building was made of railroad ties, thus the name Tie House. That's where most of Walter James' farmers used to live. It's since been torn down, but the trees are still there.

Shirl Nay's job was to feed and water the cattle, horses and sheep that were there at the Ranch corrals. He also cut and hauled hay and grew corn. The James' always had a big garden, and that was likely one of his responsibilities. They also had pigs, chickens and turkeys around. There were 3 or 4 springs large enough to be used for irrigation, but they usually ran water in ditches from the springs into a couple of ponds first, then irrigated from the ponds. Keeping ditches clean was another big job.

Some people thought the Nays were first recruited to come to Black Rock during the school year 1923-24, in order to get the number of school-age children up to 15, so the county would then be obligated to open a public school. However, when the Nays finally left in March of 1937, the *Milford News* for 3/18/1937, reported they had lived and worked in Black Rock for 11 years. That would put their arrival date as 1926.

All of the Nay children mentioned above went to the Black Rock School. There was Clinton, who may have been the oldest boy. He and Arden were sent to Milford in 1934-35 and attended high school there, then Clinton went in the Navy after that. Susie was also sent to Milford for her high school years, then she married Henry Bruvik of Stockton, California, in March of 1936. During the 1935-36 school year Merrill and Arden left Black Rock and went to Mt. Pleasant and the Wasatch Academy to attend school there. Harvey may have been the youngest, because in the 1937 newspaper article mentioned above it states: *Mr. and Mrs. Shirl Nay and son Harvey, who have made their home here for the past 11 years, have moved to Antimony where they will make their home.*

It appears they were living in Antimony and had relatives there before they went to Black Rock, because in the three months prior to their departure, one niece was killed by an accidental shooting (11/19/1936 *Milford News*), and Mrs. Nay's mother, Mrs. Homer Thompson died (2/18/1937 *MN*). These two incidents likely prompted their move back to their original home in Antimony.

Here's an interesting side-note to the Nay family. In the July 6, 1944 issue of the *Milford News*, a short article mentions Merrill Nay, who joined the Navy during the war. It stated in part:

Defying flaming oil and heavy seas, the crew of a Navy bombing plane landed in the Atlantic recently to rescue two officers and three enlisted men from a plane which had crashed in flames. Lieutenant Harold G. Olson piloted the rescue bomber landing in the rough blazing seas. Two Members of his crew, **Merrill G. Nay of Antimony Utah,** *and Charles F. Waters, Dorchester, Mass., dived into the water to rescue survivors of the crashed plane. They were awarded the Navy and Marine Corps medal.*

After the Nays left, the May 27, 1937 *Milford News* tells about the people who replaced them: **Mr. and Mrs. Lyle Kump** *and family of Mt. Pleasant have moved here recently and are living at the Walter James Ranch.*

They had two sons named Bob and Gordon, and a daughter named Sherie. This family evidently started out living at the Ranch, and in the Tie House, but later, in 1941 and 1942, they were living in one of the operator's houses down next to the railway depot. Lyle Kump was a railroad employee at that time.

Doug Denny of Milford was in Black Rock one summer and he remembered another couple who came there from just down the road a ways at Reed. This is what he had to say:

I went down there to Black Rock when I was 14 years old, and that was the first time I had ever been away from home. That would make it 1939. When I was there **Dora** *and* **Jim Smithson** *were running the hotel and store. Jim worked with the cattle just across the tracks to the east of the hotel. I remember Jim going over there every day working with the cattle. He must have been working for Walter James(?). They were running the hotel and store for AG James, that's the way I understood it. The only people I remember seeing there were some sheepmen and cattlemen. This was in the summer of 1939.*

The summer of 1939 was when Dorothy James and Al Leonard got married, then returned to Black Rock for a day or two before going east on their honeymoon. Jim and Dora must have been there watching the place while AG was away temporarily.

The Smithsons, from the Smithson Ranch at Reed, were long-time friends of both James families at Black Rock and they likely helped out for more than just one summer at Black Rock. The Smithson name pops up a lot in the Black Rock news items in the old Milford newspapers. Dan was the old man, perhaps the original settler. He had two sons, Bert and Jim. After Dan died, Bert took over the ranch, then Jim inherited it when Bert died. Jim later sold it to a man from Minersville, the present owner of the ranch. This according to Doug Denny. That ranch is still there today west of mile posts 5 or 6 on the highway north of Milford.

Before summarizing Walter James' life to end this chapter, there are several other people who had limited connections to Black Rock who are worth mentioning. In the very beginning, one of the first people to settle and homestead where the Black Rock Springs are today was **James H. Hedges**, believed to have been living in Fillmore at that time. He sold out to William Raht in 1881.

James Hedges had two sons, **Harvey** and **Allen Hedges**. It's likely neither one ever lived at Black Rock, but they always had a close connection. Both became railroad special agents, or detectives; or as some called them, railroad "bulls". Their job was to travel around on various trains looking for people who were ticket-less travelers, and to prevent people from stealing railroad property. They also kicked kids off the freight trains who were joy riding. That's how some of the people who lived and grew up in Clear Lake remembered both these men!

Not a lot is said of Harvey Hedges by the local papers, until his obituary came out in the June 8, 1944 issue of the *Milford News*. He was born in Fillmore, but raised in Frisco. He was the town marshal of Milford from 1904 until 1912, then his career with Union Pacific started. He spent much of his time in Nevada. He died at his home in Las Vegas in 1944, after 32 years with the UP.

Allen Hedges was the one whose main beat was between Salt Lake City and Milford or

Mrs. Shirl Nay and 4 Nay boys beside the Black Rock School(La Preal U. Wilson foto); and early-day newspaper foto of silent screen movie actress Betty Compson.

Caliente, Nevada, but he worked the line all the way to Los Angeles. Allen joined the UP in 1911, and was always known around Milford and vicinity as the "cinder dick". He must have been a good "dick", because he got himself shot twice and almost killed.

His first encounter took place in late January, 1919. The January 31, 1919 newspaper mentions that the hobo who was shot by Special Agent Allen Hedges was taken to Salt Lake City by Sheriff Fotheringham. His name was said to be Frank McCarty. Hedges was also shot in the hand and spent more than a month in a hospital in Salt Lake City. McCarty was sentenced to from one to 20 years for assault with a deadly weapon.

About one year later in the March 10, 1920 paper it was disclosed that McCarty was really Frank Wade. Not long before coming to Milford, he had been released from a prison in Salem, Oregon. He had served 20 years for murder.

Allen's second near-death experience took place in Caliente. The May 31, 1934 issue of the MN states that Hedges came upon an Albert Miller and his wife stealing ice from one of the railroad ice cars. There was an argument, and a scuffle and Miller drew a .38 revolver and shot Hedges twice in the hip area. Miller and wife ran, and were later apprehended without a struggle. Hedges was taken to Salt Lake City the next day by train No. 8. He apparently recovered all right, and went on to retire from the railroad in 1950 after 40 years of being a special agent.

Another rather famous person to have ties to the Black Rock region was the silent screen movie star **Betty Compson**. Her obituary was in the May 2, 1974 issue of the *Milford News*. It went like this:

SILENT SCREEN STAR PASSES

Silent screen star Betty Compson died last Thursday [April 25] at the age of 77. She was the first movie star from Beaver County. She was born in Beaver County and was raised around Black Rock and Fisco.

She worked as a nurse in Salt Lake City, before going to Hollywood in 1920 as a violinist. She starred in several silent films for the Mack Sennett Studio, and in 1929 starred in the first talking picture by RKO, "Street Girl". She married Jim Cruze, movie director.

Earlier in her life, the people in Beaver County knew her much better than when she died. In the February 22, 1924 issue of the *Milford News,* is a report about her coming back to the place of her birth to be married. That must have caused quite a stir in and around Milford. Part of that report went like this:

BETTY COMPSON TO BE MARRIED IN BEAVER COUNTY--AT FRISCO

Salt Lake's own film star, Betty Compson, is responsible for the reawakening being planned for the sleepy deserted Frisco, relic of the gold rush days. She and her fiancee, James Cruze, producer-director, plan to be married in the main street of the village.....

Miss Compson was born in the town [of Frisco]. Her father was a miner. The family moved on when the "strike" gave out, and the house where they lived stands as it was abandoned.

When Cruze led his caravan into Utah for the filming of the "Covered Wagon" [filmed near Garrison, Utah], they passed the town and stopped to inspect it. Later, after Cruze and Miss Compson became engaged, he learned it was her birth place.

It was then that they made the romantic plan for their wedding. "I have always wanted to go back", she confessed.....

A special car attached to one of the transcontinental flyers will carry a group of their intimate friends. The car will be sidetracked at Milford, Utah, the nearest railroad point to the "ghost town". Automobiles will convey the party to Frisco where an aged justice of the peace,... will be waiting to marry them. The ceremony will be performed in the middle of the town's main street. Later a westbound train will pick up the special and bring the party back to Los Angeles.

In another issue of the *Milford News* for September 21, 1933, Betty was interviewed and a long story of her life revealed. In that article she states that her father was Virgil K. Compson, a graduate of Cornell University and a mining engineer and geologist. She was indeed born in Frisco in 1897, while the James family was still residing there. It's certain that in such a small town these families knew each other.

One last famous character to have lived in the area was **Jack Dempsey**. According to a news brief in the August 24, 1939, *Milford News: As a one-time resident of Frisco and well known always to have a warm spot in his heart for Milford, Jack Dempsey is considered one of the outstanding former residents of western Beaver County and as such was mailed a special invitation to attend Milford's first Home-Coming, to be held Wednesday evening, August 6, as a timely preliminary to the 1939 Beaver County Fair.....*

Jack's reply to the newspaper editor David S. Williams was very diplomatic: *Many thanks for your nice letter and was glad to hear from you. I also want to thank you for your kind invitation to Milford's first "Home-Coming" and am happy to state that I shall be happy to attend if I am out that way.....* No word on whether or not he ever showed up.

Black Rock CCC Camp

This part begins in the fall of 1939 at Black Rock. But first a brief history of the CCC's in the Millard County region. Locally, the first camp was set up in the West Desert in Wah Wah Valley at Wah Wah Springs. It was originally scheduled to be set up near the Desert Experimental Station and near Highway 21 and Warm Point, but the cold spring water at Wah Wah was too inviting. Another camp was set up in Beaver Canyon east of Beaver. These both got started in the summer of 1933. After that date, there were spike camps set up in many locations, including on the hill just west of Milford. There were CCC camps set up throughout the state; both in the mountains, which were normally summertime camps, and in the deserts where the enrollees often spent the winter months.

One big camp was set up west of Delta at the south end of Swasey Peak and another spring called Antelope Spring. It was almost due north of Marjum Pass. That camp was first set up in the summer of 1935 and operated until the late fall or early winter of 1939, or perhaps just into the early part of 1940. Most of the enrollees were moved, lock, stock and barrel to Black Rock. No one knows the exact date when they made the move, but it's likely not everyone made the move on the same day. Also, there were other camps in the region, and enrollees were being shuffled back and forth between camps that were being abandoned or transferred, or between summer camps in the mountains and winter camps in the West Desert. The history of the Antelope Spring CCC Camp will be covered in detail in this writer's next book, **Hiking and Exploring in Western Utah's Jack Watson's Ibex Country**.

Now for the beginning of the Black Rock CCC Camp. Here is some information gleaned from the local Milford newspaper, the *Beaver County News(BCN)*. The beginning of it all was in November of 1939. In the 11/30/1939 issue of the *BCN*, an article in the news of Black Rock stated: *Mr. and Mrs. McCarty have moved into the Merrill Miller cottage. Mr. McCarty is the superintendent of the Black Rock CCC camp.* A month later an article in the 12/28/1939 *BCN* states that Captain Lawrence J. Alexander is assigned commandant of the new camp. It's not known when the buildings were brought in and erected, or from which other camp they must have come from, but by February enrollees were there, some of whom were confined to bed with the flu.

Remembering back in the story about AG's family at Black Rock in the fall of 1939 now, Dorothy & Al Leonard made a deal with 8 of the carpenters to do some remodeling on their store and beer joint. Those men were there likely in about November erecting the buildings. Also, some or all of the enrollees were there in December of 1939.

By March(3/28/1940 *BCN*) many if not most of the enrollees were moved to a new summer camp at Calleo, just east of the Deep Creek Mountains. By October, a Dr. Andrew J. Hoenes was assigned to be the camp doctor. By late January (1/30/1941 *BCN*), a new bunch of enrollees de-trained to join the rest. By July (7/17/1941 *BCN*), Del Rea Christensen was the educational advisor, assisted by Clyde Fechser. Also, Oscar Kelly had just brought a convoy of 8 trucks from the Modena CCC camp to Black Rock with 57 enrollees. Lieutenant Richard Kundle from the Modena camp was made the junior military officer at Black Rock.

Now for some stories from some who were there and remembered a little about the place. **Robert Barber** had been in the Antelope Spring CCC Camp, and got out just before that camp was moved to Black Rock. He had returned to Mississippi for Christmas in 1941, then rushed back to Utah for a new job opening right after Pearl Harbor was bombed. He was working for the railroad at Pumice, the siding just north of Black Rock. He remembers going to the Black Rock camp to visit with friends and go to picture shows at that time. Here is Barber's story about the camp at that time.

There was a hotel on the west side of the tracks, and a **beer joint** next to where the hotel was. There was a guy there named Charley Logan, a signal maintainer for the railroad. He had a car and sometimes he'd bring some of those CCC boys to town. They'd get paid off, and he'd bring 'em to town, and he'd get $8 or $10 for that. That was a lot of money in those days. He was also runnin' the beer joint after work, at night. Finally after there was a lot of drinking and trouble caused by the CCC boys, the Railroad company told ol' Charley to close 'er down. Either close down the beer joint or he'd lose his maintainer job. So he closed it down, then bid on another job down around Caliente, Nevada, so they never did have a beer joint there in Black Rock no more.

About this time, and in the October 2, 1941 issue of the *BCN*, was a short advertisement that read: *For Rent or Lease--Black Rock beer parlor and store. Apply to Mrs. Logan at the store*. This indicates they must have been living in AG's old home and had the store open for business at the time. This was about 5 months after AG & Velora James and Dorothy & Al Leonard packed up and went to Delta.

Before **Hamp Burke** died in August of 1994, he was interviewed twice earlier that same year. Here's a little of what he had to say about the CCC's and camp discipline, or the lack of it:

They had big bunk houses, offices, recreation hall, and as I remember it, they was all just set on cement blocks, about 8 or 10 feet [2-3 meters] apart. Then some just sat on top of the ground. Some of the CCC boys at Black Rock come from over in eastern Utah. And it was from a camp where the boys run it; they took some of the men and tied 'em to the flagpole and everything else. So they split the camp up and brought part of it to Black Rock. They thought they was gettin' rid of the trouble makers, but they didn't.

Here's a funny story. I was cuttin' hay in the field to the south of the camp, and some fellow came over and says, "The head man's gettin' off the train", and that was at 4 pm when that train come through. He says, "if you want to see some fun, pull up there and stop". So I pulled up and waited. When this head man got off the train, they were all there standing at attention. Then he said, "where's so and so". And the man in charge says, "they're still in the bunkhouse and they haven't come out yet". So this new leader went in the bunkhouse. And pretty soon these guys came out through the door, and the door wasn't even open. Then he said, "now if there's any of the rest of ya that think you're tough, step out. We'll see just how tough you are."

After that for about 3 months, and anytime between 2 o'clock in the morning until 2 o'clock in the afternoon, you could see these CCC boys out pushin' wheel barrows and cleaning the yard and cleaning up the junk. Sometimes he'd work 'em all night!

The CCC's built the road from Black Rock west to Crystal Peak and Snake Valley. In fact there wasn't a road west of Black Rock until the CCC's built it. They also built the road that cuts off north going to Jacky Watson's place [and to the Ibex Well], and they built reservoirs, bridges, stock ponds. They used modern equipment to do most of that work with. They had bulldozers and graders.

Oscar Kelly was there before and after the Black Rock camp was closed and he was the caretaker until all the buildings and equipment were disposed of. Oscar Kelly was a mechanic from Oasis and had joined the C's early on. He was in charge of the motor pool or garage out at Antelope Spring for several years, then was transferred to Black Rock with the rest of the camp. Oscar's daughter **Dawn Kelly Anderson,** now of Oasis, worked at the Black Rock Ranch for 2 summers and the following is part of what she remembers:

I worked down there when I was 14 and 15, during the summers of 1941 and 1942, at the Ranch for Walter and Helen James, and Benita and Hamp Burke. And mother and dad were down there the summer I was 15, the summer of 1942. The first summer I can't remember my folks being there, but they were there in the summer of 1942. I don't remember anything about the CCC camp until my folks came down there, because I was *always up there at the Ranch working. After the summer of 1942, I came back up here and stayed with an aunt and went to school in Hinckley, then before the school year was over[1942-43], my folks came back up here to Oasis. In the summer of 1943, I worked for Nina Huff in Sutherland and my folks were in Oasis then. My brother Jim was there at Black Rock and he and Ray Davis worked for Dad.*

Part of the Black Rock news in the *BCN* for June 4, 1942 states: *Once more the CCC camp here is vacated. The entire personnel and boys were moved to Simpson Springs, 60 miles[100 kms] from Tooele, where a defense plant is being erected.... O.V. Kelly, who was camp mechanic here a year ago, will move his family from Oasis as he has been appointed to care for the camp and to work on machinery in need of repair.*

From this it appears the history of the Black Rock CCC camp finally came to an end in May of 1942, then came the disposal of the buildings and materials.

Oscar's son **Jim Kelly**, now of Las Vegas(1996) remembers what happened after that:

The Grazing Service and the CCC's had been taking care of all the ranges and doing projects out there, and when the CCC's left, the Grazing Service had to take over all the water projects out in the desert. After the CCC's left, my father continued working for the Grazing Service. In the summer of 1942, he was the only person there except for myself, who was just out of high school, and another boy from Delta, Ray Davis. Then later two boys from the Beaver area came over to help us move stuff. Dad had warehouses full of sacks of cement, and stuff scattered all over the West Desert that we had to gather up.

Our work was just gathering stuff up; we had two trucks and when those boys from Beaver came to help, we hauled I don't know how many sacks of cement down and put in railroad cars. Stacks and stacks! Then Ray and I, we each had a truck, would go to the West Desert and gather up equipment from Burbank and all the spike camps. We brought all that stuff into Black Rock, then most of it went on to Fillmore. Then we finally went out and worked on several projects that the CCC's had started and hadn't finished. I worked for the Grazing Service, or somebody, and I had a hard time getting paid for a long time-- they couldn't decide who was supposed to pay me.

Dad must have left Black Rock sometime about the end of 1942, because that's when I went out to Gold Hill with Nels Bogh of Delta. The buildings at Black Rock were all there when I left and I don't know exactly where they went. But the Grazing Service did have an office and a big storage yard right there in the middle of Fillmore and all that stuff we rounded up in the West Desert and the equipment there at Black Rock was all taken to Fillmore.

The last news item about the Black Rock CCC camp comes from the Milford *BCN* dated January 14, 1943. It states: *Several Japanese from Topaz, with Mr. Lee as their supervisor, have been here several days, tearing down two of the large CCC garages. While here, two of the Japanese received minor injuries and were returned to Topaz for medical care.*

It appears little or nothing was left of the Black Rock camp soon after the beginning of the year 1943, and everything including the buildings were all taken either to the Topaz Japanese Internment Camp, which was located west of Delta, or to the Grazing Service(now the BLM) compound in Fillmore.

Walter James Dies

To close this chapter here's a quick review of the most important character in the story of Black Rock, **Walter James**. Walter died suddenly March 2, 1944. His daughter Benita was with him at the time, and she describes what happened in the day or two before that. This is part of an interview done by Gladys Whittaker on March 13, 1984:

I was with Dad when he died. He had a heart condition and didn't realize how serious it was. And he said to me one day just shortly before he died; "Well the next time I go to Salt Lake I'm going to put the ranch in the hands of a real estate dealer and sell it". I said, "Dad, you've always said you were going to stay here till you died." "Nope", he said, "I can't go to Milford and back without spending the next day in bed." He realized he was losing his strength. So he said he was going to sell it, but he didn't get to it. He went out just like you and I are talking here. All the family was grateful he went out so fast and easy. Then I had to come in here to Milford and send a telegram for a mortician who came clearn from Fillmore.

Walter's obituary appeared in the *Milford News* on March 9, 1944. It mentions a few things other people failed to mention thus far in our story:

Coming as a distinct shock to all southwestern Utah and to a large number of friends and acquaintances in all parts of the state, Walter James, 77, prominent wool grower and mining man of Black Rock and political figure throughout the state for half a century, died suddenly of a heart attack at his home Thursday of last week shortly after midnight. He had attended the funeral services of John W. Kirk, an old friend, the afternoon before his death and had greeted and chatted with several local friends previous to and following the funeral, apparently in good health and spirits and his death came as a big surprise despite his advanced age.

He was given a Masonic burial Tuesday in Salt Lake City with services in the Colonial room of the Masonic temple. Speakers were James A. Hooper, secretary of the Utah Wool Grower's Association, and the Reverend George Weber of Salt Lake City. Burial arrangements were in charge of the Joseph William Taylor mortuary, with music furnished by the mortuary quartet. Interment took place in Mount Olivet Cemetery, also under Masonic auspices.

A large number of relatives and friends were present for the services, including several from Milford, and the floral offerings were profuse.

At the time of his death, Mr. James was serving as a director of the Utah Wool Grower's Association, and took an active part in convention proceedings during the January meeting at Salt Lake City. Because he had long been associated with the group, and was a charter member, he was recently named an honorary member of the organization.

He was a member of the Elks Club of Salt Lake City, member of the Masonic and Odd Fellows lodges in Milford, and a few years ago was honored by the latter group when he was presented with a 25 year jewel.

Mr. James was widely known in mining circles of the state, having operated a number

Inez Kelly, wife of Oscar Kelly(left); and Dawn Kelly (Anderson), both at the Black Rock CCC Camp in August, 1942. (Dawn Kelly Anderson collection)

A planter or seed drill built by Oscar Kelly at the Black Rock CCC Camp, summer of 1942.
(Jim Kelly collection)

Oscar Kelly(left), then Ladd Kelly, and Hamp Burke, at the CCC camp, Black Rock, Summer, 1942.
(Jim Kelly collection)

of mines in the southern section of Utah, particularly at Beaver and Frisco and in Millard county. He also was known as an operator of butcher shops in the area, and at one time had a mercantile store in his home town. In livestock circles he was one of the best known figures and had marketed many cattle and sheep for years and had held a number of positions of trust as one of the most outstanding men of his community.

Mr. James was a member of the old Commercial Club in Salt Lake City and had attended the Congregational church most of his life.

A son of Thomas and Ann Phillips James, he was born at Baltimore, Maryland, on May 27, 1877 [actually 1866]. When he was a young man he came west to settle in Corinne[?] with his parents, who were interested in mining. Later they went to Frisco, where Mr. James married Helen Raht on January 14, 1892. He and his family had resided at Black Rock for a number of years.

Surviving are his widow, residing in Black Rock, who had been visiting in Bountiful since January; three daughters, Mrs. Merrill Miller of Bountiful, Mrs. Hampton Burke and Mrs. W.N. McMillen, both of Black Rock; one nephew, Jack B. Travers of Craig, Colorado, whom the couple reared since childhood; and two grandchildren; five brothers, John P. James and Ernest James of Salt Lake City, Dan B. James and Albert James of Milford, and A.G. James, Las Vegas, Nevada; and two sisters, Mrs. J.P. Rossiter of Butte, Montana, and Mrs. Angus McLeod of Salt Lake City.

One last noteworthy event in Walter's life should be mentioned. When the Taylor Grazing Act was passed in 1934, which regulated grazing for the first time on public lands of the west, he was on the local grazing advisory board or committee. Because of this he had the opportunity to go to Washington D.C. Here's part of an news item in the Milford paper for December 16, 1937:

Walter James of Black Rock and about ten other stock raisers of this state have returned from Washington D.C. The men were selected to attend a conference arranged by the Department of the Interior with the hope of ironing out many of the difficult and major problems concerning the Taylor Grazing Act. Fortunately, the delegation arrived in Washington on a Sunday and hence had the day to visit many points of interest in and near Washington. After the conference was completed Mr. James, Byron Howley of Richfield and others visited New York City, returning home by way of Buffalo and Niagara Falls.

Thus ended the most important chapter in the history of Black Rock.

Buildings and oil well drilling rig at the Walter James Oil Well No. 1 south of Antelope Spring, probably in April, 1926. (Kaufman collection)

Walter & Helen Raht James in about the late 1930's, and Walter James and grandson Walter James (Wally) Miller in 1927. (R. Bobbie James collection)

Frances Treweek Travers, left, and Thekla James (Miller), in front of the rock garage & wash house. About 1920.

Chapter 6
Black Rock from 1944 to 1957

The Walter James Family
With the death of **Walter James** on **March 2, 1944**, the Ranch part of the settlement of Black Rock began to change, or as some might say, go downhill from there.
Immediately after Walter's death, the family then had to settle the estate. The Ranch of course went to his widow, **Helen R. James**, and the three girls, **Benita**, **Thekla** and **Helen(Babe)**. **Jack Travers** apparently played no part in this matter. At this time, Benita and Hamp Burke were living in the Cottage and running the Ranch. Thekla and Merrill Miller, and their son Walter James (Wally) Miller were living in Bountiful. Babe McMillen and her two little daughters(Sophia and Elise) were living there at the Ranch while her husband was still in the Pacific in the Navy.
There may have been some squabbling over who got what, as is normally the case in such matters, and it went into court and was settled by making the estate into the Black Rock Ranch, Incorporated.
At the time of the court proceedings, the estate consisted of(according to courthouse records which sometimes don't tell all!) $10,143.46, 115 range cattle, 50 calves, 4 milch(milk) cows and 3 bulls. The family also fully owned about 930 acres of land, plus another 2195 acres in Millard County they owned 1/2 interest in. Some of this may have been land involving mining claims(?). They also had over 1300 acres of mining land at 1/2 or 1/4 interest in Beaver County. Walter had small plots of land scattered all over two counties, but much of it was almost worthless.
Everything was settled in court and filed on September 6, 1944. It was handled by the law firm of Irvine, Skeen, and Thurman. Their cut was $654.59, leaving $9488.87 to the Black Rock Ranch Corporation. Helen R. of course was part of it, as were Benita & Hamp Burke, and Thekla & Merrill Miller. Even though Babe was living there at the time while her husband was in the Navy, she apparently didn't want to live there. She had lived elsewhere for a number of years and *presumably* didn't want to live there in order to inherit her fair share(?). Since the other two daughters did want to live there and work the Ranch, they are the ones who remained and eventually took over the Ranch. Babe, for whatever reasons, never got any part of the Ranch, or any of the money(?) when the Ranch was eventually sold. Presumably this was because she had other plans elsewhere.
During the summer of 1944, Thekla, Merrill and Wally moved into the Big House, but in the fall of the year, Thekla and Wally moved back to a rental place in Bountiful so he could finish his last year of high school. In the spring of 1945, they moved back to Black Rock after Wally graduated from Judge Memorial High School.
Before and after Walter's death, Benita & Hamp continued to live in the **Cottage**, and Helen and Thekla & Merrill lived in the **Big House**, or the main Ranch house. Both couples worked the Ranch full time, with Helen being rather old at that point and basically retired.
Wally Miller attended Westminster College in Salt Lake for 4 years, and graduated in the spring of 1949 with a degree in business. While there he must have been a rather popular fellow, because he was elected president of the International Relations Club his freshman year, and at the end of his junior year, he was the Master of Ceremonies for the graduation of the senior class. During the summers, it seemed he was always in Black Rock helping his parents on the Ranch. During the 1949-50 school year, he attended the University of Utah doing post graduate work in business.
Babe James McMillen and her two young daughters stayed there in the Big House at the Ranch through the fall and early winter of 1945. Her husband returned from the war just in time for Christmas and got acquainted with his two daughters; 4 1/2 year-old Sophia, and 1 1/2 year-old Elise. About Christmas time, or just after, the McMillens got an

apartment in Milford. A short newspaper article mentioned that he was to spend a little time there with his family before reporting back to the naval hospital in Oakland to finish out his time. It's not known whether he actually reported to Oakland, or whether he was released from military duty while in Milford(?).

This is a good place to tell a little about Babe's husband, **William N. (Mac) McMillen** and his role in World War II. What he did and where he was located was outlined in an article in the January 25, 1946 issue of the *Milford Times*. Part of that news brief went like this:

Lieutenant Commander McMillen has been a member of the U. S. Naval Reserve since 1934. Five months prior to Pearl Harbor he was ordered to active duty. He assumed command of the USS Paramount, a coastal minesweeper, which operated in the Atlantic during the winter of 1941-42. His ship was later ordered to Panama where he operated until the spring of 1943, when he was transferred to the USS Champion, a fleet minesweeper operating with the Pacific fleet.

In August, 1944, he assumed command of the USS Ransom, another fleet minesweeper. He operated with various task groups in the central Pacific area, his principal duties being patrol and escort work in the Palau Islands. In December, 1944, in addition to his duties as commanding officer of the Ransom, he was appointed commander of Mine Division 42, U.S. Pacific Fleet.

He was a task unit commander in the invasion of Okinawa, his division of minesweepers commencing operations to clear the waters around Okinawa a week before the landing date of April 1, 1945. After the landing, the task unit continued to sweep and to perform patrol and screen duties until the island was secured.

He was in the Philippines with his ships in August when the truce was declared, and he was at once dispatched to Japan to clear the waters of Japanese mines so rescue ships could safely enter the Japanese waters to rescue allied prisoners of war. In Japan he was appointed commander of the task unit of 18 minesweepers, which swept more than 1600 Japanese mines around the ports of Nagasaki and in the strait between the islands of Kyushu and Shikoku, which leads to the Inland Sea of Japan.....

Lt. Commander McMillen was awarded the Bronze Star medal for the actions of his task unit in April at Okinawa, during which his ship shot down three of a large number of enemy planes which sank one destroyer and disabled another, who were assigned duties to protect the sweepers. His task unit rescued 300 American naval personnel from the water and delivered them safely to hospital ships with only minor damage to itself. He was again awarded the Bronze Star medal for his participation in sweeping operations with the Third Fleet in the East China Sea during July, 1945. He also wears the Naval Reserve

Looking down at the west side of the Cottage which was assembled from several old Malone cabins in 1921. (Jim Travers collection)

Honor Medal, American Defense Medal, Philippine Liberation Ribbon, World War II Victory Ribbon, and the American and Asiatic Theater Ribbons.

The next we know of the McMillens was in the summer of 1947, when Sophia and Elise spent the summer at the Ranch. It's not known exactly where the family was residing at that time, but we can presume they were living in Lakewood, Colorado near Denver, which is where they would spend the rest of their lives.

Meanwhile back at the Ranch. Because Thekla and Helen lived under the same roof, there was some quarreling and people not getting along very well with each other. By about Christmas time, 1947(perhaps as early as May, 1947?), Helen R. James left Black Rock and moved in with Babe McMillen's family in Lakewood. Babe was a registered nurse and was better able to care for her mother who was about 83 years old at the time.

Elise McMillen Brougham, presently of Wheat Ridge, Colorado, recalls a little about why her grandmother Helen R. James actually ended up living out her life in Lakewood, rather than at the Ranch at Black Rock. She told this writer, much of which came through Benita, that:

Supposedly Thekla was the bad one, although she was always nice to me. But of course we always heard this from Benny and Hampy, and they had part of the Ranch too. Grammy, that's what we little girls always called Helen R. James, was older and Thekla got Grammy to sign everything over to them, the two daughters and their husbands who were living and working at the Ranch. And then she was mean to her. Thekla kicked Grammy out of the main Big House, and so she went over to live with Benny and Hampy in the little house[Cottage]. And that place wasn't very good at that time, it just had the cook stove for heat. Then in 1947, my mother and father took her in.

Evidently, at least one daughter, maybe two(?), thought everything in the Big House should remain there as family heirlooms, to be handed down to future Ranch owners, which they probably thought at the time would always be someone in the James family. Elise goes on to mention more about the inheritance business:

My mother didn't get any part of the Ranch, and I can understand that. But, my grandmother has some nice jewelry, and according to Benny, she had to smuggle it out of

Lt. William N. McMillen (Elise M. Brougham collection)

the Big House because Thekla would never have let her take it. And we got that. Both my sister and I have this old Victorian-type jewelry. Also, Grammy had bought some savings bonds for us, my sister and I, and we got that. She didn't have that many grandkids! Also, Grammy had a house lot given to her by Raht family relatives in Seattle. She got that, then when she died, my mother (Babe) got it. Then after mother died, Dad sold that long distance. It didn't amount to much, and he probably got fleeced on the deal.

The above account by Elise is the Benita James Burke version of the whole affair. However, Nola Miller, and her now-deceased husband Walter James (Wally) Miller, always got the Thekla James Miller side of the story. As one might expect, it is exactly 180° degrees different from that told by Benita. The Millers had it in mind that Benita was the "bad one". Those reading this book can decide for themselves! Two people have told this writer that after the Ranch was eventually sold in 1957, the only time Benita and Thekla ever met was at funerals.

Helen R. James lived in Lakewood, Colorado for the next 4 years, but she did get back to Black Rock a time or two. Once she returned in the late summer of 1949, perhaps to be at the funeral of Dan James in mid-August. While there she: *was guest of honor at an afternoon tea given by Ruth Circle of the Eastern Star ladies at the home of Mrs. Jennie Martin, on Friday of last week. Mrs. James has been living in Lakewood, Colo., with her daughter, Mrs. McMillen, for some time and will leave shortly to spend the coming winter in Colorado....*

Mrs. James, for many years the gracious and charming hostess of the Walter James Ranch, is happy to be in familiar surroundings once more, at her old home at Black Rock. The James Ranch has always been noted for its generous hospitality and Mrs. James was the kind and interested friend who sent the tired and hungry traveler on his way refreshed in body and in spirit(September 15, 1949, Milford Times).

Now back to what Elise had to say about Helen, or Grammy, in the last years of her life in Lakewood: *My mom was a nurse and she took care of Grammy at home for a long time. Then finally she was in the bathroom and fell against the wall in the night, and cracked her head. So after that mother couldn't take care of her anymore, so Grammy was put in a hospital or nursing home. But she wasn't in there for very long.*

Finally on **January 3, 1951**, Helen Raht James died while living in the Dorothy Olsen Resthome in Lakewood, Colorado. She was buried along side her husband Walter James in the Mount Olivet Cemetery in Salt Lake City at about 1400 East and 1300 South. The James family has a rather large plot at Mount Olivet and four James families are buried there.

Helen's obituary, which came out in the January 18, 1951 issue of the *Milford News*, mentions some of the people who survived her. Jack Travers was still in Craig, Colorado, and with his second wife Inez; and one of Helen's two sisters Clara Raht Schindler was in Bremerton, Washington. Also, the daughter of her other sister Elise Raht Burbank, a Mrs. Margaret Burbank Scott, was still alive in Seattle.

It was later during this time period that **Helen (Babe) James McMillen** died. Her youngest daughter Elise tells us a little about how her premature death came about: *Mother died of scleroderma and it's an incurably fatal disease. It's a hardening of spots on the skin but it spreads to all the body tissues and organs. And it's fatal. It's kinda rare but people still get it. It had nothing to do with the TB she had back in 1936. She had scleroderma for 5 years before she died. She became an invalid and was in the hospital a lot during that time. Later we had a nurse come to our house. Dad was her night nurse, then we had a lady there during the day when he was at work. She had shots and everything. It was worse than these cancer deaths.*

Her funeral was held on **July 2, 1956**, so she died a few days before that. She was believed to be only 53 or 54 years of age at the time. Between Elise's memory, and what is in her obituary in the July 5, 1956 issue of the *Milford News*, here is a little more on what Babe did in the years she lived in Lakewood, Colorado.

She was an RN before she was married, but after the war when her husband came home, she stayed close to home with her two daughters. She became a volunteer person and a charter member of a sorority in Lakewood. Since this was the 1950's, and the Cold War was at its height, she was deeply involved with the Civil Defense program. While there she acted as head of the nursing service, taught first aid, and assembled a Civil Defense first aid kit which was cited by the Red Cross as a standard for other Civil Defense units.

Now back to the Black Rock Ranch. **Benita & Hamp** continued to live in the Cottage, but they had some work done on it. They had lived there since 1936. The Cottage was originally the bungalow which was built from several smaller structures back in 1921 for Jack Travers and his family.

It must have been during this time that one of the oldest professions in the wild west-- cattle rustling--took on a new look. By the summer of 1947, the state took over the road running alongside the railway line from Milford to Delta, and grading and graveling began. It was a continual job for several years until the road was completely paved during the winter of 1962-63. This improved road meant better access--better access for thieves too. In the July 5, 1951 issue of the *Milford News*, it's mentioned that: *Hampton Burke, the Merrill Millers and Walter[Wally] Miller spent several days of the past week in Fillmore, where the district court was trying two men who were caught stealing sheep from the Black Rock Ranch last March. The rustlers were found guilty.* Sheep or cattle rustling didn't happen very often, but they were caught that time.

Thekla & Merrill Miller were there in the Big House at the Ranch throughout this time period. Thekla was apparently involved with the Eastern Star organization, and became interested in growing flowers. She entered and was awarded several Blue Ribbons at the Deseret Flower Show which took place in Deseret in August of 1953. Later, in June of 1956, Thekla also attended the National Convention of Garden Clubs which was held in Salt Lake City that year. Merrill and Hamp Burke were of course running cattle, and apparently a few sheep, there at the Ranch. They did the irrigating of fields, alfalfa and pasture, and the feeding and selling of livestock. They always had a big garden and fruit trees, and apparently the women continued to do some bottling of fruit.

One thing the entire James family enjoyed doing together throughout the years from the 1920's through the 1950's, was to go deer hunting. This was always in October, and

William & Babe McMillen(left), Helen R. James, Jack Travers, and McMillen daughters, Sophia(left) and Elise. McMillen home in Lakewood, Colorado, 1949.
(Inez B. Travers Beers collection)

instead of going out camping, they normally slept there at the Ranch, then drove out during the day to hunt. Most of the time they headed southeast and hunted both sides of the Mineral Mountains which extended south from the mines at Antelope Point.

One of the men to go out with the James' and Millers was **Warren G. Allsop**. Everybody called him **Sonny,** and he was the basketball coach for Bingham High School for many years. He first got to know Merrill Miller in the CCC camp in Kamas and the Mirror Lake area in about 1935. It seems like he and some of his boys were in Black Rock almost every October until the Ranch was sold. Throughout the years Sonny remembers shooting 54 head of deer near Black Rock. For many of those years, it was legal to shoot 2 deer, which indicates it was great deer country.

Sonny remembers a little about the **post office** there in Black Rock: *Benita had the post office there for a few years, and it was up in her cottage. We used to buy all our stamps there to make it look like she was really doing business. She had it there in her home after they closed the post office down at the store & hotel.*

The Black Rock Post Office first began operating on April 1, 1891. No one is sure who the first postmaster was, but it could have been Walter James. The next one was likely AG James and he had it there in the store & hotel. The James' must have given up the job in the late 1930's or around 1940(?), then several other people had it during the early 1940's. Benita got it in November of 1945, and she had it until 1958. See the list of known postmasters on page 158. It was formerly discontinued on November 13, 1959.

Wally Miller was a student at Westminster College in Salt Lake until the spring of 1949, then he attended the University of Utah for at least one year. He then returned to Black Rock and spent some time working on the Ranch. According to some people, he worked at the Ranch, but he may have gotten a part-time job on the railroad down at the depot as well.

In the summer of 1954, Wally got a job working in an experimental program in cloud seeding. He worked for the Western Water Resources Development Company out of Denver, and his job was to go around to farmers and ranchers and sell them the cloud seeding service. He did lots of traveling with this job. He started out in Utah, then by October of 1954 he was working and living in Nevada. By March of 1955, he was living in Elko, and he spent time in southern Idaho as well. Utah, Nevada and Idaho were his sales territories.

In the spring of 1956, Wally was working in Caliente, Nevada, for the railroad. He started out at the bottom just like everyone else, on a section gang. Union Pacific was to be the company for which he worked for the rest of his life.

Oil Wells

During the summer of 1950, there were half a dozen articles about a renewed effort to drill for oil in the area south of Black Rock and Antelope Springs. This time Walter James wasn't around to promote it, and apparently no one at the Black Rock Ranch got involved. This was done by an outfit called the El Capitan Drilling Company of Russell, Kansas. The president of that little company was Floyd Spurgeon. He had studied the old logs of the original Walter James Well No. 1 and found the drillers had passed through several strata that showed signs of oil and natural gas. So in early July of 1950, they started drilling their first test well less than a kilometer northwest of the original Walter James Well. After only one week they were down 3200 feet, or very near one kilometer. Their Diesel powered rotary rig was far better than what had been used in the 1926-29 attempt.

As they went down, they began calling it the Walter James No. 1 Wildcat Well. The best description of what happened to this well, as well as giving an explanation of what was found at the original well from 1926-29, was written in the August 10, 1950 issue of the *Milford News.* Part of that news clip went like this:

The Walter James No. 1 was completed last week after perforating six different zones by the McCullough Gun Perforating Company. There were no "good shows" whatsoever, a company spokesman said, but some good saturated oil sands were recovered bearing dead oil. These sands were washed but the company was unable at any time to recover any free oil.

"The bottom hole temperature was terrific," the spokesman said, "as it was impossible to put your hand in any of the water recovered or to handle the tools immediately after they were pulled out of the hole. It is believed that this temperature was caused by a nearby volcano, causing the oil in the sands to be dead."

Incidentally, the area from about Delta in the north, south past Fillmore, Kanosh, Cove Fort, Black Rock and to near Milford in the south, is over a "hot spot". A hot spot is where the crust of the earth is thinner than in other places, allowing molten magma from below to more easily penetrate the crust. Over the last million or so years, this region has seen a number of volcanos. The Blundell Geothermal Power Plant, shown on the Area Map, is about 20 kms northeast of Milford. It was built near the center of this geothermal area. They pump water down into the top of the hot spot, which creates steam, which in turn is used to generate electricity.

After the failure of the Walter James Well, the drillers moved their rig from Section 17, T25S, R10W, to the west a ways and into Section 29, T25S, R10W. This was on the Paxton lease, just west of the highway and in the area between Malone and Reed. They drilled down to 3379 feet or just over a kilometer, but found no oil. They did however, find about 2000 feet or about 625 meters of sands and gravels which contained good water. Salt Lake geologist Mendell M. Bell, seemed to think they reached the bottom of an ancient lake bed, and that the gravels above that held an inexhaustible supply of water(8/24/1950, *Milford News*). These attempts were the third, and probably the last attempts by anyone to drill for oil in the Black Rock area.

Before the drillers left, some of the local people in Milford, including Hamp Burke and Merrill Miller, tried to get the drillers to leave their rig in place a while longer. What they wanted to do was come up with some money so that tests could be made to see how much water might be available, and what the salt content of the water might be. It was hoped that if the water was good and there were adequate amounts, it might rejuvenate the farming around the Reed and Malone areas through the use of well water. It would have been cheaper to make such tests at that time since the rig was already in place, but no money could be found on such short notice, so the drilling company moved on.

Left to right, Lemoine Dodson, Gean Shoemaker, Duane Dodson and Wally Miller at the Black Rock Ranch, Thanksgiving, 1949. (Elise M. Brougham collection)

The AG James Family

By 1944, no members of this AG James family were living at Black Rock. As of the funeral date of Walter James, we know that **AG** and wife **Velora** were living in Las Vegas, as were their daughter **Dorothy**, and her husband **Al Leonard**. Son **Ralph James** was in Chicago, Illinois, doing research on the atomic bomb.

AG & Velora and Al & Dorothy were running a little restaurant in Las Vegas. They had been there beginning in about 1942 or 1943. By June of 1945, AG was in the hospital seriously ill, but no one can remember what his problem was. He did recover, and in 1946, they all four moved to Seal Beach, California, which is just to the southeast of Long Beach. They then got involved with the Park View Hamburger stand, at 829 Ocean Avenue, near the pier in Seal Beach. AG was basically retired at about this time, but he may have helped out with the business. Al & Dorothy eventually bought a house, but AG & Velora always rented a place. Velora stayed at home and tended little **Larry Leonard**, who was just starting in school about the time they moved to California. Al & Dorothy are the ones who ran the hamburger stand, and they did that throughout this time period.

Ralph A. James graduated from the University of California at Berkeley in 1942 with a Bachelor of Science degree in Chemistry. Following graduation he joined the atomic bomb effort during the war called the *Manhattan Project*. For this work he was stationed at the University of Chicago Metallurgical Laboratory. It was while in Chicago that he married **Ramona Nieberding** on June 15, 1944.

While he was there at the Metallurgical Laboratory his principal studies had to do with the chemistry of heavy elements such as uranium and plutonium. It was while working with Dr. Glenn T. Seaborg, that he helped co-discover elements 95(americium) and 96(curium) as well as several new isotopes of plutonium and neptunium. For this he received national and international recognition, and was featured in the **July 8, 1946** issue of *Life Magazine*. The introductory part of that article went like this:

The study of plutonium's chemistry formally began in April of 1942 when a little group of Chemists led by the University of California's Dr. Glenn T. Seaborg assembled in Chicago. It was the beginning of a desperate summer for the U.S. and its allies. The Russians and

Dorothy James, Al Leonard & Larry Leonard, late 1940's. (Beryl G. Sorensen collection)

English were to fall back on Stalingrad and El Alamein; the U.S. had still to fight its defensive battles of the Coral Sea and Midway. Only a handful of scientists knew that the Allies faced a graver danger: the possibility that the Germans could make an atomic bomb. The secret campaign of the chemists was closely fitted into the magnificent structure of research and technology which led to the [atomic] bomb......

The rest of that article is incomprehensible to most of us, but it seems that Ralph was at the right place(University of California studying under Glenn T. Seaborg), and graduated at the right time(1942). His picture is seen on pages 76, 77, and 83, in the *Life Magazine* mentioned above. This event was also mentioned in the July 12, 1946 issue of the Milford newspaper.

In 1946, he returned to the University of California at Berkeley and joined the research staff of the Radiation Laboratory to pursue his Ph.D., which he received in 1948. After getting his Ph.D. he joined the staff at UCLA and taught chemistry there for 11 years, from 1948 until 1959 or '60(?). More on Ralph A. James, the small town boy from Utah who made it big time, in the next chapter.

Meanwhile back in Black Rock, AG still had ownership of their home, which was the store & hotel. The building was still there until the time period of from May, 1947, until the summer of 1948, then the store & hotel, the 2 tie houses, and all the barns were torn down so they wouldn't have to pay taxes on the property. More on tearing them down later.

From about May of 1941, when they left Black Rock for the last time, and up until sometime either in the spring of 1947 or the summer of 1948, the store & hotel building was rented out to railroad workers as living quarters. No one alive today knows who was collecting rent or showing prospective renters the place, but it well may have been handled at the Black Rock end by Benita and/or Hamp Burke(?). **Donnetta Hardy** of Delta, knows as much as anyone about what was going on at that time. Her husband Floyd Hardy, was a long time employee for the railroad, and they lived there at about this time. This is what she recalls:

I'm sure it was May 19, 1946, that we went down to Black Rock. Floyd had already

Ralph James and wife Ramona Neiberding James (Beryl G. Sorensen collection)

moved some of the furniture, because he was batching it. There was two couples at that time who were working for Floyd on the section, that were living in the old hotel. They were renting from the James' and sending the money down to Seal Beach, California. This must have been going on for several years--people renting the old hotel building and sending the rent money to California. One of the renters at the hotel was Grant Wilcock. Later he went on to be a section foreman out around Pioche and Panaca, Nevada. Still later he was killed in a car wreck out here.

Now this was 1946, and the place we were living in, which was the section foreman's house, didn't have a hot water heater along with our coal stove. So we got the address from Benita and wrote to Art[AG] James in California, and he told us to go and take that water heater out of the hotel, and we sent him $10 for it. He was in Seal Beach.

Now the story of what happened to the store & hotel and the other buildings AG & Velora James owned and had lived in since the beginning of 1917. Refer to the map on page 81. First, the **Malone School**. It had been moved from Malone up to the Black Rock townsite in about 1924, or at least some time in the 1920's, and placed on a cement foundation just north of the store & hotel. For years, both the basement and the upstairs parts had been used for storage. No one knows for sure why, but it burned down in the late summer of 1945 or maybe 1946(?). The person who knows this story best was Norman D. Hollis, more commonly known as **Dude Hollis**, from Minersville. He and his family were there from about 1930 until 1936 while his father worked on the railroad. The family moved to Milford and was living there in the mid-1940's. Here's what he remembered about the Malone School house burning down:

The Malone School burned down in 1945 or 1946. I was a young guy and I was on the Milford volunteer fire department. They were trying to get some new young talent, and train 'em. I must have been about 15 or 16 years old then and in high school. Of course when a fire was reported, then we got to leave school. Somebody on the railroad must have made a telefon call from the siding there at Black Rock, then the people in the Milford station called the fire department. We just loaded up some fire extinguishers and threw them in the back of a pickup and away we went. But it was all gone, completely burned

AG & Velora James in California in the early 1950's(Kelsey collection); and July 8, 1946 foto from *Life Magazine* of Ralph James at U. of Chicago Metallurgical Laboratory.

down, when we got there. Black Rock is in the next county, but we just went out there anyway. We didn't get out of school for that one, I think it was just prior to school starting, and it was in the afternoon about 2 or 3 o'clock. It must have been in late summer when this happened.

About this time, or just a year or so later, all or most of the buildings there were torn down. Donetta Hardy says the store & hotel were still there when they left Black Rock in May of 1947, and one fotograph from August of 1948 shows that it was gone. So sometime during this time period they were taken away. **Deon Gillen** of Oasis, who is the nephew of Velora Styler James, remembers what happened:

When he was in California, AG told us that he couldn't go back to Black Rock, but, "I've paid the taxes on it for now, but if I keep it any longer I'll have to pay more taxes. So I'd just as soon you get everything off there that is of any use to you". He was telling this to our family. So my dad and me and my brother Elmo went down there and tore all that stuff down.

When we arrived at the hotel and were tearing it down, it hadn't been broke into or anything. The windows were still in it. The barn was made of cement, so about all we could get off of that was the tin roof and the rafters. It must have been built in September of 1920, because that's the date you can still see in some of the cement there now. We had lived in one of those tie houses when we were there in 1923-24. My brother marked all the ties from that one house and he was going to bring it home and put it up, but he never did get it up. My brother's name is Elmo Gillen, and he tends the post office here in Oasis.

Tearing the store & hotel down ended a long chapter in the history of Black Rock. The original building was the old Henry Bowen Dance Hall which had been hauled down from Frisco. It was likely built in the late 1870's or early 1880's, then moved down to Black Rock in the early 1890's by Walter & Helen Raht James. All together it was enlarged about 7 times, as one can see on the floor plan.

As of about 1948, the only structures left at the Black Rock townsite were the railroad buildings, the shearing barns, corrals and boarding house, and the shipping corrals, scales & chute. It was soon after the winter of 1948-49 that the school house was taken back up

From the depot looking north at loading chutes, shipping corrals, and freight house left, and depot, ice house and shearing barns on the right. August, 1948. The store & hotel were gone at that time.
(Kelsey collection)

to the Ranch, but it's not certain what happened to it after that. Hamp Burke indicated it was torn down and the lumber used to build other structures at the Ranch. The boarding house was moved up to the Ranch and it may be the storage building in the Kaufman's barn yard(?). It's shown on the map on page 128. The shearing barns and corrals were torn down by Hamp Burke and Merrill Miller in about 1949, and the materials used to build other buildings and corrals up at the Ranch.

Now back to the AG James family in California. AG & Velora, and Dorothy & Al Leonard continued to live there in Seal Beach. Dorothy & Al ran the hamburger stand, and AG & Velora were both basically retired during the mid-1950's. It was on **July 1, 1957** that **Arthur Garfield James** died. His short obituary in the July 4, 1957 issue of the *Milford News* tells what happened, who survived him, and where they were living at the time.

Funeral services were held Wednesday at Seal Beach, California, for A. G. James, 71, who died there Monday morning of a heart attack.

Mr. James, a prominent cattleman and businessman of the Milford area for many years, was born September 30, 1886, at Oasis, to Thomas and Ann Phillips James. He married Velora Styler at Oasis.

He had lived at the old mining town of Frisco, and operated a store and hotel at Black Rock for 30 years[actually more like 24 years].

Surviving are [his wife Velora and] two children, Prof. Ralph James of Santa Monica, Calif., and Mrs. Dorothy Leonard of Seal Beach; three grandchildren; and two brothers, Ernest James of Salt Lake and Bert James, a twin brother, of Milford.

The death of AG James ended another important chapter in the history of the James family and the town of Black Rock. But Black Rock wasn't completely dead, as we will see in the next chapter.

Next is a smattering of interesting if not important events that took place at Black Rock before the Ranch was sold in August of 1957, which will bring this chapter to a close.

Sheep Shearing and Shipping Sheep

Shearing sheep continued at Black Rock after World War II, but not in the same numbers as prior to the war. Many changes had taken place in the years from about the late 1920's up through this period. Trucks were used to take supplies out to the sheep camps, so all the little sheep herder stores at Jack Watson's Ibex, Black Rock, Clear Lake and Newhouse closed down in the early or mid-1930's. The sheep numbers dropped, and with trucks and more mobile shearing equipment, it became possible to shear sheep more easily at various locations, other than at the big corrals located along the railway line.

In 1946, it was Gabriel Hoyland and his crew who sheared at Black Rock. This was a portable shearing outfit from Dillon, Montana. Mrs. Hoyland cooked for the crew in a trailer house, and that year there were many sheep being shipped from Black Rock to other points on the railroad.

By 1949, only the B.L. Larson herd was sheared at Black Rock, while the others were sheared on their own range allotments. The wool however was trucked to Black Rock and shipped out by train. In 1951, the Barton & Sons flocks were shorn at Black Rock by the portable Gabriel Hoyland outfit.

Then in spring of 1953, they had a snow storm at the height of the shearing season. That event was featured on two full pages in the Milford newspaper for May 7, 1953. Part of that article went like this:

2000 SHEEP DIE IN SUDDEN FREEZE

Losses estimated as high as $70,000 to $80,000 were suffered by sheep men in the immediate Milford area last week when sudden snowstorms and sub-freezing weather struck Southern Utah at the height of the shearing season. One herd, owned by Don Brown and Arthur Nell of Manti, lost more than 800 [newly shorn] head during a 20-hour rain and snow storm..... Alden K. Barton and Sons, running a herd in the Black Rock area, lost 300 head early in the week.

Old timers have told this writer that sheep must have a couple of days of reasonably warm and dry weather conditions immediately after being shorn. If not, sheep can die easily if they get wet right after losing their winter coats. It appears that with all the changes, including portable shearing outfits, that shearing ended at Black Rock in the early 1950's even though it's believed the barns were gone by 1949. It seems that about this same time, early to mid-1950's, shipping sheep and cattle from Black Rock also ended.

The Railroad

During the early or mid-1940's things were fairly normal for the railway workers. The depot was open and running, but there were almost no passengers, even in the mid-1940's while the war was going on. These numbers must have dropped to virtually zero at the end of the 1940's after gasoline rationing was lifted and things got back to normal throughout the country.

Floyd & Donnetta Hardy were there at Black Rock from May, 1946 to May, 1947. Floyd, who passed away in the early 1990's, was the section foreman. Donnetta, who was much younger than her husband, remembers quite a bit about what railroad life was like during that year at Black Rock:

*When we first got there, we lived in the **section foreman's house**. It was south of the depot and water tank, and just across the road to the east, and it was solid cement. Then south of that was the bunkhouse. Our house was in the first bunch of trees, then a short distance south of that was the bunkhouse. I planted those trees that you see there today; I brought 'em down from the ranch.*

When we first got to Black Rock, Bill Vestal was the signal maintainer and he lived in the most southerly of the three railroad houses. Then Gilbert McCulley lived in the north end of the depot. He was the station agent. The agent always had "trick one", or "daytime trick"; he worked the 8 hours during the day. Then there were two couples who were older people that the railroad had recruited to come back after they were retired, and they were second and third trick, or telegraph operators. I really enjoyed them because they had brought a library with them. They knew they were coming to an out-of-the-way place, and I'll bet they had 10 boxes of books. And I kept reading their books.

North of the hotel and AG James' place were a couple of houses, and I think some Mexicans lived there. They were railroad workers, but I don't think they were railroad houses. Sometimes those houses would have only one room, and when someone had a

Floyd Hardy, Fran Winfield left, Gilbert McCulley rear, George Mitchell right; in front of the Black Rock Depot, 1947. Floyd Hardy in front of their home at Black Rock. (Donnetta Hardy collection)

family it just wasn't big enough. So some families would try to find a small house and move into it.

When we were there the **postmaster** was Benita James Burke. But usually it was the agent who took the mail off the train and he'd just take it into the telegrapher's room in the depot, because someone had to unlock the mail pouch. When we were there the mail bag was just thrown off the train.

We were at Clear Lake in the snowy winter of 1948-49. The government got hold of Ray Smith of Delta, and he put his great big cat on a railroad flatcar and shipped it to Black Rock, and he went with it. He was 6 weeks out there in the desert west of Black Rock trying to clear roads, but mainly he was trying to make bedding grounds for sheep.

The railroad used water from those springs. The early ranchers had sold two of those springs to the railroad. Water was piped down to the tracks, and we had running water in our house. When we were there, they still used steam engines, and the water tank.

While in Black Rock, there would be a man come out from Milford with the pay checks, and he brought cash with him; so he could cash those checks for the men right there.

When we moved there to Black Rock, Bill Vestal was the signal maintainer but he left as they consolidated the thing and made it a longer run; a bigger area. In 1957 Floyd's brother was the foreman of a work crew at Black Rock. His name is David Hardy. There were still people living at Black Rock then, but some people were starting to drive from Milford or Delta to work.

Up to this chapter, little has been said about the workings of the railroad, yet throughout the years, more than half the population of Black Rock were Union Pacific employees. It was surely the biggest economic factor in the community. **Gilbert McCulley** of Milford was a lifelong railroad employee and he was at Black Rock a couple of times. Here's what he had to say about his work and some of the things that were happening at Black Rock at the time:

I was a telegrapher at Black Rock in 1943. That fall I went deer hunting, then left Black Rock in November of 1943 and went into the army. I got out of the army in 1946. I was a telegrapher, then the agent and operator. I was the agent there in the winter of 1948-49.

In the old days, the **agent** was technically the one who had the power. He was the railroad's representative for each station or town. He was also the one who ran the shipping. If you were going to ship something you had to get a bill from the agent. He

Gilbert McCulley hands message to train engineer, with Donnetta Hardy sitting, and George Mitchell to the far right. (Donnetta Hardy collection)

Black Rock Railroad Depot Floor Plan--1926 to 1972

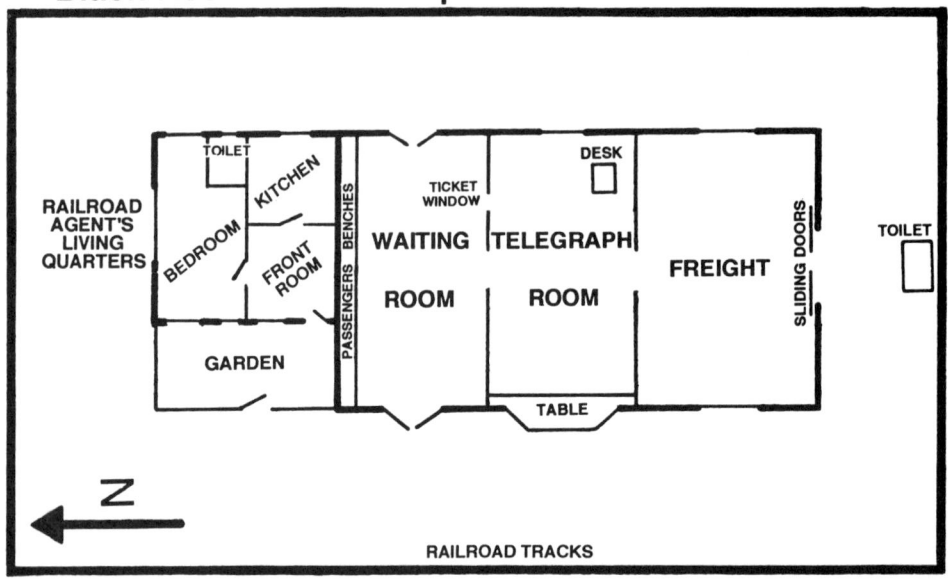

was the one to order a car to come so you could ship. A box car or whatever, would be set on a side track for a certain time. You'd load it, and bill it, then the agent would call into Milford or Salt Lake and have the car picked up. But the main thing the agent did at Black Rock was to issue **train orders**. East-bound trains have priority over west-bound trains. The east-bound trains were even numbers, and the west-bound trains were uneven numbers. Originally the train orders come from the **dispatcher** in Salt Lake over the wire with the old Morse Code.

As an agent we also had to make the section foreman and the signal maintainer a **lineup**. In other words, a lineup of trains coming, so they knew when to put their motorcars on the tracks. You see, in those days you didn't have signals, at least you didn't run trains by signals. So the agent wrote out a train order for the crews.

Now every 5 miles [8 kms] you had a side track, a place where trains could meet and pass each other. So your signal maintainer and section foremen, they had to have this lineup to go by, which was about when these trains was going to arrive. So they could watch out for 'em. That's what we agents did, was make train orders, and they also shipped things out from the station.

I was agent there at Black Rock, and my big business was shipping pumice from the first side tracks to the north which was called **Pumice**. The billing had to be done at Black Rock, which was a billing station. There were billing stations only every 30 or 40 miles [50 to 65 kms]. Clear Lake had a station, but they didn't do any billing. All they had to do was the train orders.

Byron Ray was my big shipper out of Black Rock. He shipped pumice out of Pumice. Also he shipped a lot of sheep--sheep in and sheep out. In the 1940's, Carl Neilson shipped his sheep in during the fall and out in the spring. And we'd ship anywhere from 80 to 100 cars a day sometimes. They'd come in sometime after October 15th, and there was an agent there all winter and throughout the spring. This was up to about 1950 when I left.

The **signal maintainer** was one of the later people hired. In the early days, back in the 1920's or earlier, you didn't have signals. So when they finally got signals, which had to be maintained, then you got a signal maintainer. They came in some time in the late

1920's. So all the information the signal man got about coming trains was from the operator, and on Morse Code. Telefons came later.

[The **section foreman** was in charge of the section gang or crew, and they maintained the rails and couplings, etc. He took his orders from the **roadmaster** in Milford. The roadmaster would come out on the trains or in a motorcar and look for bad spots, then he'd report the bad spots to the section foreman, and the gangs would then go out and fix it. Donnetta Hardy].

For the **motorcar**, they weren't supposed to handle them with less than 3 men. Usually they had more than that, but 3 was minimum. Now sometimes we'd have a storm out there on a weekend, and David Hardy the section foreman, usually had just one man with him, so he'd come and get me to be the third man. Three men could lift that motorcar on and off the tracks. And every so far along the tracks you'd have your motorcar setoff. They had a regular setoff place. And we'd patrol the tracks to make sure there wasn't any washouts or anything. Now on those motorcars, you always had one man looking back to look for an approaching train, whereas the rest of the men would be looking foreword all the time. I would say they made the change over from **handcars** to motorcars sometime in the 1920's. It was when I was a kid they made the change over.

At Black Rock, the railroad had all the water it wanted, and all the ranch got was what was left over. I tried to have a garden and a little lawn around the depot, but Benita would come down, and boy, she would raise all kinds of hell with me about watering that lawn. That was because I was using some of the water they wanted up at the Ranch.

But the thing that really hurt 'em up at the Ranch, was when the railroad went to the **Malley engines,** which used more water. The Malley was the big steam engine which had two sets of drive wheels, instead of just the one set. The other type engines are what we called the **Mike engines**, which have only one set of drive wheels on both sides.

The Malleys, which had the two sets of drive wheels, were called 3500's and 3800's. The 3500's had the smaller drive wheels, and they'd pull the freight cars or trains. They had smaller wheels, and they were slower, but they had more power. Then you had the 3800's which had the bigger wheels, and they'd pull the passenger trains. The Malleys used a lot more water than the older engines.

Now in Delta, they would drain those water tanks fast, then the engines would have to wait a while for the tank to fill up. But that Black Rock tank would fill up just like that, so the railroad was having all their Malleys fill up at Black Rock. That's the only reason they'd stop at Black Rock was to fill up with water. And of course the Burkes and Millers was hurtin' for water up there at the Ranch because the Malleys was usin' so damn much water.

The advantage of using the **Diesel engines** wasn't for the pulling power or the speed, it was the maintenance part. Now they used to have trains No. 103 & 104, the high speed passenger trains. Those trains would come from Clear Lake to Black Rock and their ordinary time was about 16 or 17 minutes, I think(?), and that was around 34 miles [55 kms]. Now if they was in a hurry and running late, they would do it in about 15 minutes, or about 130 miles an hour [210 kms]. And it didn't matter if it was Diesel or steam.

Now when I was at Black Rock they were going through the transition from steam engines to Diesel. Sometimes the No. 103 or 104 passenger trains would have Diesel, and the next time they would have a steam engine. It was a pretty fast change over, it might have been 5 or 6 years, something like that. The change came fast especially after World War II. When I left Black Rock in 1949, or the first part of 1950, they were pretty much running on Diesels.

When I lived at Black Rock, I used to use the old **Cellar** which used to be on the north side of the old hotel, for a chicken coop. Some guy was leaving and he didn't have room to take his chickens with him, so I bought them for very little money. I had screen wire around it because the coyotes and cats would come down around there. So I locked them up and closed the door at night to keep the coyotes and cats away from the chickens.

When I was there, instead of the railroad having their fences up, they had these guys herdin' cows to keep 'em off the tracks. I guess the Ranch lost lots of cows over the years, being hit and killed by trains. It was after the war that they done away with those drovers.

When I first went out there to Black Rock in about 1943, we didn't have electric lights; we were using **kerosene** or **coal oil** in what we called **Aladdin lamps**. And then when they started to hire the women, which was during World War II, the first thing they did, not just at Black Rock, but with the whole railroad, was to upgrade living quarters, toilets and things like that. Now we always had electricity there at Black Rock, but they only had it at the depot and used it to run certain things like switches or something like that. It was the women who demanded more and started using the power. It cost the railroad quite a bit more to hire women than it did the men. I'm blaming the girls, but they had some help!

Electricity had been used a little bit there at Black Rock up to the time I went into the army. Sometime earlier, one of the signal maintainers there went up one of the power poles and ran an electric line into one house. But all he run on that was his refrigerator. So I think after about 1946, power came to all the houses. Then we all had electric lights.

The power line was run right down along the railroad all the time, because it run the signals. But it was a private line, that's the reason the Ranch couldn't tap into it, and it didn't have that much power anyway. The power they had was low grade. They didn't have all the big transformers and stuff to upgrade it.

In the real early days, the operators made their own battery for electric power to run the telegraph. It didn't take much power to run them. In the depots they had the big glass vessels and they used what was called blue vitriol. That's your copper, and you made an acid which was kinda like a battery. You had to redo those every so often. These would all be in the depots.

When I started on the railroad you didn't work 5 days a week like you do now; you worked 7 days a week and you worked 'till you died! We had an agent up at Garfield who was 93 years old. And the guy over in Pleasant Grove was 96 years old, and a lot of other guys was 70 and 80 years old.

Floyd Hardy left in 1947, then David Hardy came up from Reed and took his place as section foreman. Floyd was a little older. The station was open every day, but there weren't many people getting on the trains. Most of them were sheep herders, or the sheep owners. When they'd come in on the train, if somebody wasn't there to meet 'em, then I'd take my car and drive 'em out to their camp, out in the Cricket Mountains, or wherever they had to go. I didn't charge them to do that, but they were awfully good to me. I had lamb to eat all the time. About the time I'd finish one leg of lamb someone else would come in and bring me another one. Mutton isn't my favorite meat but I ate it.

During the war, they had a hard time finding people to help 'em on the Ranch, so Hamp and Merrill used to come down and get me to help 'em. They had a 3 man bailer and there was only 2 men there. So I'd go up and help 'em on the bailer when they was bailin' hay.

Walter James told me about the winter of 1898, or it might have been 1899(?). That was the year it froze the cows to death standing up. He said that was the coldest winter he had ever seen. Also, 1932 and 1936 was bad around here. It froze up the railroad and they had to have the snowplows out to get the trains through.

I was there during the winter of **1948-49,** with the heavy snow. The sheep were snowed in and I had to do a lot of talking with Fillmore and the BLM, and tell 'em how the sheep were. I took 54 inches [1.30 cms] of snow off the platform at Black Rock. I measured it every day.

The thing that made the winter of 1948-49 so bad was the wind. It was cold and there was a lot of snow too. When it snowed it was more like frost than regular snow; didn't have a lot of moisture in it. But in August of 1949, there was still snow at Black Rock. It was up there in the rim rock, along that black rock bench north of Black Rock. That's the only time in my life I saw snow in the valley in August.

Even though there were few if any passengers using the depot during this time period, there must have been enough cattle and sheep and wool shipped out of Black Rock to still justify its existence. From what McCulley has stated above, and what was found in some news clippings from the Milford paper, it seems that the depot may have been closed part of the year. But it seems to have always been open during the winter and spring months, at least up until this chapter ends in August, 1957. With the road between the Delta area and Milford being completely paved as of the winter of 1962-63, more people began driving to work from Milford and Delta, as Donnetta has stated above. Slowly, but surely the need for a station or depot and a full-time crew stationed at Black Rock became less and less.

Another reason why there was less need for work crews at Black Rock was the coming of Diesel engines. Throughout the years, and while using steam engines, Black Rock was a very important water stop along the Salt Lake to Los Angeles route. With the transition to Diesel engines, the need for this waterhole was simply not needed. The transition began in the early 1940's, and sometime between 1950 & 1952, all engines on this line were Diesel powered.

Other Events at Black Rock

Some other interesting events happened at Black Rock that are worth mentioning. Since the mid-1860's, the route between Delta and Milford has been used by a few people to get from northern Utah to southern Nevada. The Mormons used this approximate route to run a stage coach line from Pioche and Panaca, Nevada, north to Salt Lake City. But the reason it never got popular as a land route was the lack of water.

However just after the turn of the century, the railroad people found it to be the best route for them when they laid tracks south from Northern and Central Utah all the way to Southern California. There were mountains, but they were a lot lower than the ones just to the east. By 1929 and because of the existing railway line, this corridor became part of the main transcontinental air routes which went right along the tracks from Salt Lake City to Los Angeles. At first it seems to have been a mail route and there were 2 to 4 planes passing this way each night. Milford had an airport and was an important refueling place for a while. The airport also had a beacon which helped guide planes at night.

Black Rock also got into the act. According to Frances Rogers Green, the daughter of Dalles Rogers, and school teacher Rose Rogers: *There was some kind of a* **signal light** *for airplanes out there somewhere. It wasn't Dad's job to turn that light on and off every night, but who ever did it was sometimes on vacation, so then my dad would do it. We'd take our dinner and all go out there, and he would climb up this big ladder and turn the light on. When we'd do that we'd always go in the James' truck, so it was quite a ways*

Typical motorcar from 1950's. David Hardy is 2nd from left. (Ida Hardy Beitz foto)

from Black Rock, but I can't remember which direction it was.

La Preal Utley, who was the school teacher at Black Rock from 1932 to 1934, also stated it was one of AG James' jobs to look out for a light set up to guide airplanes on night flights. Later in time this route became a favorite route for small private planes making the flight from Salt Lake to LA. In the early and mid-1950's, Black Rock had several visitors who "dropped in". Perhaps the first plane to land at Black Rock was mentioned in the Milford paper for January 3, 1952. Some guy evidently got cold and landed on the road next to the depot. After getting warmed up, he continued on to Milford and to points unknown.

A news clipping in the April 9, 1953 paper mentions that, *A Piper Cub plane landed at the gates of the Black Rock Ranch Tuesday. It was piloted by Herb Vesper of Ely, Nevada. Mr. Vesper and his companion, a photographer, landed at the Bert Smithson Ranch [to the south] where dinner was served by Mrs. Smithson, then they flew here.*

The next aircraft landing wasn't so happy. On October 16, 1954, three people were killed north of Black Rock when their plane crashed. The site was about 150 meters west of the highway and a couple of kms south of the Continental Lime Plant, which is near mile post 40. It was just west of where the old Bloom siding used to be. The victims were Theodore Paul Gurschke, his wife Barbara and daughter Deborah from Las Vegas. The cause of the wreck may have been that the pilot "lost his horizon" because he wasn't "checked out" for night flying and apparently went into a spin heading straight for the ground.

Here are a few details from the October 21, 1954 issue of the Milford newspaper:

Mr. Gurschke filed a flight plan with the Delta CAA communications station at 7:14 pm [Saturday], about four minutes before the crash. He was flying at 14,000 feet [4267 meters]....

The wreckage was spotted about 9:15 am Sunday by two private search planes, after an all night search by Milford officials had failed.... First to reach the scene were Cassady [Cap] Petersen, from Ephraim, and Lester Poulson, who were herding sheep in the vicinity. A note dropped from a CAP plane instructed the two men where to find the wreckage. Mr. Petersen rode his horse to the highway, about a mile east, to direct rescue personnel, and Mr. Poulson remained at the crash scene.

Carl Boyter of Milford was there and he picks up the story later that day:

Benita & Hamp Burke, at the Black Rock Ranch, 1950's. (Elise M. Brougham collection)

We heard about the thing and they took us up there by motorcar. Dick Murdock was the foremen at Reed, and I worked for him. When we got there everybody was dead and I think they were killed instantly. David Hardy and his Black Rock crew got there right after we arrived. I didn't see any sheep herders but there could have been some there before we came.

We arrived there at about 1:30 in the afternoon, and Murdock told me I'd better save a little bit of my lunch because it looked like I was going to have to be the one to stay out there with the plane. I didn't have any blankets or anything, I just had to keep walking back and forth all night long to keep warm. I made a fire for a short while but there wasn't enough brush to keep a fire going. I was the only one there that night. I just watched over things until everybody came by the next day. They got the bodies then. My foreman came and got me and by about 2 pm I left to go home. At the time I was stationed at Reed.

The Black Rock Ranch is Sold

This chapter ends with the sale of the Ranch. By about the winter of 1956-57, Thekla & Merrill Miller, and Benita & Hamp Burke were living at and working the Ranch. The third daughter Helen (Babe) James McMillen, was living in Lakewood, Colorado, and had nothing to do with Black Rock or the Ranch. No one alive today(1996) knows for sure, but apparently the two couples weren't getting along that well together. Several people have stated that Hamp and Merrill got on just fine, and Benita got along well with Merrill, but Thekla and Benita had disagreements as to what to do with the Ranch and how it should be run. Remember, there were two couples there, and this was a time when perhaps this ranch wasn't big enough to support them both. It wasn't as easy at that time to make a living ranching as it had been earlier. Some wonder why an agreement couldn't have been made so that one couple could buy out the other, thus keeping the Ranch in the James family. Evidently a compromise couldn't be reached, so the decision was made to just sell the Ranch and part ways.

An ad was placed in the Los Angeles Times by a small real estate company in Milford run by Gene and Elmer Kirk. **Victor** and **Dorthea Kaufman,** and sons **Jim** and **Joe** of Porterville, California, saw it and came up to have a look. Vic and Dorthea were interviewed several times, beginning in 1994. Here's part of what they said about finding the place in 1957:

When we first came here, which was at Easter time in 1957, the real estate man brought us out and she [Thekla or Benita?] told us to get lost. The place was advertised in the Los Angeles Times and we came over here to find out about it. Gene Kirk was the real estate man in Milford, and he worked with his brother Elmer Kirk. It would have been Gene Kirk who put the ad in the newspaper. They had several places for sale at the time. One was south of Milford, and then he mentioned that he had one up north with a spring that runs 3 second/feet of water. Now if you've got water, whether or not it rains, you can do something. So when we saw the place, we just fell in love with it. It was and is a lonely place.

According to Vic Kaufman, it was August 5, 1957 when the Ranch was sold, but courthouse records indicated it was August 20 when it was first filed and recorded there. The exact date is not important, but it was **August, 1957** when they bought it. The news was made public in the Milford newspaper on August 29, 1957. Here's what that article said:

BLACK ROCK RANCH SOLD TO CALIFORNIAN

The famous Black Rock Ranch, 20 miles [32 kms] north of Milford, has been sold to Victor A. Kaufman of California. Mr. and Mrs. Merrill Miller and Mr. and Mrs. Hampton Burke, sons-in-law and daughters of Walter James, original owner of the combined Black Rock Ranch acres recently completed the sale through Kirk Reality Co. of Milford.

Involved were more than 5200 acres of privately owned land, range rights, 350 head of Hereford cattle, 50 head of purebred sheep, and water rights to Black Rock Springs. Purchase price was $140,000.

This ended about 56 years of ownership by the James family, and 76 years of joint ownership by the combined Raht-James families.

Black Rock depot and school left, shearing barns on the right. February, 1949.
(Carl Nielson foto, Kelsey collection)

Big Spring, Black Rock Ranch, 1949. Old ruins to the left, maybe from 1870(?), and the headhouse which covers the Big Spring to the right. (Carl Neilson foto, Kelsey collection)

Owen Gregerson's French-designed bulldozer at the Black Rock Ranch, February, 1949.
(Carl Neilson foto, Kelsey collection)

Reed Erickson left, at the Carl Nielsen(right) sheep camp, February, 1949. At Sand Wash, near Jack Watson's Ibex. (Carl Neilson foto, Kelsey collection)

Chapter 7
Black Rock from 1957 to 1996

The Kaufman Ranch
   The Black Rock Ranch was sold to **Victor A.** and **Dorthea S. (Dot) Kaufman** in August of 1957 which is the beginning of the last chapter in the history of Black Rock. Vic and Dorthea were interviewed in May and June of 1994, then Dorthea was interviewed in February of 1995. Finally Jim Kaufman and his wife Cynthia were interviewed in January, 1996. Below is an edited and combined version of all these interviews which tells the Kaufman's story of the Ranch:
   When we bought the place **Merrill** and **Thekla** lived here in the **Big House**, and **Hamp** and **Benita** lived over there in the **Cottage**. There were some hard feelings in the family, that's why they sold the place. When we actually bought the place in 1957, Thekla and Merrill moved to Bountiful, and Hamp and Benita moved in here and lived in the Big House until we moved here in March of 1960. It took us that 3 1/2 years to finalize our business down near Porterville, California, before we could move up here.
   Our one son Jim went to Milford High School for 2 1/2 years but our other son Joe stayed with his grandmother and graduated from Porterville Union High School in June, 1960. During his college years, Joe came to work on the Ranch at Black Rock each summer and every school vacation. After earning an engineer's degree at Fresno State College, he went to work for Ford Motor Company at Pico Rivera. After 12 years the plant as Pico Rivera closed and he went to work for Hughes. He and his wife Barbara and two girls spend their vacations helping at the Black Rock Ranch. They hope to retire here.
   When we bought the place, we put it in our names, then when Jim came back from his tour of military duty, he decided to stay here and make a living, then we incorporated it into Kaufman & Sons. That was around March, 1967.
   We love this big old house and have done some remodeling on it. Monte Work and Seth Jackson drove down from Delta every day to remodel our kitchen. We hired some Porterville friends and put a brick porch around to the north and west sides of the house. With the help of friends, one a plumber and carpenter, the other an electrician, we did the rest of the work ourselves.
   Through the years before 1950, other changes had been made. A screen porch from the east side of the house was moved to the north side and some windows and doors inside the house were changed. A two-story room was added where the east porch once was. Later, Benita made the downstairs room into a sun room and the upstairs part furnished sleeping quarters for the extra help. During the "hay lift of 1949", Benita said 27 sheepmen were snowbound here at the Ranch. They needed the sleeping quarters that year!
   Just to the north of us here and by the Tie House Spring was another house. The **Tie House** was built of railroad ties but it had a problem with the flooring. We decided to use the roof from that house for the garage we built at the Big House. We carefully saved all the lumber from the Tie House. Right there below the Tie House Spring was another house and it was made of lumber. Apparently that was the old **Stahl's place** many years ago. It had been moved from down by the Big Spring up there just below the Tie House. Nobody was living in them at the time and they were both empty.
   In between the Big House and the Cottage was another building and we think that was called the **Bunkhouse(?)**. It had a partition in the middle, and it might have been used as a school house or bunkhouse. It still had paper chains for decorations in it when we tore it down. It stood where the apple trees used to be between the Cottage and the Big House.
   Jim and I [Cynthia] got married in November of 1973. At that time I was working for Mountain Bell in Cedar City. I was driving to Cedar City to work each day and Jim was

always working here at the Ranch, but driving from Milford. Well, I drove to work at Cedar for about one year, then I took a one-year maternity leave when Kristen was born, and then I never went back to Mtn. Bell. Then we decided to live out here. At first we were just going to clean the **Cottage** up and move in, but then when we came in and started cleaning things, we decided to remodel it. We thought we were going to move in during the spring of 1975, but by the time we got through remodeling it was like December of 1975 before we got in.

Benita told us there were a lot of abandoned homesteader's houses located out to the south and southeast of Black Rock. People had gone off and just left them. This was the Malone area. A while after they left, her dad Walter James brought them in here and put them together. Our kitchen was one of those small houses; someone said it was a two room house at one time. The living room was another house, and then out on the back end was another small room, like a little porch. When we got here we opened it up and made a bigger room there. Earlier it had been Benita's post office.

When we came here we tore out all the interior walls and put new sheet rock and insulation in it. The beams here in this frontroom came out from the depot. It had a real low ceiling, and so by making a cathedral roof it made it feel much bigger. And that's when we made the loft up there in the north end. We have a bed there, but because of the heat going up it's so hot you can hardly sleep there, even in winter time. Our son Ben stores his drums and other things there. Below that were two bedrooms added onto the north end of the house. Before we came, you had to go from the livingroom into one bedroom, then into the other bedroom just to get into the bathroom. So when we remodeled it, we changed that and put the little hallway in.

There was a wood stove in the kitchen, and there was a hot water reservoir on the side of it. They didn't have a regular water heater, they just heated it from the cook stove. There weren't a whole lot of cabinets in the kitchen, but those they had were real high because Benita was so tall. The sink and side boards were higher than standard height. She didn't want to bend over.

Those rooms on the west end are all from our 1975 remodeling. There's the new hallway, a bedroom, a bathroom, storage room, and the garage; then upstairs the girls have their bedrooms. Also there's a storeroom over the garage.

In the frontroom here we use this Stoker Automatic coal stove. We bought it in Cedar City and had it installed. This is the only heat we've got in the house. If it gets really cold, then we put a fan on the side of the stairs and it blows warm air down the hallway and into those back bedrooms. We keep the doors open all the time. In the bathroom over there, we do have a little electric heater, but we seldom use it. We use propane in both houses to cook with and to heat water.

Benita had a **wash room** and shower out there in that small building just south of the Big House. That was in the east end. There was a **meat room** or cold storage room, and an **ice room** in the middle, and the **garage** was on the west end.

There was a **pond** just west of the Big House when we came. We got rid of it in about 1960. It was shallow and it had trees all around it. [They used to have ducks and geese on it and ice skating parties in winter]. It was always full of leaves, and it took a corner out of the field that wasn't doing any good.

We have a garden and we grow everything; carrots, beans, potatoes, zucchini, cucumbers, banana squash. The kids always had pumpkins to sell in the fall, but when the price went below 6 cents, forget that! I [Cynthia] can a lot, and I go to Hurricane to buy fruit. We can peaches, pears, cherries, and then green beans, I put them in bottles, and then we put corn in the freezer. We make our own pickles, and our own pickled beets. The pear tree and the apricot tree died here a few years ago because of the cold winter.

The **Big Spring** is south of us here, about a city block or so. Some people have called that the Railroad Spring. The railroad had an 8 inch pipe running from that headhouse where the spring is, all the way down to the railroad depot and the water tank. There also used to be about a 4 inch pipeline running from the **Tie House Spring**, and it looked like it went down to the shearing barns. It was on the north side of the county road and it

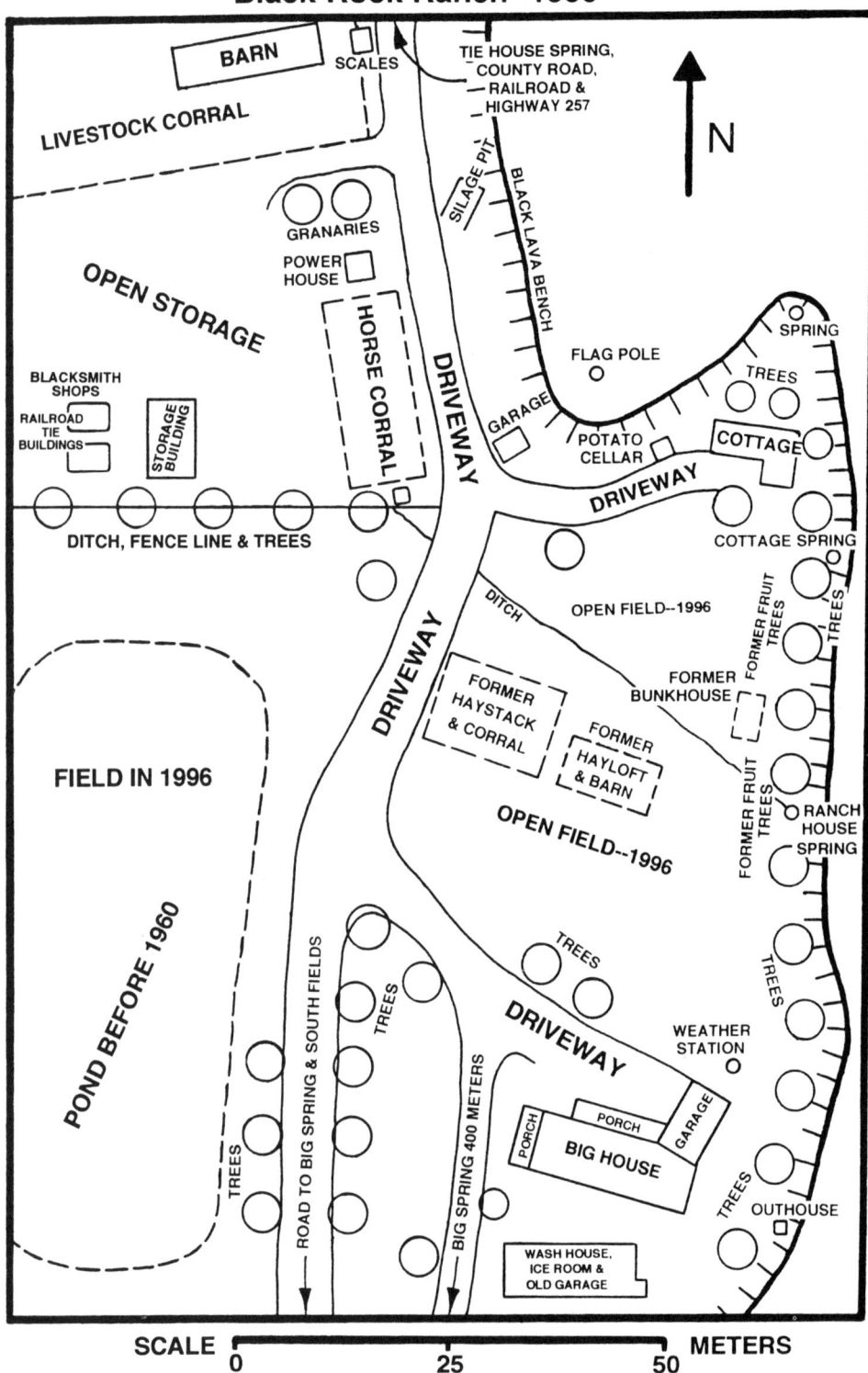

Black Rock School & 1908 Ranch House Floor Plan(1996)

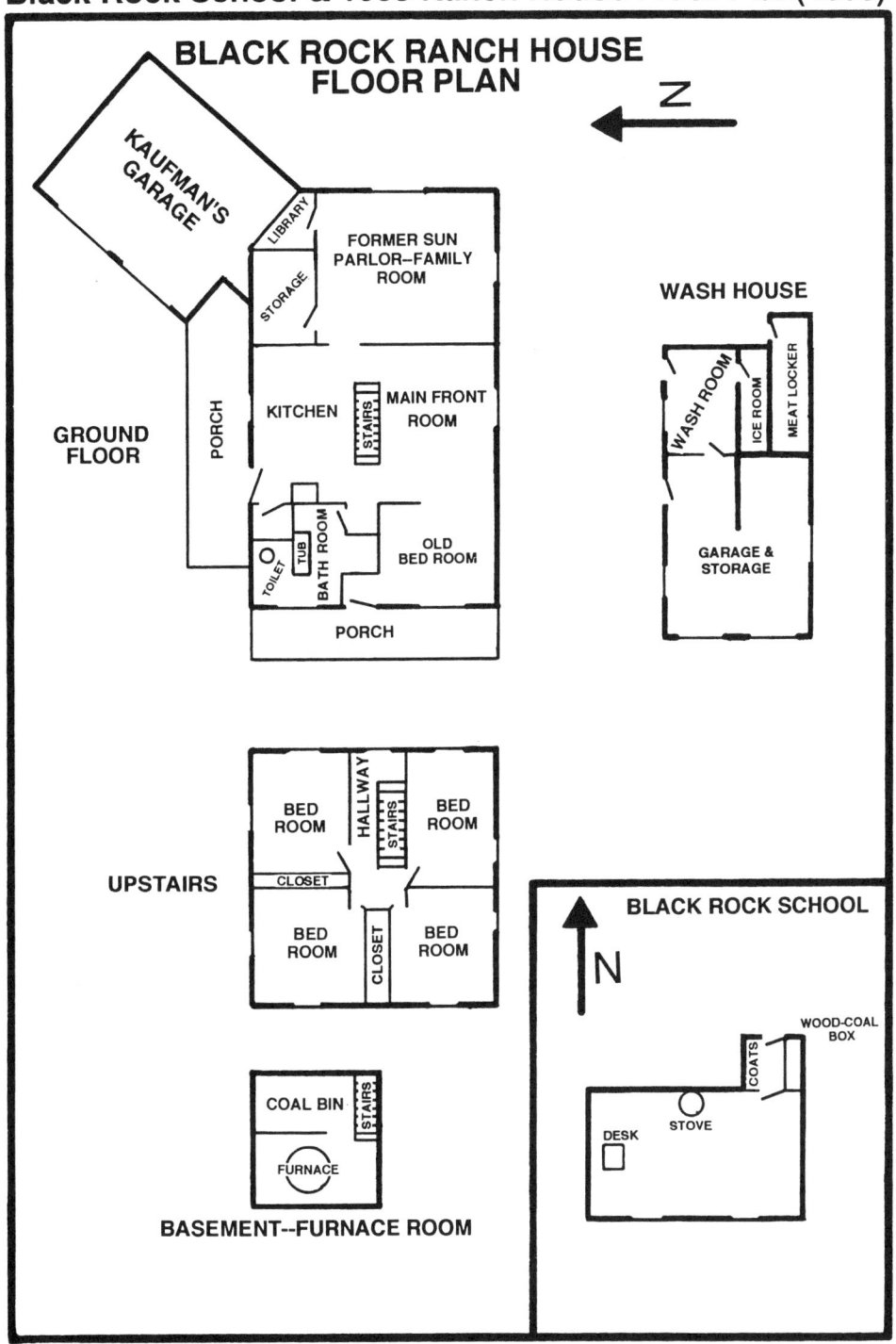

crossed through that wash. When they closed everything down and moved the houses away from down along the tracks, then we turned the water off that ran down there from the Big Spring. I believe that was sometime in the spring of 1993. From that time, all the water the railroad had owned reverted back to the Ranch.

When we first came here we tried drilling a well to see if there was water going straight down. We had come with a sprinkler system and so we drilled down a ways, but we didn't find any water down below. It turned out all we had was surface water, just that which comes from the springs The object was to try to put sprinklers in to irrigate with. All we do now is flood irrigating.

The James' tried to get the water from the Big Spring up to here, but that wasn't working with open ditches, so we put in the cement pipeline. We now pipe water from the Big Spring north to the Little Reservoir just west of the Tie House Spring, and from that pond we do most of our irrigating. With the water in that Big Reservoir, we irrigate fields and pasture down below. The discharge on the springs is about 3 second/feet. You can irrigate quite a bit with that. We raise enough feed for the cattle. We feed the calves until they're 550 or 600 pounds [250-275 kgs], so it works out pretty good.

We have a little over 9000 acres of private land; that's land we own. That's before we even do our leasing. We irrigate about 200 acres, and we do that from the ponds, gravity flow. We built that pond or **Little Reservoir** up at the gate back in the 1960's after we tore down the old Stahl's House. At that time it was all open ditch irrigation. The **Big Reservoir** was there when we came, but there were no Russian olives down there then. We think the Big Reservoir was built about the time the CCC's were here(?).

To do something with the water in the winter time we built **5 more little reservoirs** going south along the lava bench from the Big Spring. The water is all in gatted pipe when we irrigate and we do it 24 hours a day. You have to or you fall behind. We drain the land around these fields, otherwise they'd be water logged. Before, you couldn't raise anything on it.

When we bought the place there were no fences in the area east of the depot. The sheep used to trail in here to the reservoir and back out and there was big sand dunes in

From the Big Spring looking west where the Stahl's house used to be. Old stone cabin ruins on the right. February, 1949. (Carl Neilson foto, Kelsey collection)

The Tie House with Dorthea & Vic Kaufman, 1960's. (Kaufman collection)

Looking west over the Black Rock Ranch barnyard toward the Big Reservoir beyond.

there. The sheep don't come in here now, but the sheep herders get their drinking water here. They come in with a barrel and fill up. We dug up the **CCC camp foundations** out in that field and dragged them over to the north of the county road.

Bird watchers come up here occasionally. We get 'em from back east, and from California. I guess this place is on some bird watchers hotline. We start getting Canada geese in here about the middle of October, and a lot of them will stay part of the winter. And we have a few that stay the year-round. They see the big pond and land for a while to rest. Sometimes they come right up here on the lawn. They know we don't hunt 'em, and nobody is allowed on our land to hunt them.

Our drinking water comes from the spring behind the Big House. Some have called that the **Ranch House Spring.** We have a small pump in the basement which gives us a water pressure. There's a "Y" in the line, and one goes over to the other house where our son Jim lives. But we have plenty of pressure even when the pump isn't working. The James' never put a bathroom in the upstairs, and I guess they didn't because they didn't have the water pressure. There was however a dry sink upstairs.

This place had electricity from **generators** when we came. A 10 KW generator is down there in that shop by the corrals, and then there are two of them up here; one is pretty well worn out. So we have three, two are standby's. They're all Diesel motors, old Wittes. That's the whole thing, motor and generator. You can't buy them new anymore, and the one down there is worth about $10,000. Somebody is making parts now down in Texas. When we first came, there were some little gas generators already here. I think they had planned before W.W.II to bring the big power line over the top into Milford and through here, so the house had some pretty good wiring. We put in a lot more outlets when we tore away the old plaster. We built the little house for the generator about 3 or 4 years ago.

The scales over in the barn yard were already there, but we put the building around it. It's that little gray house made of lumber.

We run cattle west to Red Knoll, but we can go to Cove Fort on the east. We graze a lot down where Malone and Reed used to be, and then we lease some Indian tribal land over by the freeway. It stretches for about 25 or 30 miles [40 or 50 kms] east and west. We generally keep about 300 cattle. That's the number of cows the BLM allows us to graze on public land.

Sometimes those military jets fly over us down real low, maybe training to escape radar(?). They haven't been doing it lately, but when they do, it panics the cows and sometimes they'll go through a fence.

In about 1960 or 1961, the road was finally paved all the way from Milford up to the cattle guard north of Black Rock a ways. Then in the winter of 1962-63, Jim got a job on a road construction crew. He worked for Sumption Construction Company and they paved Highway 257 out here all the way up to mile post 40, which is where the Continental Lime Plant is today. With that part done, there was a paved road all the way from Milford to Delta.

The transcontinental telegraph line was still used until 1963 or 1964. It ran north and south about 5 miles [8 kms] east of our ranch. When the microwave system was put into use, they pulled out the poles. Where the line crossed private land, the owners could have the poles. That's where the big ones for our power lines came from.

When we first came here in 1960, I guess every railroad house down here by the tracks was full. There was two **bunkhouses**, and there was a Texan living in one. We called him Tex. And there was a little apartment on the north side of the station or depot for the **agent**. The Walkers were there; they had lived in Nephi and had a restaurant there.

Trains 5 & 6, one going north, one going south, were stopping here. They were the mail trains. We had wonderful mail service then. At that time the engineers and the trains were still stopping down here for inspections. Then there was a gradual decrease in the number of people living here. The families with children didn't want to stay out here because there was no school. They lived in Milford or Delta. The husbands would come down and stay during the week, then they'd go home on weekends

The Cottage at the Black Rock Ranch as it was in the summer of 1995.

A 1995 foto of the front of the Big House.

Hattie and **Scotty** were the black couple there. He was on the section crew. He worked on the line straightening the rails. He got to drinking toward the last but he was so comical when he wasn't drinking. Hattie made the most beautiful pies you ever saw. That couple was here until the mid or late 1960's sometime. Hattie and Scotty lived in the first house to the north, that's where Crystal Peak Minerals office used to be until recently. [More on Hattie and Scotty later].

Dale Jones and his wife were just starting out when we arrived, and he was the **section foreman**. Dale lived in the second house. I think he still works for the railroad, he worked his way up and he's an official now. He had one of those cars that rode on the tracks. The **signal maintainer** lived in the third house, the one to the south.

The railroad started moving people out of Black Rock when they started welding tracks together into quarter-mile [400 meters] sections. They had special gangs come in to do that work. I guess the section foreman is in Milford now and they go all over in pickups. But they were still using the motorcars on the tracks when we first came.

Then they decided to get rid of most of those buildings. We bought the **water tank** first; we bid $25 to a Mr. Larkin, who was superintendent of the railroad. We kinda thought we'd be ignored. But anyway, he accepted the bid just like that. But as soon as the water service of the railroad heard that we had acquired it, they came out and gutted the inside and took all the valves and cut the pipes and everything. The crew had taken it for their own use. So we wrote another letter to Mr. Larkin, then the water service crew out of Milford came back and brought it all out here. That little round trough you saw as you came into our place was part of it. We cut the water tank up into sections, and welded it back together again and made it into watering troughs. We have a pretty good shop out here, and a welder. We do everything out here.

Then we bid on the stock yards **[shipping corral and loading chutes]** and the railroad included a pre-cast cement **bunkhouse** that was further south. It was in panels of pre-cast cement, and that was the southern-most building out there. A fellow by the name of Johnny Boyles lived there. We had to take that bunkhouse down when we bought the stockyards. We didn't want it, but the railroad wanted it taken out too. We took the corral and loading chutes down and lifted the poles out with a tractor.

Then we asked the railroad about the **depot** and we got to bid on it. It was a nice depot. It had a tile roof, and they designed it southwestern style, with stucco on the outside. The depot had a little waiting room, and then in the back, where the freight came in, was another big room.

We tore down the depot in 1972. By then, they never used it and they were paying taxes on it, so they sold it. We tore it down and used the lumber on other things. The room at the back of this house is made from that lumber. It was good lumber, nothing was wrong with it. But it took us a long time to tear it down, and oh did they hound us! We bought it and were supposed to get it out or torn down by a certain date; we had just a few months. But we did it ourselves, so it was slow.

On both sides of the depot, east and west sides, they had a nice ceramic sign with the name, "The Union Pacific Overland Route" on it. Then one morning we went down there and looked around and the Overland Route sign on the west side was gone. The other one is in our son's yard in California; he's a steam train buff.

Somebody came out and dismantled the **section foremen's house**. Somebody else got that one. Then there were **two motorcar houses**; the signal maintainer had a motorcar house and the section foreman had one. They were two galvanized metal sheds. There was also a coal house near the water tank and an underground gasoline fuel tank there for the motorcars. A regular contract crew came through and removed that fuel tank.

The **ice house** went to somebody up in Delta. And all those houses had good sized **coal houses** behind them with doors that opened up so you could pitch coal inside. They jacked those up with four handyman jacks and put a hay trailer under 'em and they went to Delta.

There was also a big **outhouse** for men and women south of the depot; in-between the depot and water tank, and it had a coal house in the back of it. It was kind of funny what

The west side of the Black Rock Depot, with semaphore. (Donnetta Hardy collection)

Tearing the Black Rock Depot down in 1972. (Kaufman collection)

happened to that. When they tried to remove that one with the four handyman jacks, they never checked to see what was in the attic before they got it on the wagon. It was full of tile which was left over from the depot, and pipe from the water line. And when they turned a corner, it just went crunch! They were taking it to Delta or Deseret. They were railroad employees, but they had bid on those buildings and they took them away on their own time. All this was done in the early 1970's.

We have been taking care of the **weather station** for 36 years. Each month they give us a form to fill out and then we send that in once a month. The James family must have been taking weather records for 40 years before we got here. The weather bureau could tell you all the figures. We don't get paid, we just do it on a volunteer basis.

The **Malone Reunion** used to be on Memorial Day each year. The old people who had lived at Malone would come back here for a reunion. Malone was south of us about 4 miles [7 kms]. They had some nice houses there. Malone was on the east side of the highway, and Reed was on the west side. There were flowing wells there, that's how they irrigated; but when they built the Minersville Reservoir that dried up all the flowing wells. Not too many years ago, they closed all those little roads crossing the tracks to Malone. When we first came here, they called one road Orange Boulevard, because there were so many people who came up from Orange County in California. Most of the people who came to the reunion were also from down around Orange County. Julia Oliver, the Helwigs, the Averys, all of them are gone now,

It was in about 1968 when Mr. and Mrs. Clark, Clark's brother Marvine and his sister Unice drove in on a Memorial Day weekend. They had been up to Delta to put flowers on Mr. Scott's grave, and they came in to see if any of the James' still lived here. So we started having the reunions beginning in about the late 1960's and they stopped in about 1990 or 1991. It went on for about 20 years. I got so I [Dorthea] couldn't handle doing the reunion. The last year there was about 75 to 90 people showed up and we had cars parked along the road clearn down to the cattle guard.

Most of those homesteaders turned out to be successful people. And there's a few of the kids or grandkids who still come back on Memorial Day weekend. One family used to fly over here from London, England.

Mr. and Mrs. Walter James must have been well-liked people, because I've never heard anything bad about either one of them. The kids who worked during the summers for Mr. James while they went to school, used to come by and see where they once worked.

In closing the Kaufman's story of Black Rock and the Ranch, Dorthea wrote a letter about one of the early homesteaders to this area named **Lester Alluisi.** He had taken up a homestead near Black Rock in the mid-1910's and in the summer of 1916 had plans to open a garage in Garrison with L.G. Clay. According to the 7/21/1916 Fillmore newspaper, he had received his auto mechanic training in the Fiat shops in New York City before coming west. In the late 1960's, it was Lester who spearheaded the drive for the Malone Reunions at the Black Rock Ranch. Here are some of the things Dorthea remembered about what Lester Alluisi told her:

The Tie House Spring got it's name from the tie house Lester Alluisi built. He was a race car mechanic from New York and came with Fiat to race between LA. and Phoenix in 1912. He heard about the cheap land in Utah and eventually had a homestead out here. He helped Walter James and also did assessment work for absentee farmers. He married the girl who is standing by the mercantile store in the picture [that shows the post office & hotel--page 45]. Their daughter was a Pan Am stewardess and went down with a plane in the Pacific in the 1930's. Their son was employed by Pan Am and during W.W.II was a mechanic on Air Force II. Lester went to France during W.W.I. That time counted toward his homestead [requirements]. We later bought Lester's old homestead. He got the last of the homesteaders together for our Memorial Day reunions, but Lester died before our first one. He was a remarkable man & a good friend.

To recap a little, the depot was shut down for good about the time the Kaufmans came to Black Rock. For a few years before that, it seems to have been open only in the winter and spring and just for a few months each year. That was during the early or mid-1950's.

The completion of the paving of State Highway 257 running from Milford to Delta in the winter of 1962-63, allowed workers to live in surrounding towns and drive out to Black Rock to work on the rail lines. By the mid or late 1960's, only a few people lived in the railroad buildings near the highway. All the buildings at the Black Rock townsite were gone by the early 1970's except for the three homes east of the depot. Those three houses, which were once used by telegraph operators and the signal maintainer, remained at Black Rock for about another 20 years, or until 1993. More on when they left later.

The Original Settlers Die

It was during this time period, after the Ranch was sold to the Kaufmans, that the last of the James family, who had lived and worked at Black Rock, began to die. **Albert or Bert James** finally passed away on June 17, 1961. **Ruth (Bobbie) James**, the woman who married Dan James' son Tom, is still alive in 1996, and here's what she remembered about Bert:

Bert or Albert was the one who didn't get married. He used to go around with one girl either before or after the war, but he never did get married. He was an old bachelor and he lived over across the tracks in a little shack. And he had this cabinet in there that had belonged to the grandparents, Thomas and Ann Phillips James. He got it when they died. When he had it in his place it looked pretty cluttered with everything on it.

Bert used to come up to our place every Sunday and have a bath, his annual bath; or he'd go to my mother-in-law's, or to my sister's place. He didn't have a place to bathe in that shack of his. We'd always have Sunday dinner and he'd always come up on a Sunday and have dinner with us. We were about the only family he had, at least around close. He was a nice old fellow, but he used to be quite a drinker in his day, I understand. Bert is buried in the Milford Cemetery.

Ernest James died on March 29, 1966, but his life was discussed earlier. With the deaths of Bert and Ernest, we see the last of the Thomas and Ann Phillips James children pass away ending an important chapter in that family's history.

Next to go was **Velora Styler James**. Her niece Mildred Gillen Fitch, presently of Ventura, California, remembers a little about Velora's last years, and about **Dorothy & Al Leonard**, and their son **Larry Leonard**:

Aunt Velora and AG stayed right there in Seal Beach until AG died in 1957. Dorothy & Al also stayed there and they were really busy because they had that little business right at the pier and everybody would come down to the beach and go swimming, and then they'd come over to the stand and get hamburgers, or what ever it was they sold. That kept them real busy; they were working all the time. I think Dorothy had a couple of girls come in to help her in the hamburger stand, and then I think Velora took Larry under her wing.

Velora stayed there in Seal Beach, then she was sick for quite a while, then she moved over with Dorothy after Al died on August 18, 1964. He was on the city council when he got cancer and he was so sick he couldn't do anything, then they appointed him an honorary mayor of Seal Beach. This was just a short time before his death. That was in Seal Beach, both couples always lived in Seal Beach.

Then after Al died, Velora moved over with Dorothy and Dorothy took care of her until she passed away on February 21, 1968. Before Velora died, she and Dorothy got into classes where they were doing crafts and mosaics and things like that. Both AG & Velora are buried in the Rose Hill Memorial Park, in Whittier, California.

After Velora died, Dorothy went to work over in Pasadena for a while, then she sold her house, and moved into a retirement center called Leisure World in Seal Beach. It's still there today. In 1988 or 1989, Dorothy developed lung cancer and she was in and out of the hospital for about 2 years. She died on May 16, 1990 in Seal Beach.

Larry Leonard apparently never married. He died in San Clemente, California, late in the year 1993, under mysterious circumstances, at least that's what everybody who knew him states. Someone stated it was some kind of an accidental death(?).

Ralph James, the son of AG & Velora James, is perhaps the best known person ever to be born and raised in Black Rock. To summarize his life, he graduated from the University of California at Berkeley in 1942, then worked on the Manhattan Project at the Metallurgical Lab, University of Chicago, from 1942 until 1946. He then got his Ph.D. in chemistry from the U. of California in 1948. After that he was a chemistry professor at UCLA for 11 years altogether. In 1956 Ralph received a one-year Guggenheim Fellowship to work at Birmingham University in England. Later he became assistant to a Dr. Kane, head of the radiation laboratory's chemistry department at the Lawrence Laboratory in Livermore, California until his death on February 24, 1973. He was only 52 years old when he died.

Ralph married **Ramona Neiberding** on June 15, 1944. They had two boys; **Marshall James**, born on March 23, 1945, and **Brian James**, born on March 19, 1948. They are both married; Marshall lives and works in Los Alamos, New Mexico, Brian lives in California. Ralph's wife Ramona died November 28, 1981. They are both buried in Alamo, California.

Meanwhile in Colorado, **Helen (Babe) James McMillen** died in 1956 as stated in the previous chapter. Her husband **William N. McMillen** then married Geraldine Flynn of Lakewood within about a year of Babe's death, in 1957. Their daughter **Elise McMillen Brougham** tells what happened to him after that:

My dad, Bill or Mac McMillen had his own company, the Gas Equipment Company, of Lakewood and Wheat Ridge. He sold bottled gas and the kind of equipment for bottled gas, couplings, etc. He was a wholesaler in bottled gas. He started it himself and was lucky and it turned into a pretty good business.

Then dad had a stroke in his office while doing his taxes. He then called his 2nd wife Geraldine, but he had slurred speech. She went there and put him in the car and drove him to the hospital. While there he had a massive stroke, and he never regained consciousness. But he smoked, and I guess that's what did him in. He was 61 years old at the time.

Mac McMillen died on March 19, 1974. He and his wife Helen (Babe) James are buried in the Crown Hill Cemetery, in Wheat Ridge, Colorado.

Hamp Burke(Hazel Burke Bullock foto); and Sophia McMillen(Babe's daughter) at the Big Spring, 1977. (Elise M. Brougham collection)

Elise McMillen later married **John Brougham** and they have two boys, **Joseph** and **Patrick**. They live in Wheat Ridge, Colorado. The oldest daughter of Babe James is **Sophia McMillen**. So far she has not married. She presently lives in Honolulu, and is a librarian at the University of Hawaii.

Jack B. Travers died in Craig, Colorado, in 1955, and his story is in previous chapters. However, his 2nd wife **Inez Bertoldi Travers** married a man named **James Beers**, and they are both still alive as of 1996. They live in Craig, Colorado. She was born in 1914, which made her 24 years younger than Jack. They never had any children.

However, Jack did have two boys by his first wife, **Frances Treweek**. They were **Jack Travers, Jr.**, born in 1918, and **Walter James (Jim) Travers**, born in 1920.

Jim Travers was still alive in 1996 and living in Kanab, Utah. He didn't know all that much about his dad, but here is some of what he did remember about his father Jack, his mother, his step-father, and brother:

When my parents split up, we were living in Ely, then me and Jack Jr. and mother went to California. We must have moved to California in about 1925, or maybe a little later. We went to Caliente first, that was the closest place to catch the train. They had a stage, which was actually a bus then, and we went over to Caliente, then got on a train and went to LA.

In California, my mother Frances Treweek managed to get herself a job, and we lived with my aunt, mother's sister, in LA. And they raised my brother and me. I went back to Black Rock quite a few times when I was in my teens. I drove back to Black Rock one time with Babe James. She picked me up in California and she had a little ol' putt putt Chevrolet, and they didn't have air conditioners in those days. I can remember coming through that California Desert, and it was so damn hot we couldn't breathe! I was 14 or 15 or something like that when we did that trip.

My bother wasn't as interested in Black Rock like I was. I went back to Black Rock during a lot of summers. I just played around, I had a little .22 and I shot the hell out of everything. I still have that little old .22. My dad bought me that for my birthday in Ely, and I couldn't have been but 5 or 6 years old; and I still have the thing. We were in Ely when Dad and Mom split up.

When I was probably 13 or 14, my mother remarried. That was in the early 1930's. And she married quite an outstanding guy; in fact he is the man who built the steel mill there at Provo, which was Columbia Steel. He built it and was president, and they built the iron mines, and they got the whole thing going, and then they built a steel mill in Torrance, California.

*His name was **Don Botchford**, and he was a wonderful guy. Then he was involved in building a reduction facility in Vancouver, Washington, and everything was going along just keen and he died. I was 19 years old, so that would have been in 1939 when he died. We lived in Beverly Hills when my step-dad was alive. He was president of Columbia Steel.*

After my step-dad died, my mother became a dental technician, and she worked for a dentist--like a dental assistant. And we lived in West LA. Then she went along and got old and up & died. As I vaguely remember, she was 80 something at the time.

*I didn't know a lot about my dad **Jack Travers** except that he was quite a football player at the University of Utah. He had a heck of a foto album, and Inez got it, it had all his football pictures in it. Dad was an educated man, he wasn't a typical Utah sheepherder!*

*My brother **Jack Travers, Jr.** was a damn smart guy, and he went to college at the New Mexico Military Institute. And he was a football player there and did quite well. Then when he came home from NMMI, he went to work for North American Aviation. And he was an A & E mechanic, which is an airplane & engine mechanic.*

Then the war started on a Sunday [December 7, 1941], and he and I went down to enlist on Monday [December 8, 1941]. My eyes weren't good so they wouldn't take me, but they took my brother. And he was only in there a week or two and he was First Class Aviation mechanist mate, which was one step under Chief. He had the experience with airplanes, and he had the military experience at college and all that sort of thing, so he went right up the ladder.

Right after the war he got married, then I remember he worked for North American for a while. He went to England for North American and was at Farnbough which is at Wright Field in England,. He left Mary, his wife, at my place pregnant, and their first kid was born with him absent. About that time he also worked for Autonetics, and he was head rep in Engman Field in Florida. His wife Mary had some sort of an accident and was killed, then in 1987, one of his kids called me up and said, "I've got some bad news for you, your brother just died about an hour ago." He lived in Fort Walton Beach, Florida when he died.

My brother Jack Travers, Jr. had two kids. The first one was named **Jim** and the second one was named **Jack**. Now I don't know where they are and I haven't heard from 'em for 5 or 6 years. I have no idea where they are or what they're doing.

Later on in the war, they relaxed their regulations a little bit and I **[Jim Travers]** joined the air force, and I became a crew chief on a C-47 transport. And I went to Iwo Jima, and I was wounded there in ground action, and I went to Okinawa and all over that area. I was there for two years. And then when I came home, I got mixed up in automobile racing. I'd always been interested in hot rods and all that sort of thing. So when the war was over, I went to work for a fellow named Howard Keck, and he owned the Superior Oil Company, which was a very, very big outfit, but you didn't hear about them, because they weren't marketers, they were producers. Later on they sold the company to Socony for 4 point-some-billion dollars. So it wasn't a penny ante organization!

And we went to **Indianapolis**, and we won there twice. I was the chief mechanic and manager. Me and Frank Coon were partners at this time. Bill Vukovitch was the driver and he won twice for us, and then the next time he was killed in a hell of an accident while he was leading the race. That was at Indy. The first year we went there was 1948, and we went there with this Keck car. We won the race at Indy in 1953 and 1954, and the last time we were there was 1956.

Anyway, we went to Indy and did quite well. Then we went to work for Ford Motor Co.

Jim Travers, left, and Mary & Jack Travers, Jr., and Jack's son Jim. (Inez B. Travers Beers collection)

and while working for Ford, they asked us about the name of our outfit and I just said **Traco**, after **Travers & Coon**. So they financed our company, and we started buying machinery and all kinds of stuff. That was the beginning of Traco. So everything was lovely with Ford then all of a sudden they and GM and all the other big companies decided they were going to get out of racing. This was stock car stuff, and we did run Daytona. Anyway, they jumped out overnight. That left us hanging, the end of it. Then everybody got canned who was involved with Detroit.

So then we got mixed up with this guy Ravetlow, who was Barbara Hutton's and Woolworth's millionaire, and we built cars for him.

Then we left him and went to Champion Spark Plug Company. Up to that point this was Jim Travers & Frank Coon. We were reps out in the field, covering races. And we also built engines in our shop, for people who were being financed by Champion.

Then that folded up and we started building engines for people all over the world; England, Germany, Australia, Mexico, everywhere! For a while, we were the biggest company in the world building auto racing engines. Not long ago, Open Wheel Magazine had a two-month article about my life.

That story about Jim Travers' life appeared in **Open Wheel Magazine** for the months of **December, 1995**, and **January, 1996**. In this writer's interview with Jim, he forgot to mention a few other important things about his auto racing career. According to the December issue of Open Wheel:

Few today know that Jim Travers was involved in developing the first injector with Stu Hilborn, or that he and Frank Coon brought the first one to the Speedway in 1949. Few recall that they designed the first roadster; that they were the first to bring scales to the Speedway to aid in chassis setups; that they developed ram-tuned induction for the Offy; or that they honed the concept of fast pit stops to a fine art.

Fewer still recall that this was the same Travers and Coon who, upon their retirement from Speedway competition shortly after Vuky's tragic 1955 crash, built the Traco engines that for a time dominated almost every form of racing throughout the world, culminating in a 500 victory for Mark Donohue in 1972.

The winning Indy 500 racing team. Left to right, Jack Beckley, Frank Coon, & Jim Travers, with Bill Vukavitch in the car at the Indy 500 track in 1953 or 1954. (Jim Travers collection)

After Indy and while involved with Traco, Jim lived in Del Ray and Culver City, California. Jim was so busy, he forgot all about marriage. In 1964, at age 44, he did take the plunge, but he probably should have stuck to racing & cars, because that one ended with him kissing his "X" and "about a million bucks good-bye!"

Jim now lives in Kanab, and certainly doesn't look his 75 years. He's retired from racing machines, but he now spends all his time with an animal protection group and the **Best Friends Animal Sanctuary** north of Kanab. The telefon book lists him as Walter J. Travers, but everybody still calls him Jim.

After the Black Rock Ranch was sold in August of 1957, **Thekla & Merrill Miller** stayed there for maybe a month, then they moved back to Bountiful, where they had lived for several years before Walter James died in March of 1944. This time they bought a home instead of renting. It was in Bountiful they lived until each of them died.

Thekla had a stroke and they put her in a hospital, but she died a day or two later on August 19, 1972.

Merrill went back to work for the Forest Service and he eventually retired from there in about 1968. At that time he had worked for the Forest Service for 20 years over a 35 year period. He started his career in the CCC's in 1933.

Wally Miller's widow, **Nola Miller** had this to say about Merrill: *He got emphysema and it was in about 1977 or 1978 when we had to put him in a nursing home, because he said he needed constant skilled care. He was in the Hillheaven Nursing Home. He was there for a total of 4 years. Merrill maintained that he got it from fighting forest fires, but I think he smoked like 3 packs of Camels a day for a long time. Merrill died on August 24, 1981 of emphysema. Thekla and Merrill are both buried in the Bountiful City Cemetery.*

After working in the cloud seeding program for about 3 years, **Walter James (Wally) Miller** got a job on the Union Pacific Railroad in about 1956. From working on a section crew gang in Southern Utah and maybe Nevada, he then landed a job as clerk in the roadmaster's office in Delta. He was there for several years, up into the 1960's, then moved to Salt Lake and was working with engineers in the maintenance department of

Jim Travers, 1996; and Wally Miller & wife Nola, about 1990. (Nola Miller foto)

Union Pacific. Nola Miller takes up the rest of his story from there:

In about 1964, which was about 10 years before we met, he had a bad flare-up in his ankle. Walt (Wally) went to a doctor named R.O. Johnson who caught ostiomylitus in his arm from Walt. While in this relapse, he had to get part of a new ankle bone from the bone bank. They wouldn't use one from his own body because they were afraid it would still have the ostiomylitus in it. So they got a bone from the bone bank and transplanted it to this ankle in 1964. After that he wore slip-on shoes that he didn't have to tie so his leg didn't have to bend so much. Around home he wore thongs a lot. Also, in the early part of our marriage, he had a couple of flare-ups; his ankle would swell up and get red.

Originally I was from Salt Lake. When Walt and I were married I was a divorced woman with 6 kids and one grandchild, and Wally said, "that's what I want." My oldest daughter was married at that time and she had a little girl. We were married February 12, 1976, in the Skaggs Memorial Chapel, which is in the First Baptist Church on 13th East and 8th South, in Salt Lake. He was 49 years old when we got married.

Walt was diagnosed with emphysema on November 12, 1984. He told me he had smoked since he was 10 years old! He retired from Union Pacific on July 31, 1985. He was 58 years old when he retired, after about 29 years with the UP. He would have had 30 years in had he not been off work when his ankle flared up back in 1964.

In 1991, he also got prostate cancer. It contributed to his death, but it wasn't the final cause. Walter James Miller died November 19, 1992.

As soon as the Ranch was sold, **Benita & Hamp Burke** stayed there and worked for the Kaufmans for about 3 1/2 years. When Thekla & Merrill moved to Bountiful, then they moved from the Cottage into the Big House. Benita continued to write the Black Rock news items in the Milford paper as long as she was there. During that 3 1/2 years, the Kaufmans were coming and going, to and from California. They were trying to finish up their business down there before making the final move to Utah. To have Benita & Hamp there was the best thing that could have happened to the Kaufmans, because they knew the ranching business in that part of Utah as well as anyone.

By November, 1958, Hamp had to be hospitalized for something, but apparently it wasn't anything serious. About this time Hamp hired **Art Talbot** to work on the Ranch and he and his wife **Darlene** lived in the Cottage. In March of 1959, Benita resigned as postmaster of Black Rock, after serving for about 16 or 17 years. She took over that job in 1942, left it for awhile in 1944, then got it back again in 1945. She held the job until 1959, then **Darlene Talbot** took over as postmaster at that time and she lasted for 6 months or so.

The last noteworthy event concerning Benita & Hamp's last days at Black Rock had to do with the post office. In the November 19, 1959 issue of the Milford *Beaver County News*, under the Black Rock news it states:

Mrs. Hampton Burke returned home Nov. 7 after spending three weeks touring the Eastern and Southern States. She traveled on a chartered bus carrying postmasters and friends to Washington, DC., where they attended the National Postmaster's Convention.

The tour also included viewing Niagara Falls, Ontario, Canada; seeing the original cast present "My Fair Lady" in New York, and many other interesting sights....

Friday, Mrs. Art Talbot was here attending the closing of the Black Rock Post Office, thus terminating the only means of communication for this community.

The **Black Rock post office** was officially **closed** on **November 13, 1959**. It had run continuously since April 1, 1891. It's not known for sure who the first postmaster was, but it may have been Walter James. After that it was likely AG James, then after four different people had it, Benita James Burke got it until Darlene Talbot came along. See the list of known postmasters on page 158.

According to Vic & Dorthea Kaufman, they moved into the Black Rock Ranch permanently in March, 1960. Then Benita & Hamp moved back into the Cottage for a few months. The last Black Rock news item in the Milford paper was October 6, 1960, and that was written by Benita. Then in the February 2, 1961 paper was a article stating: *An open house was given in honor of Mrs. Hampton Burke Monday afternoon at the home of*

Mrs. L.G. Clay. The occasion was in observance of Mrs. Burke's birth anniversary and to welcome her to Milford. The Burkes had been living in Black Rock but have moved into Milford. Thirty eight Milford friends called during the afternoon.....

It's not certain, but it appears they left the Black Rock Ranch for good some time around Christmas 1960, thus ending about 60 years of James family , and 80 years of Raht-James family occupation.

Once they moved into Milford Hamp remembered: *I worked around doin' nothin', then I got a job with the lumber yard and they finally made me manager of it. That was the hardware store and lumber yard there in Milford.*

During the winter of 1995-96, Dorthea Kaufman recalled a little of what she remembered about Benita & Hamp:

We never knew the reason they sold the Ranch. It must have hurt Benita deeply, because she was the "son" Walter James never had. She helped him with the sheep herds & later the cattle. She could ride the wildest, meanest horse, yet she could be the most attractive woman in any social gathering with her golden hair, lovely smile and beautiful carriage.

When we knew Benita while she lived here at the Ranch, she was usually in a sun dress, winter and summer. She'd go down and get the mail off the mail train, and she'd wear a sun dress, which was sleeve-less. But she wore jeans when she was riding. She would never go to town like I do in jeans. When she went to town, she always dressed up.

She had a stroke and was in the hospital about a month before she passed away. Hamp would come to see her with tears in his eyes. He depended on Benita a lot, and she sure depended on him. She died in a local hospital in Milford. She never was in a care center; and she was healthy until she had that stroke, or whatever. She could still talk. We were there one evening, and Hamp came to visit with her. She'd wait to hear his voice, and of course when he'd come in the door, everybody could hear it; you knew Hamp was comin' in, everybody making a fuss over him.

You'd say it was an unusual marriage, but it was a good marriage. They never did have kids--I think she was too old by the time they were married. But Hamp just loved children, and children just loved him. Back in those days when he was at Black Rock, kids would ride back and forth between Delta and Milford, and they'd wave hello to Hamp when

Benita J. Burke, and Ring the dog, February, 1949. (Carl Nielson foto, Kelsey collection)

they'd see him putting the mail on the truck for Benita.

Benita died November 5, 1984. She was nearly 91 years old. Hamp later married **Rosalie Koch Cook** of Milford. They went to Pioche, Nevada, and were married on December 3, 1985. They were married about 8 years before Hampton Burke finally passed away on August 8, 1994. He was 83 years old and the last of his generation to go. They are both buried side by side in the Milford City Cemetery.

Vic and Dorthea Kaufman mentioned the names of Hattie & Scotty above. Their real names were **Edward** and **Hattie Scott**, but everybody just called him **Scotty**. Many people in the Milford area remembered this couple for two reasons. The first reason was, they were the only black people to live in this part of the country. Donnetta Hardy of Delta recalls that: *Scotty worked for Floyd Hardy at Clear Lake. Floyd had an all-Negro section gang, about 4 or 5 men, and I think Scotty was with that bunch. This was in June of 1947. We left Clear Lake in 1952, then Scotty apparently moved down to Milford.*

According to Richard Jefferson of Milford, Hattie & Scotty lived together in Milford for several years; he worked on the railroad, and she did house cleaning and things like that. After a year or two, Scotty got bumped out of Milford and went to Black Rock. They were there beginning some time in the mid-1950's and Benita J. Burke, who was writing the Black Rock news for the Milford paper, mentions their names many times. Hattie worked for Benita for a while up at the Ranch and everybody who knew her, said she could bake the best pies in the world. Hattie also had family members in the Southern California area.

Scotty worked on the section gang maintaining the rail line. He also went fishing almost every weekend. He went out to Pruess Reservoir near Garrison, and Minersville Reservoir. He also tried to transplant fish to the ponds at Black Rock, but he never succeeded. The Fish and Game Department got on him for that, but they never did anything about it.

The second reason people remember this couple was because of an incident that took place on September 12, 1965. The Milford newspaper, the *Beaver County News* for September 16, 1965 had the story:

HATTIE SHOOTS SCOTTY

Beaver County's only Negro family became embroiled in a family argument last Sunday

Hamp Burke and 2nd wife Rosalie K. Cook, mid or late 1980's. (Hazel Burke Bullock foto)

afternoon, and the husband wound up in the hospital and the wife in jail.

Hattie Scott, [age 53] wife of Edward "Black Rock Scotty" Scott, [age 50] fired five bullets from a .22 pistol at her husband, at their home in Black Rock, 20 miles [32 kms] north of Milford, but only one of the slugs did major damage. Scotty was shot in the left forearm, left bicep, and a bullet lodged in his chest near the heart.

After the shooting he started for Milford, driving his own car, but after five or six miles hailed a tourist who drove him to the Milford Valley Memorial Hospital. After preliminary examination and X-rays, Dr. D.A. Symond and Lyle Wiseman transported the injured man to a Salt Lake hospital for specialist surgery, hanging a bottle of whole blood on a broomstick outside the car so transfusions could be administered en route.

Tuesday the bullet was removed with a bronchoscope. It had lodged in the lung in such a position that chest surgery was not necessary. Scotty is recuperating satisfactorily.

Mrs. Scott, charged in a Millard County justice court with assault with a deadly weapon was released on $5000 bond, posted by Milford friends of the couple. Her preliminary hearing has been set for 10 am Wednesday, Sept. 22, in the court of Fillmore Justice of the Peace Eugene McBride. She is represented by Joe Jackson of the Milford law firm of Cline & Jackson.

According to Richard Jefferson, Scotty had gotten drunk and was trying to beat up Hattie. It was Milford Mayor Ray Kaiser who bailed Hattie out of jail, and a collection was made to raise money for her defense. Most everybody in town donated $5, because they were a well-liked couple. In the end, Scotty never pressed charges, and Hattie was apparently put on some kind of probation and never went to jail. They later lived together for a while, but then they parted company. She went to California where she eventually died. Scotty went to Salt Lake City where he was a member of the St. John's Masonic Lodge. He has since passed away, but it wasn't too many years ago.

Crystal Peak Minerals

In 1987, new life came to Black Rock. It wasn't exactly a resurrection, but at least there was a little activity in town, which at the time consisted of three old railroad houses and a

Section gang & railroad officials and a motorcar bus. The black man on the left is Edward Scott, or Scotty. Probably in the late 1940's or early 1950's. (Ida Hardy Beitz foto)

doublewide mobile home. It was the coming of **Crystal Peak Minerals**, an outfit which did exploratory research work in mineral extraction on the Sevier Dry Lake bed west of Black Rock. **Larry Sower** of Milford is the one who ran, or helped run, this company, and here's what he had to say:

*Sevier Lake, except where the river comes in on the north, never had any water flowing into it and there was never any Indian stuff left around the shore. The first recorded history I've been able to find on Sevier Lake was from **G. K. Gilbert's** travels from about 1873, I believe. He rode in through Black Rock Pass where the new road is now, which is just west of Black Rock, and camped there on the old Lake Bonneville Bench or Beach, which sits right there in the pass. He was the first to look at the lake in terms of mineral content. He sent one of his crew out there on snowshoes and collected a brine [salt water] sample. And that was the last sample taken until the 1920's.*

During World War I the price of potash went up over $400 a ton because at that time we got all our potash from Germany. So there are a lot of old projects out there on almost every terminal salt lake bed in the Great Basin, except Sevier Lake, and I think the conditions there were a little more than anyone wanted to look at at the time.

The lake bed is extremely flat and has a little over 130,000 acres, and even just a couple of inches [5 cms] of water can cover about 1/3 of the lake bed. And the lake physically moves almost the entire length of the lake bed depending on which way the wind is blowing. One day you'll look at it and it's all stacked up on the south end, and the next day it'll be stacked up on the north end.

In the mid-1980's it was full and about 12 feet [4 meters] deep. That was as deep as it got after the DMAD Dam's spillway broke and Gunnison Bend Reservoir was breached and the river flowed uncontrolled into Sevier Lake for about 18 months. Then it dried back out by about 1989 or 1990. Sevier Lake is a mud lake, it's not a hard pan like Pine Valley or Tule Hardpan. The brine or salt water in it is somewhat similar to the Great Salt Lake, but there are some distinct differences. First of all, being a dry lake, the brine reserve is down in the lake bed itself.

*The modern-day exploration of Sevier Lake started in about 1977 with a geologist by the name of **Murray Godbe**. It was his grandfather who was involved in the smelter up at Frisco, and his father was up in Park City, and it was one of his ancestors who was involved with the Godbeites in Salt Lake in the 1870's. The Godbe's are a long line of mining people.*

But in 1977, the price of uranium was going through the roof and Murray's thought was that with all the uranium in the upper drainage in the Sevier River, and since it bordered on the Colorado Plateau, that some of that may have been washed and deposited down there somewhere. As it turned out, as with most of these big brine reserves, there was no mechanism in the lake to concentrate uranium or any of the other metals. But it did become readily apparent that there was a very large reserve of very high quality brines in the lake bed. Within the last 30 years, technology has been developed to produce potash, magnesium, common salt and other minerals from these types of reserves. So from about 1977 to 1982, they were in the exploration phrase, then the floods started coming in about 1983, through 1986.

Now I had worked for a similar extraction operation on the Great Salt Lake minerals and the company hired me at that point to come in and put a production facility together on the Sevier Lake. So we started out very quickly and we had plans to get something going there. It turned out to be similar to the mining industry, with the ups and downs of the industry and the difficulty in finding investment dollars, and we just never could pull it together. But before all was said and done, and with over 15 years that we were out there, and between Murray and myself, we spent about $8 million trying to put something together. But it's a world class reserve of potash and other saline minerals, and at some point in the future somebody's going to do something with it.

Now we drilled to a depth of nearly a 1000 feet [300 meters] with brine all the way, so there's an immense amount of salt brine minerals in the lake bed. We drilled 3 deep holes; one was out on Needle Point(middle of the lake on the west side), one was on the

Drilling rig stuck on the mud flats of Sevier Lake bed, about 1990. (Larry Sower collection)

Crystal Peak Minerals office at Black Rock. (Larry Sower collection)

east side, and one on the southwest side of the lake bed. Then we drilled every quarter section out there to get under Federal potassium lease laws. We needed to demonstrate the reserve on every quarter section. So we had something like 860 holes drilled out in the lake. We had to use track machinery; Thiokol machines, like snowcats, to go out with a portable rig on the back of it.

I've seen sheep out there on the lake which have gotten stuck and died in place, so we had to develop lots of ways to use high-flotation equipment just to work out there. I've had to pull people out because they went in over their knees. I had to go out and pull 'em down, then roll'em out. So we had to work on great big wooden mats while drilling. Typically they were constructed out of big ponderosa pine logs. I've got lots of pictures of equipment stuck out there.

Initially we were going to use collection ditches, which are just deep ditches dug with drag lines out through the lake bed, then the brine seeps in, which is very similar to the Bonneville operation up there at Wendover. And in the longer term develop wells on the lake bed to pump brine up into large solar ponding operations. I used to work over in Potash, near Moab, and that's how they do it.

This would have been a potassium sulfate operation; but the mineral content of this brine is a little different than that in the Moab area. If we were extracting it now, it would be used for fertilizer. With potassium sulfate you can also produce magnesium, similar to what Amax does up on the Great Salt Lake. Also, lots of common salt. The idea was we were going to run a rail line in there to connect it with Black Rock eventually. With our plans the total investment in the project would have been about $60 million.

We've pulled out now and finished reclamation on it. But at some point in the future somebody will return, because it can be developed into a world class operation. We spent 8 years on the project altogether. I'm a chemist, and a specialist in brine chemistry.

Our offices were at Black Rock. We leased those three houses out there from the Union Pacific and our lease agreement called for us to get rid of them if or when we left the place. So we demolished one, and then Dick Rollins of Milford picked up two of 'em and moved them into town here, for just the price of movin' 'em.

Last Residents

It was during the time Crystal Peak Minerals had their office at Black Rock that the last railroad employees actually lived there at the townsite. Jim & Cynthia Kaufman remember several of the last full-time residents:

Delbert Carrington and his wife lived down there while their little boy went to kindergarten; they drove back and forth to Milford. Then when their boy got in the first grade, they moved into town because they didn't want to drive.

Then there was the Mexican family. His name was Juan. Their little girl went to school with our little girl in Milford and we drove them back and forth to school. After they moved away, Rulon Hardy's boy came, and he lived in that new house. They brought a new doublewide trailer house out there, and he stayed there. They originally brought it in for the section foreman. That doublewide was set down just south of the three houses. Then when Hardy moved out, Doreen and Roger Nelson moved in. They were Navajo's from New Mexico.

The guy who stayed there last was a Mexican from up north who rolled up the fencing, took the hot water heater, took the washer, dryer, and the stove. On a weekend he went back and he cleaned the place out. And he rode right up here with LaVar Davis, and La Var asked if we had seen anything happening down there, and right there was the guy who was doin' it and employed by the railroad! That doublewide first came here sometime in the early 1980's.

Larry Sower goes on to say that: We went to Black Rock in 1987 and there were 4 buildings there at the time. The 4th building was a doublewide which is now at the Union Pacific Railroad Club House down here by the tracks, by the Lions Car. There was a line crew out there and a fellow by the name of Max Sanchez was living out there at the time. Max was the last guy to live at Black Rock down at the railway tracks. That doublewide was moved to Milford in the late 1980's. The three railroad buildings were taken out of there some time in the spring of 1993.

One of the last things to take place at the Black Rock Ranch was the installation of a new radio-telefon. Jim and Dorthea Kaufman tells about that:

*We got the **telefon** from **Crystal Peak Minerals** in May of 1993. They had used our trailers to haul things, and they traded the telefon for the use of our trailers. They needed trailers to haul their equipment from over at Sevier Lake to Milford. They had no trailers, so they used our flatbed outfit to haul all their pipes and railroad ties, and anything else they had over there, and they took it to town. They had to clean up everything and haul it away. Later they had an auction and sold everything.*

Then they closed their office here and opened another office in Milford until they had everything settled. They used our horse trailer to haul all their office desks and chairs and everything from the office down here into town. They had one of our trailers for almost a month, and I had done a few things for them with the tractor too, so in exchange for that they said we could have the radio-telefon. We just traded services.

So one time when the power company was working on the east side not far from here they come through with the truck one day after work. The truck they had came with a big ol' trailer and post hole digger. They pulled the thing out down there at the railroad, laid it on the trailer, and brought it up here. It was a big 60 foot [20 meter] log, it was almost from one end of the driveway to the other. So they started with the post hole digger and dug the hole, then put the pole in. I think it took less than half an hour from beginning to end. The other end of the radio-telefon hookup is right on top of the airport beacon tower in Milford. If they hadn't done it, we couldn't have afforded it. We have wires from the pole and antenna into each house. We have the same number at both houses.

Perhaps the last noteworthy event to happen at Black Rock was the death of **Victor A. Kaufman**. He passed away on January 19, 1995 and he was 81 years old. Dorthea states:

Vic's funeral was in the Methodist Church in Milford. The new Presbyterian minister was one of those who helped give the service, and the dinner afterwards was in the Baptist Church. Southern Utah Mortuary handled the funeral from Cedar City.

Presently, Dorthea is still at the Ranch and in the Big House. Her son Jim and his family live in the Cottage, which is a lot bigger now than it used to be. According to Dorthea:

***Cynthia Freeman**, Jim's wife, moved up from California and lived in Parowan with her family. She finished high school there, her last one or two years. **Kris** is their daughter, she's the oldest, and she is in college at Southern Utah University at Cedar City. In the spring of 1995, she is 20 years old, but will graduate this year. **Benjamin** is 17 in the spring of 1995 and in high school in Milford. **Kelli** is in the 7th grade this year. Then **Kari** is in the 5th grade, she's 10 years old.*

Kris used to drive the others to school each day, now Benjamin takes the other kids to school in Milford. The school gives them mileage for one round-trip per day. Ben picks up the mail each day as well.

At this time it's unclear as to what might happen at the Black Rock Ranch in the future, but it seems Jim & Cynthia will continue the Kaufman name for some time to come. Jim's brother **Joe Kaufman** lives in southern California. He has a wife and 2 children, both girls. They usually spend their vacations at the Ranch, and may some day retire there.

Maps & Things to See Near Black Rock

For those interested in looking around the old townsite of Black Rock and/or some of the nearby mining areas discussed in this book, the first thing you'll need is a good map. Probably the single best one which shows most of the places of interest, especially around Black Rock itself, is the USGS topo map titled **Richfield**, at 1:100,000 scale. This map shows Black Rock, Interstate 15, Sulphurdale, Cove Fort, the north end of the Mineral Mountains and Antelope Point, Antelope Spring, Twin Peaks, and as far north as the Continental Lime Plant near mile posts 40 & 41. It also shows Big Sage Valley and one of Walter James' mines there, believed to be in Section 34, T21S, R10W. Get there by turning west from Highway 257 near mile post 39.

To visit the Sevier Dry Lake Bed, you'll need the map titled **Wah Wah Mtns. North**. This map also shows Jack Watson's Ibex, Crystal Peak, the old abandoned townsite of Burbank, and Garrison on the Utah-Nevada state line. Also, this map shows the north end of the San Francisco Mountains and Frisco Peak, and the Beaver Lake Mountains & Mining Districts in which Walter James and his brother's John and Dan had mining interests.

A 3rd map titled **Beaver,** shows the majority of the Mineral Mountains, Minersville, and the Rocky Ford Dam & Minersville Reservoir which proved to be the last nail in the coffin for the settlers and dry farmers at Reed, Malone and the Beaver Bottoms. And last, a 4th map covering interesting sites in this region is titled **Wah Wah Mtns. South**. This one shows Milford, Frisco, part of the Beaver Lake Mountains, the Star Range, and it stretches west to the Nevada state line. It also shows most of Pine Valley and Mtn. Home, and the Wah Wah Valley and Mountains. All four of these USGS maps are at 1:100,000 scale and for sale wherever topographic maps are sold. To go with these, you'll also need a Utah state highway map.

Now for things to see. The only things left to see along the railroad tracks on the east side are some cement foundations and a few trees. Immediately next to the tracks is a large elevated area, and that's where the depot once stood. South of that where two clusters of trees are today is where the bunkhouse and section foreman's houses used to be.

On the west side of the tracks and to the north a little are some old fences outlining barn yards, two walls of the cement barn that AG James built in September, 1920, and the roof-less **Cellar** which is made of black lava rocks. It was built sometime in the 1890's. Also, there's the cement foundation which once held the Malone School, parts of an old chicken coop, and an underground cellar or two. There are some shrubs still growing where the store & hotel used to be, and one old straggly tree. There is nothing where the shearing barns used to be, except manure.

AG's old place sits on two different sections, and as of 1995 no one had paid taxes on that ground. It was still in Larry Leonard's name, but he has since deceased. It's private land, but no one could possibly object if you stop and walk around the place. Same with the area where most of the railroad buildings once stood. You can also walk east from the tracks to see the only grave at Black Rock. See the Black Rock Townsite map on page 81.

If you drive east of Black Rock on the main graveled county road in the direction of Cove Fort, you could also explore around Antelope Spring, where the old stagecoach station used to be. That old station was first set up in about 1870. South of Antelope Spring is where a number of wildcat oil wells were drilled, including the original Walter James Well No. 1. Further east and at the north end of the Mineral Mountains, one could walk a couple of kilometers and explore around several old mine shafts and adits(tunnels). Walter James and his brothers were there first around 1900. If you do visit these old mines, you do it at your own risk!

One of the more interesting places to visit, although it's quite a ways from Black Rock, is the old abandoned townsite of Frisco, and the abandoned railway grade. Seen there are some old kilns for making charcoal, lots of old mines, the foundations of old buildings, and best of all the cemetery, where one of the James boys is buried. Get to Frisco via Highway 21 running west out of Milford. Most of the things to see there are located between mile posts 62 & 63.

Those living at the Black Rock Ranch would appreciate your honoring their privacy.

Vic & Dorthea Kaufman at their Black Rock Ranch, 1991. (Kaufman collection)

Jim & Cynthia Kaufman family, 1993. Children from the left are: Kari, Kelli, Ben, and Kristin. (Kaufman collection)

Joe & Barbara Kaufman family, 1987. Kendra, behind, and Kaci. (Kaufman collection)

Government trappers park their sheep wagon and trailer where the Tie House used to be.

What's left of the old cement barn built by AG James in September of 1920.

The cement foundation of the Malone School; and the old Cellar beyond, which was just north of the store & hotel. It was built of black lava stones no later than the mid-1890's.

Another look at the east side of the Cellar.

These are two of the last houses which were at Black Rock until May of 1993. In January, 1996, they were located just southwest of the Milford Airport.

The only grave at Black Rock, with the trees in the background showing where the depot and bunkhouse used to be located.

Rocky Ford Dam and Minersville Reservoir. The building of this dam put the Reed and Malone settlers out of business by stopping spring floods & drying up the Beaver Bottoms.

Another look at the shearing barns which were located on the east side of the tracks.
(Kelsey collection)

Location unknown, but the three James girls are there. Thekla is in the rear, Benita is to the left, and Babe is in front on the left. Merrill Miller is behind Babe. Early 1920's. (Jim Travers collection)

Known Railroad Agents at Black Rock

This is an **incomplete** list of known agents at the Black Rock Depot. These names were found in old newspapers from Milford and Fillmore and in the section titled **Black Rock**. Some of these people were **relief agents**, but most were considered **full-time agents.** Some dates indicate when they arrived, others indicate when they left.

Date There	Agents Name	Date There	Agents Name
June 1915	W. D. Livingston	April 1943	Dale V. Bradley
November 1915	A. J. Sieber	November 1943	Mrs. G. A. McCulley
January 1920	Mrs. Jack Chapman	May 1946	R. D. Christensen
November 1921	D. H. Pellee	December 1946	W. R. Peck
December 1921	M. P. Tyree	July 1947	Ken McKay
July 1928	Mrs. Sam Forbes	1947-1949	Gilbert McCulley
December 1928	Estella Forbes	November 1949	Robert Wright
January 1930	Mr. Morrell	November 1949	Stewart Rowberry
March 1932	D. M. Carroll	March 1950	Charles Fleming
July 1934	W. J. Sturdavant	July 1951	Paul Folger
August 1934	H. H. Rowberry	August 1951	Jerry Wilkins
September 1934	W. H. Morgan	February 1954	R. L. Kishall
November 1934	W. J. Sturdavant	April 1954	Ivan Pierce
September 1937	W. J. Sturdavant	June 1956	Spencer Preece
August 1938	Hugh Woolsey	April 1957	M. Dahl
July 1941	W. J. Sturdavant	June 1958	Sam Miller
January 1942	J. W. Storrs	June 1959	Mrs. Pearl McDonald
November 1942	Lew Kaiser		

Known Postmasters at Black Rock
Post Office operated from April 1, 1891 to November 13, 1959

Postmaster's Name	Date of Service
¿Walter James?	¿April 1, 1891 to December, 1916?
Arthur Garfield (AG) James	¿December, 1916? to about May, 1941?
William J. & Della Sturdavant	Ending July 16, 1941
Victoria G. Beckstead	July 16, 1941 to November 25, 1941
W. G. Storis	November 26, 1941 to August 13, 1942
Benita James Burke(acting)	August 13, 1942 to March 7, 1944
Dale V. Bradley(salary $360/year)	March 7, 1944 to November 30, 1945
Benita James Burke	November 30, 1945 to March?, 1959
Darlene Talbot	March?, 1959 until November 13, 1959

Mail Messengers 1941-1959	Leave Replacement Postmasters 1941-1959
Merrill Miller	Thekla James Miller
Bertha J. Burke	Hampton (Hamp) C. Burke
Benita James Burke	Mildred G. Miller

(Postmasters Salary: 1945, $432/year; 1949, $954/year; 1956, $1223/year)
Part of the above information compiled by Byron C. Muir; Milford, Utah

Further Reading

A Century in Meadow Valley [Panaca, Nevada], 1864-1964, by the Panaca Centennial Book Committee, Ruth Lee & Sylvia Wadsworth, co-chairmen, Panaca, Nevada, 1966.
Diary of Abraham A. Kimball, Late 1880's, B.Y.U. Library, Special Collections, Provo, Utah
Early History of Millard County, and its L.D.S. Settlers--1851 to 1912, Ladd R. Cropper, MS Thesis, B.Y.U.
Encyclopedia of Western Railroad History--The Desert States, Donald B. Robertson, Caxton Printers, LTD., Caldwell, Idaho, 1986.
History of Lake Bonneville, G. K. Gilbert, USGS Annual Report, 1881.
Life on the Black Rock Desert--A History of Clear Lake, Utah, Venetta Bond Kelsey, Kelsey Publishing, Provo, Utah, 1993.
Lincoln County, Nevada: 1864-1909 History of a Mining Region; James W. Hulse, University of Nevada Press, Reno, 1971.
Los Angeles & Salt Lake Railroad Company--Union Pacific's Historic Salt Lake Route, John R. Signor, Golden West Books, P. O. Box 80250, San Marino, Calif., 91108-8250.
Men Who Made Good in Nevada, Goldfield News, 2nd Annual Edition, 1906-1907.
Millard and Nearby, Frank Beckwith, Art City Publishing Co. Springville, Utah.
Monuments to Courage--History of Beaver County, Aird R. Merkley, DUP of Beaver County, Milford Press, 1948.
Newspapers--Millard County Progress(Fillmore) and **The Chronicle**(Delta), Old newspaper articles from 1909 to mid-1940's). **Beaver County News**(1916 to 1925), **Milford News**(1926 to 1955), and **Beaver County News**(1956 to the Present). Old newspapers from 1916 to early 1960's.
Postal History of Utah--1849--1976, Ted Gurber, J-B Publishing Co., Crete, Nebraska, 1978.
The Historical Guide to Utah Ghost Towns, Stephen L. Carr, Western Epics, 254 S. Main, Salt Lake City, Utah, 84101.
They Answered the Call--A History of Minersville, Utah, Gillins & Robinson, Minersville Centennial Committee, 1962.
Union Pacific Country, Robert R. Athearn, Rand McNally, & Co.
Utah--Story of her People--1540-1947, A Centennial History of Utah, Milton R. Hunter, Deseret News Press, Salt Lake City, 1946.
Volney King: Millard County 1851-1875, Utah Humanities Review, Volume 1, Number 1, January 1947, University of Utah.
100 Years of Millard County History--1851-1951(Milestones of Millard), DUP of Millard County, 1951.

Other Guide Books by the Author
(Prices as of January, 1996. Prices may change without notice)

Climber's and Hiker's Guide to the World's Mountains, 3rd Edition, Kelsey, 928 pages, 447 maps, 451 fotos, ISBN 0-944510-02-7. US$34.95 (Mail orders US$37.00).
Utah Mountaineering Guide, and the Best Canyon Hikes, 2nd Edition, Kelsey, 192 pages, 105 fotos, ISBN 0-9605824-5-2. US$9.95 (Mail orders US$11.50).
Canyon Hiking Guide to the Colorado Plateau, 3nd Edition, Kelsey, 288 pages, 116 maps, 159 fotos, ISBN 0-9605824-1-5. US $12.95 (Mail orders US$14.50).
Hiking and Exploring Utah's San Rafael Swell, 2nd Edtion, Kelsey, 160 pages, 35 mapped hikes, plus lots of history, 104 fotos, ISBN 0-944510-01-9. US$8.95 (Mail order US$10.50).
Hiking and Exploring Utah's Henry Mountains and Robbers Roost, *Including The Life and Legend of Butch Cassidy*, Revised Edition, Kelsey, 224 pages, 38 hikes or climbs, 158 fotos, ISBN 0-944510-4-3, US$9.95 (Mail orders US$11.50).
Hiking and Exploring the Paria River, Updated Edition, Kelsey, 208 pages, 30 different hikes from Bryce Canyon to Lee's Ferry, 155 fotos, ISBN 0-9605824-7-9. US$10.95 (Mail Orders US$12.50).
Hiking and Climbing in the Great Basin National Park--*A Guide to Nevada's Wheeler Peak, Mt. Moriah, and the Snake Range*, Kelsey, 192 pages, 47 hikes or climbs, 125 fotos, ISBN 0-9605824-8-7. US$9.95 (Mail Orders US$11.50).
Boater's Guide to Lake Powell, Updated Edition, with hiking emphasised, Kelsey, 288 pages, 256 fotos, ISBN 0-9605824-9-5. US$12.95 (Mail Orders US$14.50).
Climbing and Exploring Utah's Mt. Timpanogos, Kelsey, 208 pages, 170 fotos, ISBN 0-944510-00-0. US$9.95 (Mail Orders US$11.50).
River Guide to Canyonlands National Park & Vicinity, Kelsey, 256 pages, 151 fotos, ISBN 0-944510-07-8. US$11.95(Mail Orders US$13.50).
Hiking, Biking and Exploring Canyonlands National Park & Vicinity, Kelsey, 320 pages, 227 fotos, ISBN 944510-08-6. US$14.95(Mail Orders US$16.50).
Life on the Black Rock Desert, *A History of Clear Lake, Utah,* Venetta B. Kelsey, 192 pages, 123 fotos, ISBN 0-944510-03-5. US$9.95(Mail Orders US$11.50).
China on Your Own, *and The Hiking Guide to China's Nine Sacred Mountains*(3rd and Revised Ed.), Jennings/Kelsey, 240 pages, 110 maps, 16 hikes or climbs, ISBN 0-9691363-1-5. US$9.95 (Mail Orders US$11.50). This is out of print, but I have a few copies left.

Distributors for Kelsey Publishing

Primary Distributor All of Michael R. Kelsey's books are sold by this company. If you'd like to order any book, please call or write to the following address.
Wasatch Book Distribution, P.O. Box 11776, 268 S., 200 E., Salt Lake City, Utah, USA, 84111, Tele. 1-801-575-6735, or for bookstores, 1-800-786-6715, Fax 1-801-575-6834.

Some of Kelsey's books are sold by the following distributors.
Alpenbooks, 3616 South Road, Building C, Suite 1, Mukilteo, Washington, 98275, Tele. 1-206-290-8587, or 1-800-290-9898. Fax 1-206-290-9461
Canyon Country Publications, P. O. Box 963, Moab, Utah, 84532, Tele. 1-801-259-6700.
Canyonlands Publications, 4999 East Empire, Unit A, Flagstaff, Arizona, 86004, 1-602-527-0730.
Crown West Books(Library Service), 575 E. 1000 S., Orem, Utah, 84058, Tele. 1-801-224-1455.
Northern Arizona News, 1709 North, East Street, Flagstaff, Arizona, 86004, Tele. 1-602-774-6171.
Many Feathers, 2626 West, Indian School Road, Phoenix, Arizona, 85012, Tele. 1-602-266-1043.
Nevada Publications, 4135 Badger Circle, Reno, Nevada, 89509, Tele. 1-702-747-0800.
Mountain 'N Air Books, 7251 Foothill Blvd., Tujunga, California, 91042, Tele. 1-818-951-4150, or for bookstores, 1-800-446-9696
Peregrine Outfitters, P.O. Box 1500, Williston, Vermont, 05495-1500, Tele. 1-802-860-2977, Fax 1-802-860-2978.
Recreational Equipment, Inc.(R.E.I.), P.O. Box C-88126, Seattle, Washington, 98188, Tele. 1-800-426-4840(or check at any of their local stores).

For the UK and Europe, and the rest of the world contact:
CORDEE, 3a De Montfort Street, Leicester, England, UK, LE1 7HD, Tele. 0116-254-3579, Fax 0116-247-1176.